THE END OF ALLIANCES

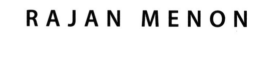

RAJAN MENON

THE END OF ALLIANCES

OXFORD
UNIVERSITY PRESS

2007

OXFORD
UNIVERSITY PRESS

Oxford University Press, Inc., publishes works that further
Oxford University's objective of excellence
in research, scholarship, and education.

Oxford   New York
Auckland   Cape Town   Dar es Salaam   Hong Kong   Karachi
Kuala Lumpur   Madrid   Melbourne   Mexico City   Nairobi
New Delhi   Shanghai   Taipei   Toronto

With offices in
Argentina   Austria   Brazil   Chile   Czech Republic   France   Greece
Guatemala   Hungary   Italy   Japan   Poland   Portugal   Singapore
South Korea   Switzerland   Thailand   Turkey   Ukraine   Vietnam

Copyright © 2007 by Oxford University Press, Inc.

Published by Oxford University Press, Inc.
198 Madison Avenue, New York, New York 10016

www.oup.com

Oxford is a registered trademark of Oxford University Press

Library of Congress Cataloging-in-Publication Data
Menon, Rajan, 1953–
The end of alliances / by Rajan Menon.
p. cm.
ISBN 978-0-19-518927-8
1. United States—Foreign relations—1989– 2. United States—Foreign relations—1945–1989. 3. Alliances.
4. Strategy. 5. North Atlantic Treaty Organization. 6. United States—Foreign relations—Japan. 7. United
States—Foreign relations—Korea (South). 8. Japan—Foreign relations—United States. 9. Korea (South)—
Foreign relations—United States. I. Title.
E895.M46 2007
327.73009′05—dc22   2006020664

1 3 5 7 9 8 6 4 2

Printed in the United States of America
on acid-free paper

To Cathy, with love

Preface

A mong the central tenets of Buddhism is "impermanence," which means just what it says: that all things in life are constantly changing and, as such, are transitory. At first blush, the insight that everything we have or like or are comfortable with proves fleeting is simple, but deceptively so, for it is hard to live by. Much as we claim to relish new circumstances and ideas, there is a part of us (indeed a large one) that is pleased with (or resigned to) what is and wants to believe that what is will remain more or less as it is. And why not? The objects, people, conceptions, institutions, and circumstances of our present provide predictability and order, and assurance that what we believe is correct, and that tomorrow will be a variation on today. We are understandably attached to life as we know it. In the Buddhist perspective, however, attachment, extraordinarily tough to overcome, is the taproot of suffering.

In *Bring Me the Rhinoceros*, his book on Zen koans, John Tarrant presents the parable of a moth flying into a candle's flame, because it is working "from an erroneous map." Humans, too, he explains, rely on maps to navigate life, but a particular map can cease to be a reliable guide. One can then discard it, "even though it has been a nice map and worked well for fifty years or five minutes." "The other path," says Tarrant, "is the one in which the more doubts you have about a map, the more strongly you insist that it is accurate. This is the moth's path."[1]

What follows is not a treatise on Buddhism. Yet what does run through this book is the centrality of contingency in spite of our tendency to cling to the familiar, mothlike behavior. Despite our preferences and our resistance, what seems firm and fixed is neither, for change intrudes. Borrowing from philosopher of science Thomas Kuhn, I refer to the rise of new ideas and practices that upend existing modes of thought and conduct as "paradigm shifts." Such stark shifts occur routinely in life, and this is no less true of the history of nations. Mountains of books tell of societies that experienced dramatic change in their internal order and external orientation, even as well-informed observers thought it impossible.

One is reminded of Lenin's observation, not long before the 1917 Bolshevik Revolution, that while a socialist revolution in Russia was inevitable, it would not happen in his lifetime, or of the legions of seasoned Soviet experts who were caught completely off guard—as I was—when the Soviet Union fell apart. Or consider how Germany, which acquired a reputation for aggressive nationalism and militarism during the first half of the twentieth century, is now wedded to peace, commerce, and stability, or how China, once zealous about exporting socialist revolution, now focuses on exporting goods to capitalist markets.

The United States is not, of course, headed for revolution, let alone collapse. But I do believe that it is in the early stages of a paradigm shift in grand strategy, one that will advance for a decade or so before its reality becomes apparent. By "grand strategy" I mean quite simply the ideas that leaders use to understand and relate to the world, the various means and ends they pick to act within it, and the institutions they create to help achieve their objectives. Grand strategy is multifaceted and certainly not reducible to military might, but it does include it.

All countries perforce have grand strategies, whether successful or not, and those of great powers have kept scholars busy for centuries. Countless tomes have been written just on the grand strategy of the United States after World War II—one country in a blip in time. Innumerable things have happened in the world over the past sixty years. The United States has been involved in a welter of issues so complex that any single formulation or framework does violence to specificity and complexity. Yet at the end of the day, one must generalize to comprehend the flurry of disparate events. Relating them to American grand strategy helps us organize and interpret them.

The term that best describes postwar American grand strategy is *containment*, and I'll use it often in this book. Containment, a highly successful strategy, rested on the premise that the Soviet Union, by virtue of its ideology and power, presented the principal challenge to the interests of the United States. These interests encompassed the physical security of the United States and its economic needs and values, but also the security of countries that, from Washington's viewpoint, were essential to a world order and a balance of power favorable to America's concrete needs and its ideological precepts. The contest between the United States and Soviet Union, which journalist Walter Lippmann christened the cold war, was the defining external reality for Americans between the late 1940s and 1991, the year the Soviet Union disintegrated. But that rivalry also shaped the political contours of the world in general, just as the lives of all Greeks in the fifth century BCE were molded by the rivalry between Athens and Sparta.

The goal of containment was to fence the Soviet Union within the borders and spheres of influence it held as it emerged from World War II, on the theory that the expansion of either would alter the global balance of forces, thereby harming American interests. Significantly, containment was a radical departure from the strategy the Republic had followed since its formal establishment in 1783. In the name of containing the Soviet Union, the traditional aversion to permanent alliances was cast aside, and the United States formed a multiplicity of military pacts and deployed many thousands of troops overseas. The result was a global military-intelligence complex that some consider a form of empire.

In this network of alliances, three were far and away the most important in terms of the economic and military resources and the personnel the United States committed to them. These were NATO (the North Atlantic Treaty Organization) and the pacts with Japan and South Korea. Successive American leaders and strategists considered these parts of the world to be pivotal to the contest with the U.S.S.R. because of their economic potential, location, and population size (these individual criteria did not, of course, apply in equal measure to each locale). American policymakers pledged to protect them through open-ended alliances and deployed troops on their territories to back promise with power. These areas were ravaged and weak, having been the centers of the carnage and destruction of the war; in the estimation of American leaders, they were unable to defend themselves and thus were susceptible to Soviet coercion or, in the minds of some, even conquest.

Yet long after the revival of Europe, Japan, and South Korea—which have long since become the principal centers of wealth and technological innovativeness in the world and our economic competitors as well—the United States continues to deploy military forces there. The proposition that this should continue indefinitely is widely accepted within the foreign policy establishments of America and its allies—so much so that it is rarely questioned. Indeed, it remains the framework through which world politics is understood and foreign policy is formulated in America, the overarching strategic conception to which we have become accustomed, indeed attached. George W. Bush's policy of "regime change" may seem a departure, but it too has been implemented, in Afghanistan and Iraq, within the institutional framework and philosophy of containment.

Containment was a strategic success for nearly fifty years following World War II. Europe, Japan, and Korea received American protection, all three reached unprecedented heights of prosperity (security and prosperity being two sides of a coin), and the Soviet Union collapsed in 1991, inaugurating a unipolar world in which, to borrow Michael Mandelbaum's analogy, the United States is a latter-day Goliath.[2]

But with the Soviet Union gone, and with America's allies having long since become wealthy societies in their own right, what is the justification for continuing the traditional strategy? In mainstream foreign policy circles our alliances in Europe and the North Pacific continue to have totemic significance. I have found it rough sledding when it comes to persuading scholars and policymakers that these structures are fast becoming obsolete. Oddly, even though I am advocating a major change in our defense policy, our military officers seem much more open to it. In general, however, the thesis that we must, and eventually will, reassess the value of our alliances invites the raising of eyebrows, and, on occasion, even the rolling of eyes.

It is of course quite possible that I am wrong—our map may still be valid—but we shall know soon enough, I believe within a decade. Meanwhile, at the very least, we should debate whether "containment-plus"—placing our military resources in the three places where they have been for more than half a century, and continuing to guarantee the security of cold war allies—remains sensible. I am convinced that it does not and that the United States will inevitably move toward a new grand strategy, one shorn of formal alliances. We are, in short, due for another paradigm shift. This is not as outlandish a claim as it might seem, for great powers have regularly changed course. Containment is itself an example in that it departed from the long-established national consensus about what the United States should seek in the world and how.

The shift I foresee will result from changes in our interests and changes within Europe, Japan, and South Korea that will alter their attitudes toward the U.S.-led military pacts they have belonged to for the better part of a generation.

I should be clear on one point since it may prove to be the major misunderstanding about this book. I am not predicting, let alone advocating, isolationism. Such a policy would be neither feasible nor desirable—for the United States or for the world. (Nor, beliefs to the contrary notwithstanding, has the United States ever adopted such a policy in any strict sense of the term.) Despite missteps and blunders, some of which have cost us and others dearly, America remains a force for the good. There are, however, many ways to engage the world, and to pursue our interests in cooperation with other states, individually or collectively. Military alliances are not indispensable for a vigorous and effective foreign policy. The path the United States chose and remained on for most of its history is proof of that, and one does not have to delve too deeply into history books to find other examples of successful strategies that did not turn on military alliances.

Since its founding, the United States has aligned itself with many countries—with the combination of partners varying, depending on the issue—and it will continue to do so. But *alignment* is a supple and creative mode of statecraft; *alliances*, by contrast, can become rigid— and limiting as a result. The distinction between the two strategies is important to the case I make.

Given the strategic realities of the new century—revived allies, a vanished Soviet Union, a depleted Russia, the rise of terrorism as a central threat, the overextension of our armed forces—I believe that our alliances in Europe and Asia are dispensable. What's more, they have become impediments that inhibit creative strategic thinking at home, while infantilizing our partners who live under the American shadow. I reject the notion that the end of alliances will bring misfortunes. Forced to develop the strategies and capacities needed for their own security, America's allies will respond effectively. They lack neither the intelligence nor the means to do so; what they do lack, on account of their comfortable reliance on American power, is the will.

The end of alliances does not, however, mean the end of comity, let alone the onset of enmity, between us and our allies. There are many issues on which the United States will and must cooperate with them— but also with new states that have become important players on the world's stage—and convergent interests guarantee that there will be such cooperation, though not, as the war in Iraq demonstrates, agreement on all major issues.

Why this future will come to pass and what it implies for us and for others is the subject of the chapters that follow.

Acknowledgments

I have accumulated a great many debts and been shown many kindnesses by friends and colleagues while writing this book. Not all of them are likely to embrace my argument, and I know for certain that some do not, but their willingness to offer encouragement, to listen to ideas in progress, and to read drafts (some in very early form) means all the more to me because of that. It is with pleasure and gratitude that I say thank you to all my interlocutors.

Melvyn P. Leffler, now at the University of Virginia, has been my close friend for almost thirty years, starting with our years on the faculty of Vanderbilt University. Mel, one of America's best historians of the cold war, has read a large proportion of what I have written over the years and was once again kind enough to set aside his own work to read drafts of the first three chapters. Many of the changes I made in response to his observations and criticisms, especially in the second chapter, required considerable effort. But it was worth it. I hope he thinks so, too.

My friends Michael Mandelbaum (School of Advanced International Studies, Johns Hopkins University) and Anne Mandelbaum have offered support and advice in so many ways and on so many matters that I cannot record them all here. Michael's aphorisms on the task of writing, some derived from Satchel Paige, have been both humorous and helpful, and his own stellar achievements as a scholar are an inspiration. Anne has been a trusted and ever-reliable source of counsel about writing and about life.

Alexander Motyl (Rutgers University) has been a valued friend and critic since we first met long ago at Columbia University's Harriman Institute. He has been unfailingly generous with his time, interrupting his scholarship and prose fiction writing (and painting) to read my work, sometimes when it was still in a raw state. We have had less time for our customary conversations over dinner or lunch because of this book, and I look forward to resuming the routine.

Without S. Enders Wimbush, I might never have left the vineyards of Soviet (and later, Russian) studies to explore new vistas. He has thus influenced the writing of this book more than he knows—or perhaps would care to take responsibility for. It was through the projects I worked on with Enders (at Science Applications Corporation International, Booz Allen Hamilton, and the Hudson Institute) that I came into contact with a brilliant group of people who have influenced my thinking on various issues: Victor Cha (Georgetown), Thomas Christensen (Princeton), Nicholas Eberstadt (American Enterprise Institute), Hillel Fradkin (Hudson Institute), Aaron Friedberg (Princeton), Graham Fuller (now retired from the National Intelligence Council), Husain Haqqani (Boston University and Carnegie Endowment for International Peace), Ross Munro (Foreign Policy Research Institute), Dmitry Ponomareff (Office of the Secretary of Defense), Ashley Tellis (Carnegie Endowment), and Arthur Waldron (University of Pennsylvania). My work with Enders also introduced me to Andrew Marshall, director of the Pentagon's Office of Net Assessment. I have worked with Marshall on many projects over the past decade, and I know of no better strategic thinker. He has served in our government with distinction under various presidents and unfailingly welcomes and inspires unconventional thinking, even when it does not accord with his own views.

The End of Alliances began as an op-ed piece for the *Los Angeles Times* and was later transformed into an article for *World Policy Journal*, before Oxford University Press offered me a contract to write a book expanding its thesis. I have been fortunate to have the help, advice, encouragement, and sharp eyes of many people. Sue Horton, editor of the "Sunday Opinion" (now "Current") section of the *Los Angeles Times*, ran the piece as a nine hundred-word essay, and, while she remained at "Sunday Opinion," edited many other pieces of mine, teaching me much about writing and thinking in the process. Others at the *Times* have been terrific editors and critics, in particular Nick Goldberg (editor of the daily op-ed page and now also of "Current") and Ann Brenoff, who commissioned my first article for the *Times* and then edited more of them than anyone else at the paper.

The *World Policy Journal* is the best place to turn for interesting essays on world affairs, and that is largely due to the acumen and skill of Linda Wrigley, its managing editor until 2006. Nicholas X. Rizopoulos, Linda's husband, is without a doubt the keenest critic I know.

Nick Rizopoulos also runs the Foreign Policy Seminar at the Carnegie Council for Ethics and International Affairs, a weekly forum where some of the most creative thinkers present their work—and are then subjected to a thorough but always (well, mostly) cordial grilling. The suggestions I received when I presented "The End of Alliances" there in article form were invaluable, and I wish to thank, in particular, Nick, Linda Wrigley, Mark Danner, Michael Eliot, and the late and much lamented James Chace.

At Oxford University Press, I was very lucky to have Dedi Felman as my editor. She took an early interest in this project, offered her wisdom and encouragement at every turn, and commented on draft chapters with patience and acuity. I am grateful to have had the chance to work with her. Every writer should be so lucky. My thanks as well to production editor Gwen Colvin, assistant editor Michele Bové, copyeditor Renee Leath, and to David McBride, who replaced Dedi following her departure.

Lehigh University has provided me a congenial and supportive intellectual home since 1985. I am particularly indebted to Anne Meltzer, dean of the College of Arts and Science, and Henri Barkey, chairman of the Department of International Relations, who arranged a course reduction for the spring semester of 2006 that helped me complete this book amid an avalanche of administrative obligations.

During my most recent leave from Lehigh, as a Carnegie Scholar, I spent an academic year as senior fellow at the Council on Foreign Relations, where I began to work on this book. I thank Leslie H. Gelb, then the Council's president, for his hospitality, and Max Boot, senior fellow at the Council and a leading scholar of military history, for stimulating conversations. I am also grateful to the president of the Carnegie Corporation, Vartan Gregorian, who has been a friend and an inspiration to me for many years, as he has been to countless others. I wish to thank others on the staff of the Carnegie Corporation: Deana Arsenian, Neil Grabois, Stephen Del Rosso, Patricia Rosenfield, and David Speedie.

I am thankful to Ted Halstead and Sherle Schwenninger of the New America Foundation for inviting me to join NAF, a hive of creativity and unorthodoxy, as a fellow. Sherle read early drafts of the Europe and Japan chapters and has supported my other professional ventures in many others ways. Michael Lind, New America's resident polymath, offered valuable comments on the first two chapters.

NAF attracts truly outstanding research assistants, and I was fortunate to have the help of several. My thanks to the resourceful and eagle-eyed Erica De Bruin in particular, and to Swati Pandey and Robynn Sturm. Each, I am happy to note, has gone on to bigger and better things: Erica to the Council on Foreign Relations, Swati to the *Los Angeles Times*, and Robynn to Yale Law School. Sameer Lalwani, also of NAF, tracked down critical polling data and articles relating to South Korea and I thank him as well. Finally, my thanks to Douglas Greenfield for his timely and essential assistance.

Several friends, who are the foremost authorities on the countries they write about, read and commented on the NATO, Japan, and Korea chapters. My sincere thanks to Jim Auer (Vanderbilt) and professors Robyn Lim (Nanzan University, Japan), Sean Kay (Ohio Wesleyan), and Richard J. Samuels (MIT) for their kindness. I appreciate Jim's help all the more given that we see the U.S.-Japan alliance through very different eyes.

Upon entering graduate school, I encountered two outstanding teachers, professors Oles Smolansky and Roger Kanet. Their example inspired me to enter the academic profession and their assistance enabled me to stay within it. Thank you both.

A number of friends have influenced my thinking on a great many issues and so have shaped this book indirectly. In particular, I am indebted to professors John Oneal (University of Alabama), Jack Snyder (Columbia), Hendrik Spruyt (Northwestern), John Steinbruner (University of Maryland), Thomas Weiss (Graduate Center, City University of New York), and Charles Ziegler (University of Louisville).

Barry Magid, founding teacher of the Ordinary Mind Zendo in New York, has added to my understanding of many things, in many ways, and other members of Ordinary Mind, particularly Cathie Newman, have provided valuable, if quiet, fellowship.

I've saved the best for last. My daughters, Lekha and Zoë, are used to entering my study (diffidently) and finding an absentminded father, but they have never been absent from my heart. When their peals of laughter ring through our New York apartment, book writing is placed in proper perspective, and I am reminded of what really matters in life.

I owe my wife, Cathy Popkin, far more than I can record in a few lines. Her love, patience, intelligence, and belief in me have been constants. Without her, I would not have begun to write this book, much less finished it. More important, life would not be joyous and full. (I would also have taken myself much too seriously.) Despite the demands that teaching, research, and administrative responsibilities at Columbia University place on her time, she helped me with her sage advice and superb critical eye. She is quite simply the best writer I know, and the best at getting people to write better. To her, I dedicate this book.

Contents

THE END OF ALLIANCES

The Impermanence of Paradigms

1

The United States is moving toward a slow, little-noticed, but far-reaching change in the way it engages the world. This reorientation will shred many of the assumptions, theories, institutions, and prescriptions that now seem so rock solid, precisely because they have proved so enduring and reliable in the past. Together, these conceptions and structures served, to use a term that Thomas Kuhn has made commonplace by now, as a paradigm, a framework within which it was possible for Americans to think about and act in the world—and effectively so.[1] Yet paradigms become limiting with time, out of kilter with a reality that changes relentlessly and strains their confining categories. Eventually, the march of time creates new circumstances for which they are ill-suited and inevitably they are superseded by new paradigms.

Impermanent Paradigms

To return to a theme I adumbrated in the preface, this displacement of the old by the new does not occur easily. Inevitably, there is resistance to the idea that existing modes of thought and action no longer suffice—that they will be and must be transcended. When it comes to assaying what the future holds, we are, to one degree or another, prisoners of our past. This is but natural; theories and practices that are familiar by virtue of having been tried and tested tend to be better guides than conjecture. Yet there are breaks in continuity; previous patterns, no matter how comfortable we have become with them, do not extend limitlessly forward. There are changes, sometimes gradual, at other times sudden. This is readily apparent in politics, where, most of the time, it's a safe bet to say that tomorrow will be a variant of today. Neither can one sensibly plan ahead on the assumption that what lies ahead will be unlike what now exists. However, as each of the great revolutions of the last 250 years has demonstrated, sudden, unexpected change can upend what seemed, in the political sphere, axiomatic.

Assume that we were to board a time machine and make three stops: France in 1780, Russia in 1900, and the Soviet Union in 1980. In all three instances, we would encounter people who point out the inadequacies, perhaps even the bankruptcy, of their respective political systems. But in none of these locations would we encounter a prevailing opinion that foresees the imminent and utter destruction of the existing order. Yet that is precisely what soon happened in each of these countries: France in 1789, Russia in 1917, and the Soviet Union in 1991. What had been was a poor guide to what would be. The forces that produced each of these transformations did not appear like thunderbolts; they had been at work for years, perhaps even decades, but were little noticed because they were screened out by the dominant intellectual frames of reference.

A rather different, less jarring category of change is exemplified in the realm of science and technology. At the outset of the Industrial Revolution, it would have been impossible to envision the wonders of today. We can now change the genetic structure of crops to transform their resilience and yield. Breakthroughs in our understanding and mapping of the human genome have raised the possibility of human cloning and, in the process, raised ethical quandaries that had hitherto never been contemplated or even foreseen, save perhaps in science fiction. The inventors of the steam engine and the internal combustion engine believed that they had compressed time and space to an extent never before imagined, and they were right. But they would be struck dumb by the gadgets that have been invented since then that are now so routine and unremarkable and that have redefined communication and travel. Consider what these inventors from a bygone era would say if they were to visit us and be confronted with fax machines, personal computers, the Internet, mobile telephones, and jet aircraft. What they would see also amounts to a revolution, a sharp departure from the past. There is, though, one difference relative to the political transformations I discussed earlier: the former occurred suddenly and swiftly, even though they were the result of conditions long in gestation; the latter, though by no means less consequential, unfolded over a long time span.

So what does all of this have to do with the disjuncture that I foresee both in America's foreign policy and, because the United States remains a peerless power, the larger political world that it inhabits? We are, I believe, in the early stages of what will prove to be a thoroughgoing redefinition in the means and ends of American statecraft: a total reordering of the way we deal with others and others with us. This slow-motion shift is hard to discern. Attempts to identify its nascent signs are not infrequently received with profound skepticism (or so my experience has been when I have presented the ideas underlying this book to experts in international relations). One reason for this could be that the changes I anticipate are in fact not taking place, and will not take place, and that the tools and goals of American foreign policy will not be all that different, in a strategic as opposed to a tactical sense, than they have been for the last sixty-plus years. To admit that, of course, would be to beg the reason for writing this book. While I am certainly willing to concede that my prognosis may be faulty, or perhaps premature, ultimately I am convinced that the tectonic movements that lie ahead seem impossible now precisely because they are, if you will, out of paradigm. That is why I have written this book.

Containment as Grand Strategy

If one of my themes is that we are about to enter a new phase in American foreign policy, a second is that the paradigm that has defined our thinking about world politics since the end of World War II tethers us to traditional conceptions that will prove obsolete. The familiar framework I have in mind is the product of the grand strategy that the United States has relied on for over a generation: containment and its various subordinate manifestations. Containment has proved itself as a marvelously successful strategy for assuring American primacy in the world and for facing the challenges of the state—or, as some believe, the empire, and an evil one in Ronald Reagan's famous formulation—that was America's principal nemesis: the Soviet Union. No better proof of this is needed than to point to the obvious: the Union of Soviet Socialist Republics is no longer with us. Despite books that proclaim that "we all lost the cold war" and decry the tension-filled, resource-wasting period that marked the competition between the superpowers from 1945 through 1991, no one, least of all those in Russia today, has any doubt about who the victor was.[2]

The United States emerged victorious for many reasons. Its economy, we now know, was about 40 percent larger that that of the Soviet Union. That meant that in an extended test of endurance lasting almost half a century, the United States had resources to draw on that the Soviet Union simply did not. The Soviet Union was also outclassed in another respect: it was not merely a matter of how much its economy produced in comparison to the United States, but *how* it produced. From at least the early 1960s, the Soviet economy's rate of growth began to decline, and the trend continued almost without letup. There were many reasons for this, of course, but one was the inability to shed an "extensive" approach to economic development and to master an "intensive" one. The former was wonderfully, if brutally, successful in promoting the transformation of what, at the time of the 1917 Bolshevik Revolution, had been a largely peasant economy with islands of industry into a modern one featuring railways, dams, steel mills, automobiles, and ships. Had it not been for this achievement, the Soviet Union would not have been able to fight Nazi Germany virtually single-handedly for several years and then vanquish it. In the last decades of the twentieth century, however, the name of the economic game changed. What mattered now was what economists call "factor productivity," or output measured per composite unit of labor and capital. Growth under these circumstances depended on technological innovation, and, despite occasional flourishes such as Sputnik, the Soviet economy proved to be spectacularly non-innovative compared to other industrial powers, which is what ultimately mattered. By the time of the computer revolution and the rise of robotics, this limitation became undeniably clear. While the Soviet military-industrial complex, coddled with the country's best brains and massive investments, proved an exception for a time, by the 1980s, Soviet senior generals were warning of the dangers of falling behind technologically because the Soviet Union was trailing in what would later come to be known as the "Revolution in Military Affairs."[3] On the economic front, therefore, the Soviet Union operated with deficiencies that were quantitative (the size of its gross national product, or GNP) and qualitative (a dearth of technological creativity); in both arenas the United States was in an altogether different league.

The problem was worse than that. If your adversary's wealth and technological abilities exceed yours, one way out of the bind is to gather to your side others who can help close the gap. The Soviet Union was singularly unfortunate in this respect; the United States thoroughly blessed. The Soviet Union's principal allies, members of the Warsaw Pact alliance that it led, were the states of Eastern Europe. There, not even East Germany, economically the most advanced Soviet ally, could do much to help cut the American economic and technological lead. Worse, beyond Europe, the quasi allies courted by the Soviet Union relied on its largesse; Cuba and Vietnam alone received billions of dollars a year in aid and subsidies.[4] The United States, by contrast, presided over an alliance network that yielded an embarrassment of riches. Its allies were the world's wealthiest and technologically most vibrant states: Britain, Germany, Japan, and France, among them. Starkly put, the Soviet Union was running a fool's errand. It was incapable of winning the contest with the United States, either one on one or alliance to alliance. It had pitted itself against the world's richest and most technically advanced adversaries, and the outcome, though long in coming, was a foregone conclusion if the historical record is any guide.

In the military domain, the Soviet Union and its allies had the advantage over NATO in the quantity of major weapons (tanks, artillery, and armored personnel carriers, for example), but the qualitative edge was held decisively by the West.[5] Moreover, containment forced the Soviet Union to stretch its forces across several azimuths. In the west, it faced NATO, fortified by the permanent stationing of many thousands of American troops during the cold war. On its southwestern and southeastern periphery stood the Central Treaty Organization (CENTO) and the Southeast Asia Treaty Organization (SEATO), respectively.[6] On its eastern perimeter, adjacent to the vast, thinly populated Russian Far East, itself thousands of miles from the major centers of Soviet power in the west, were the American alliances with Japan and South Korea. Each country hosted tens of thousands of American troops and served, as Soviet strategists were wont to put it, as gigantic platforms from which the United States could project its power onto the eastern extremities of the Soviet Union. Then there was the American alliance with Australia and New Zealand, or ANZUS, which stood athwart the major sea-lanes of Southeast Asia and the South Pacific and offered the American navy bases, supply stations, and an array of surveillance installations. And these were just the major components of an American basing complex that spanned the world. As if this were not enough, the strategic encirclement created by containment tightened once the Chinese quarreled with the Soviet Union in the 1960s and soon thereafter entered into an unspoken alignment with the United States against the common foe. Soon, the Kremlin was forced to position more than one hundred thousand troops along the Sino-Soviet frontier, creating a new military front that placed additional strain on Soviet resources.

A final, but no less important, aspect of containment was nonmaterial; that is to say, it concerned the battle in the arena of ideas. Here, there was a reversal of roles. For a number of years following the Bolshevik Revolution, the Soviet Union offered an ideological alternative to capitalism, one that many were drawn to because they considered it idealistic, heroic, and fundamentally more just, all of which made Soviet communism a transnational movement, or as it came to be known "an ideology in power." In the 1930s, capitalism seemed a synonym for impoverishment, unemployment, injustice, and ruined lives, and the monstrous fascist regimes in Italy and Germany were regarded as its evil culmination. In those troubled times, the Soviet experiment gained many converts in the West and elsewhere; the magnitude of the atrocities then being perpetrated by Stalin was either unknown, or was explained away as the necessary price for utopia. During the cold war, the Soviet Union continued to inspire—this time as a model of how the newly independent, formerly colonial countries of Asia and Africa could industrialize rapidly. They were drawn to the Soviet Union because, unlike the Western powers, it was untainted by colonialism, a quality widely attributed to its having transcended capitalism.

But the ideological appeal of the Soviet model, while it was never extinguished, had fizzled by the 1980s at the latest. The Soviet Union invaded Hungary in 1956, Czechoslovakia in 1968, and Afghanistan in 1979 to rescue unpopular socialist regimes; and it pushed the Polish authorities to impose martial law in 1981 to quash the anticommunist Solidarity movement. These deeds made it seem scarcely different from other great powers. The freewheeling debates within the Bolshevik Party, meanwhile, were but a memory, having long since been replaced by the arid catechism of Stalinist ideology and a repressive, stultified one-party dictatorship. What once was hailed by many as a revolutionary power had become a bureaucratic behemoth led by a coterie of old men. As for the promise to create an economy of super abundance, a boast that became a motif of Soviet leader Nikita Khrushchev, it too seemed like hot air by the 1970s. By then, the Soviet Union evoked images of scarcity, shoddy goods, and interminable lines for all except a privileged, entrenched communist elite. Western capitalist democracies were hardly free of blemishes, but they offered freedom and prosperity. That was something the Soviet Union could not do without becoming something other than itself. The very fact that the main adherents of hard-core socialism by the late 1970s were Albania, Cuba, Ethiopia, and North Korea itself spoke volumes.

The collapse of the Soviet Union is often attributed, simplistically, to the policies of Ronald Reagan. In fact, it was the culmination of many problems that had been left untended for decades. Paradoxically, Mikhail Gorbachev's efforts to address them through *glasnost* and *perestroika* set in motion forces whose synergy induced the very unraveling that the reforms were supposed to avert; revolutions, as Tocqueville noted in his classic account of the French Revolution, occur not when conditions are terrible and seemingly unchangeable, but in periods when efforts to change the status quo pry open a Pandora's box.[7] What has not been given enough emphasis in accounts explaining the Soviet collapse was the extent to which détente and the Helsinki Accords ventilated the system, exposing Soviet citizens to the reality that the West was leaving their country in the dust. In 1983, on his first visit to the West, Mikhail Gorbachev, who had yet to climb to the pinnacle of power, was struck by the magnitude of the gap while visiting a five-thousand-acre farm that, to his amazement, was, thanks to leading-edge technology, operated by a handful of people. It was during that very trip that Gorbachev and his reform-minded confidant Aleksandr Yakovlev, then Moscow's ambassador to Canada, decided that for the Soviet Union, reform was not an option but a necessity.[8]

Containment as a Security Blanket

In light of containment's longevity and track record, it's not hard to see why there is such strong resistance to viewing the alliances with Western Europe, Japan, and South Korea as anything other than pivotal. Nor is it difficult to understand the deeply rooted belief that America's strategy following the cold war will be a variation of what preceded it—that NATO and the alliances with Japan and South Korea will prove malleable enough to be adapted and remade to suit a world without the Soviet Union, and that new unifying purposes will be found to keep these pacts relevant to the times and therefore central to American foreign policy.

One reason for this belief is sheer longevity. The prevailing concepts, theories, and institutions that underlie American grand strategy were all forged during the cold war. They have shaped how an entire generation of Americans, experts and nonexperts alike, see the world, and how they define their goals toward it. These intellectual constructs have become comfortable, like an old pair of shoes, and it's hard to discard them; indeed the thought of trading them in for something different may not even arise, so habituated have we become to their feel.

A second reason is the success of containment. It had a well-articulated purpose, a clear strategy for assailing the chinks in the armor of the Soviet system; as a result, it held a disparate and extensive alliance network together. It is hard to imagine therefore that what was relied upon for so long and to such good effect should be abandoned. Surely what is called for is adaptation, not abandonment. It seems indisputable that the pillars of the policy, the principal alliances, must be preserved so that the United States continues to lead while Europe, Japan, and South Korea continue to be grateful and dependent consumers of the security Washington provides.

Yet the historical record is clear. States do discard existing grand strategies for new ones, regularly and often over a relatively short stretch of time, chiefly because the strategic environment in which they operate changes dramatically. I'll make this point at some length in the next chapter with reference to the United States by showing how containment and membership in long-term alliances have been but two of America's stances toward the world beyond. For now, I want to offer two examples that demonstrate that great powers routinely abandon what appear to be well-established conceptions of the means and ends of statecraft when the conditions that produced them start fading away, and that paradigm shifts are common in the realm of strategy.

Britain's Twists and Turns

Consider, to begin with, Britain. Britain was never a superpower in the sense in which that term came to be used after World War II. But from the end of the Seven Years' War in 1763 (and perhaps even earlier, but certainly after that date), which settled the question of whether Britain or France would be the dominant global power, until the decade or so before World War I, when Germany and the United States were overtaking Britain in key ingredients of national power, Britain's power was unrivaled. Its navy was second to none; it played a pivotal role in maintaining equilibrium in continental Europe's balance of power; its plentiful capital served its economic and strategic interests; and its empire spanned the globe. The swings in British strategy are therefore instructive for assaying the American future.

Until the twentieth century dawned, Britain had a well-articulated grand strategy, one that was both elegant in its simplicity and unquestionable in its effectiveness. Britain maintained a fleet that achieved mastery of the sea, dominated the maritime trade routes, and ensured access to its far-flung colonial constellation. The campaigns Britain fought between the Seven Years' War and the battle of Waterloo were, in large measure, about thwarting France's efforts to contest British naval supremacy. Britain's success in this rivalry guaranteed that it would be the preeminent colonial power and the leading trading state as well, and that it could prevent any adversary from contesting its primacy in both the possession of territory abroad and in overseas commerce and investment.

While Britain invested considerable efforts and resources into achieving naval dominance, the same was not true when it came to land warfare. Britain had a relatively small population and could not raise massive armies of the sort fielded by Austria-Hungary, France, Prussia (and, after 1870, Germany), or Russia. Yet it had an abiding interest in preventing any mainland European state from becoming the unrivaled master of the Continent; control over Europe would not only ensconce a hostile state adjacent to the British Channel, it would also provide a rival the resources necessary to build a navy equal to Britain's.

Britain devised an elegant and effective strategy, one tailored to its naval dominance and its inability to muster a large army, to protect its interests and to thwart the challenges to Europe's balance of power— and thus to British global hegemony—mounted successively by the Hapsburgs, Louis XIV, and Napoleon.[9]

The British used their unrivaled wealth to bankroll European coalitions that checked would-be hegemons. The idea was to help tie up challengers on land, while Britain attacked them at sea, cutting off the colonial possessions that added to the adversary's wealth, prestige, and ambition. When necessary, Britain intervened in Europe's wars with its own forces, as it did in the campaigns led at different times against France by Marlborough and by Wellington. As a rule, however, it eschewed wars in Europe, fearing that they could, by requiring the deployment of troops, drain British wealth while trapping it in quagmires. Why not, instead, help others to do what is in the common interest and that you are not well-equipped to do? While relying on others, however, the British avoided formal, long-haul alliances. This policy came to be known as "splendid isolation" during Lord Salisbury's tenure as prime minister, but its underlying logic can be traced further back in time.

As the curtain was closing on the nineteenth century, the circumstances that enabled this long-established and celebrated strategy were dissipating. This forced Britain to take a different tack. There has been some debate over whether the new course really amounted to a revolution, or in the Kuhnian parlance I have used, a paradigm shift. To some, the new policy, which, as we shall see, led to a deeper and far more formal British entwinement in European affairs, was not a drastic change: they maintain that Britain had been engaged in managing the balance of power even earlier and never stood apart. True, but the relevant questions are how the British conceived of and executed that management once the new century began, and whether they did so in a manner distinct from past practice.

By then, several developments had rendered the old policy if not obsolete, then certainly increasingly unsuitable. Britain's standing in the global balance of power began to slip. Its margin of superiority in the key elements of power was diminishing rapidly, in no small measure because others began to emulate some of its policies and because the spread of its technology and capital created new centers of power: the United States, Japan, and Germany. The last of these states became an increasing, and ultimately the preeminent, source of worry. After 1898, Germany was determined, Bismarck's counsel about moderation notwithstanding, to become the dominant state on the Continent and to rival Britain's long-established naval superiority. Before the magnitude of the German challenge became apparent, the British sought an alignment with Germany to check the French, who were still seen as their key competitors in critical regions. But that overture, which spanned the years from 1898 to 1902, was abandoned when the Germans insisted that Britain join the Triple Alliance consisting of Germany, Austria-Hungary, and Italy, a combination whose very purpose seemed to be to promote the project of German supremacy in Europe.

A clear sign that Britain was coming to realize the limits of splendid isolation was its decision in 1902 to form an alliance with Japan to balance Russia. But the British were quick to see that their foremost problem was the German challenge. To counter it, they signed an alliance with France, regarded hitherto as their foremost rival in Africa and the Middle East—the foe, not the friend. The result was the 1904 Anglo-French Entente Cordiale, which aimed to end Anglo-French rivalry. But the transformation in British calculations went even further. In 1907, Britain concluded an alliance with Russia, which, until recently, had been seen as a threat by virtue of its designs on the Balkans (then slipping away from the grasp of the Ottoman Empire), the Turkish Straits, Persia, and Central Asia. The culmination of these two alliances was the Triple Entente, which faced the Triple Alliance, and not only dragged

Britain into the depths of the Continent's conflicts, but did so through formal alliances, which had hitherto been avoided as unsuited to and unnecessary for Britain's objectives abroad. Until 1907 it was possible to insist that the 1902 alliance with Japan was not a drastic change in British strategy inasmuch as Britain still refrained from entering into formal alliances in Europe, but by 1907, Britain's break with its long-held and successfully executed strategy was clear and indisputable.

My goal here is not to provide an A to Z account of British diplomatic history but to show, as a means to substantiate the overall argument of this book, how America's immediate predecessor as the foremost global power refashioned its grand strategy once it recognized that the circumstances that enabled the strategy's success were being transformed. Lest this example be considered an aberration, it's worth at least encapsulating some others that show Britain engaging in this selfsame process of reassessing and revamping the principles and practices it had relied upon to apprehend the world and to further its interests within it.

Indeed, there is an even more consequential example than the one I just offered relating to the jettisoning of splendid isolation. And that is Britain's shift after 1918 from a policy of weighing in intermittently to prevent Europe's domination by any one power or coalition to a very different approach, which has since been disdainfully labeled "appeasement."

It is hard to quarrel with the judgment that the latter was a wrong-headed policy that aggravated the threat Nazi Germany posed to Europe by boosting Hitler's confidence that he could achieve his goals by milking the European powers' determination to avoid yet another conflict after the Continent had just been decimated by four years of brutal, unrelenting war. Yet it was hardly unreasonable for Britain to pursue this policy. No state in Europe was eager to stop Hitler in his tracks immediately through a swift resort to force, even though he was then operating from a position of military weakness. For one thing, while in hindsight his aim to demolish the status quo and to replace it with a German empire is clear, at no time did Hitler, in making his demands, announce that as his objective; on the contrary, he presented each territorial claim

The Impermanence of Paradigms

as a discrete one, framing it as reasonable in light of Germany's wounded nationalism: so it was with his rejection of the strictures the postwar settlement imposed on German military power, the *Anschluss* with Austria, and the claim on the Sudetenland. European leaders, who lived in the shadow of the Great War, could be forgiven for believing that each demand could be accommodated through diplomacy. We know now that they were dead wrong, but the relevant question is whether they could have really been expected to know that at the time. "Appeasement," derided in textbooks and classroom lectures today as an admixture of foolishness and spinelessness, reflected the fervent desire of ordinary Europeans to prevent another war and to make big compromises to do so. It is well to remember that Neville Chamberlain, who now appears in the pages of history as the embodiment of pusillanimity, was feted as a hero when he returned from Munich, having cut a deal with Hitler at Czechoslovakia's expense.

What this encapsulation of Britain's response to Germany until 1939 (when Hitler invaded Poland, revealing what he truly was, an imperialist, not a mere nationalist) illustrates is that London abandoned one strategy—which was appropriate for its time—that it had used to preserve equilibrium in Europe for another that was dramatically different in means and ends. The new approach, moreover, was not fleeting: it remained in place for most of the 1930s, until Winston Churchill—who had been a lonely voice, a Cassandra, warning about Hitler's true aims—became prime minister.

For over a century before World War I, Britain bestrode the world unchallenged, its stature symbolized by the colonial real estate it had amassed in all corners of the globe. But drained by World War II, Britain, whose margin of advantage over the United States and Germany was narrowing already by the late nineteenth century, had become a second-rank power. It reacted to the new status by altering its strategy once more—and drastically. It continued to maintain the balance in Europe, but in a wholly new manner. Accepting its diminished position, Britain became a loyal member of the multilateral alliance led by the United States and stationed a permanent contingent of troops in West

Germany. Each aspect of this strategy was new—the subordination of Britain's security to the United States (a former colony, no less), the long-term adherence to an alliance with numerous members, and the open-ended deployment of military units on European soil. Certainly no Victorian diplomat would have foreseen such a turn.

But the changes in British strategy after World War II extended beyond the Continent. Given its waning power and the upsurge of anticolonial nationalism (itself a product of the new technologies and ideas that imperial rule had introduced into colonies), Britain relinquished its empire. For over a hundred years, these possessions had been sources of wealth, symbols of Britain's peerless power, and emblems of its image and self-image. But beginning, ironically enough, with India, the celebrated "jewel in the crown," the colonies were evacuated, not as a matter of magnanimity but of necessity and undeniable new realities of power. Just as most people in 1980 would have ridiculed the prediction that the Soviet Union would abandon its East European empire in 1989 without firing a shot and itself unravel quickly and virtually bloodlessly soon thereafter, few in the Victorian establishment would have foreseen, much less approved of, such a revolution in British statecraft, so confident were they of Pax Britannica's indestructibility.

From War to Peace in Europe

The experience of Britain is instructive for the United States because it shows a state that long dominated the international system making several sharp, and unexpected, turns in strategy. But paradigm shifts can also be illuminated by going beyond individual instances involving preeminent powers and examining dramatic, unexpected changes in the political order of an entire region. Perhaps the best recent example here is what has happened to Europe over the past fifty years. Again, no one pondering the world in the nineteenth century would have anticipated what, by any standard, is an astonishing development: Europe's success in reinventing itself from the cauldron of war that it had been for multiple centuries to the community of peace that it has become since 1945.

Before 1945, Europe without war was unimaginable; now, war within Europe is unimaginable.

Think of Europe's blood-drenched past. The Continent's wars were perennial and protracted, so much so that some even carried numerical designations: the Hundred Years' War; (1337–1453) that pitted France against England; the Eighty Years' War (1568–1648), which was centered in the Low Countries and bled, as it were, into the Thirty Years' War (1618–48), which was fought mainly in the German principalities; and the Seven Years' War between France and England (1756–63). Then there were the wars of revolutionary and Napoleonic France (1792–1815). None of these compared in the scale and scope of their destructiveness to the two world wars, which demonstrated the dark side of the surge of technological innovation released by the Industrial Revolution. While this is a partial listing and omits many other major European wars, it suffices to make the point of how violent a place Europe had been for at least 600 years prior to the end of World War II.

Apart from the regularity of Europe's wars, the number of lives consumed by them, even allowing for the difficulties in providing exact counts and differences among the authoritative accounts, is mind numbing. The Hundred Years' War claimed 185,250 lives on the battlefield alone. During the same period, with a substantial share of the losses no doubt accounted for by the Black Death (which swept Europe within the same time span), France's population was reduced by six million, or one-third.[10] Between 15 and 20 percent of the population in the Germanic territories died as direct result of the Thirty Years' War, or from the epidemic of typhus and plague spawned by its side effects; the total number of deaths attributed to that war is seven million.[11] The Seven Years' War killed 1.2 million soldiers and civilians, while the wars associated with the French Revolution and Napoleonic Empire took three million lives, a third or so accounted for by the revolutionary wars.[12] The worst was yet to come: fifteen million people died in World War I and fifty million in World War II.[13] In short, Europeans seemed fated to be trapped in the slaughterhouse of war.

Remarkably, Europe has freed itself from what seemed an unbreakable cycle. Since 1945 it has become a zone of peace; war between traditional antagonists, Britain and France and France and Germany, is well-nigh unimaginable. Germany, which has been widely blamed for World War I and that certainly was the state singly most responsible for World War II, is now deeply embedded in the pacific structures and processes of the European Union (EU). As its reaction to the American invasion of Iraq in 2003 showed, it stands at the forefront of those European states opposed to wars waged without the United Nations' authorization. The stereotypes of Teutonic militarism have long since dissipated. Few in Europe fear a return of German expansionism. Indeed, Americans on the right now deride what they consider German pacifism and its spread across Europe.[14] Europe's transformation into a community of peace provides yet another example of how historical continuity gives way to new trends that seemed scarcely possible.

Making the Case

The examples I have discussed should establish that while tomorrow generally resembles today when it comes to the grand strategy of states, fundamental changes and unanticipated paths are common. This applies to the United States as well. I believe that we will witness a new turn in American strategy—one that abandons cold war alliances and the military commitments associated with them. However much we may revel in American exceptionalism, a change of course would hardly be abnormal by historical standards. Nothing immunizes the United States from the paradigm shifts that remade the foreign policies of other great powers.

This observation does not in itself establish that American statecraft is headed for a new turn; that particular task lies ahead and constitutes the bulk of this book. As a prelude, I should clarify what I am arguing and what I am not. The title *The End of Alliances* should not be construed to mean that I believe that alliances, a mechanism through which states pursue both defensive and offensive goals, are about to become an anachronism. Alliances will be a part of states' repertoire so long as they must rely on their wits and resources to secure their safety, so long as there is no international analogue to national governments and police forces, and so long as there are revisionist regimes bent on remaking an existing order. This is as axiomatic now as it was during the Peloponnesian War.

Nor—and this bears repeating—do I maintain that the United States will turn isolationist. The United States has never been detached from world politics and the label of "isolationism" that is routinely affixed to particular phases of American foreign policy is a misnomer. Even if it were possible to do so, a retreat into "Fortress America" is hardly the sole alternative to a strategy resting on fixed alliances and the permanent positioning of thousands of troops overseas. For most of its history the United States engaged the world while shunning alliances, but it changed course after 1945, adopting a strategy of permanent alliances. Both were ways of engaging the world. My argument is that America will change course yet again, not that it stands on the threshold of disengagement. The advent of an American-dominated "unipolar" world has been both celebrated and condemned but this book is not a prognostication of, or a prescription for, a go-it-alone policy. Not only is that politically, economically, and militarily unfeasible, it is also unnecessary. Through contingent alignments and specific coalitions created for particular ends, the United States can act in concert with other states to realize shared goals, avoiding isolationism, alliances, and unilateralism.

The rest of this book is organized as follows. Chapter 2 delineates the major periods of American foreign policy. It is not an exhaustive history of American foreign policy, but rather a survey intended to show that the United States has, for much of its history, deliberately avoided alliances on the grounds that they do not add to security but subtract from it. The alliance-driven strategy of containment is, therefore, an aberration, not the norm. Chapter 3 assesses the prospects for NATO and concludes that it is adrift and cannot be redesigned to serve new ends. Chapter 4 examines the Japan-U.S. alliance. I argue that it, too, is becoming obsolete, that Japan is capable of devising an independent defense strategy, and that its choices do not boil down to minimalism or militarism. Chapter 5 considers the alliance with South Korea. I dispute the common view that South Korea cannot defend itself against North Korea unless American soldiers remain on its soil, and I identify changes within South Korea that will eventually undermine the alliance. Chapter 6 ties the threads together and then outlines a new grand strategy for the United States.

Alliances and America's Grand Strategy   **2**

We are so habituated to the ideas and institutions linked to containment that they persist even though the problem that produced them, the challenge of Soviet expansion, has ceased to exist. Given that the majority of Americans now living were born during the cold war, it is worth keeping in mind that an alliance-driven policy began to guide America's foreign relations only at a late stage in the country's history. For 169 years, from the Declaration of Independence until the end of World War II, the United States avoided long-term alliances. The founders of the Republic and the generations that followed them would have been surprised to see that the United States had changed course. For them, foreswearing permanent alliances and entanglement in faraway conflicts had been article of faith and part of the American identity.

Yet not long after the defeat of the Axis powers, the United States undertook to protect most of Western Europe, Japan, and the Republic of Korea (which I refer to hereafter, using common parlance, as South Korea), adopting extraordinary and unprecedented measures to that end. America entered into open-ended alliances with states deemed crucial to the struggle against the Soviet Union, deployed hundreds of thousands of troops in a constellation of bases abroad, sold billions of dollars worth of armaments to allied countries, and collaborated routinely with allied intelligence agencies. This strategy, which enmeshed the United States in the defense of Western Europe and Northeast Asia, has continued for more than sixty-one years.

Activism without Alliances

The jaundiced view toward permanent alliances that characterized American thinking on foreign policy was not linked to "isolationism."[1] The founders of the Republic had indeed warned against being sucked into faraway conflagrations, and they would have taken a dim view of campaigns designed to remake entire countries in the name of abstract principles. But they were offering a way of being in the world, not a plan for avoiding it, which, in any event, would have been impossible in any literal sense. They did not equate a rejection of permanent alliances with a rejection of diplomacy, commerce, or even war. The United States was active in the world from the start in numerous ways and it certainly was no stranger to war, which forged the nation in the first place.

By the time of American independence, ships had long since begun to bridge continents, trade had become international, and Europe's powers ruled a sprawling network of colonies. The United States was a latecomer to overseas empire, but it traded extensively with Europe, Latin America, and China, and maintained many diplomatic missions besides. The waves of immigrants that reached America's shores, first from western and northern Europe, then from other parts of that continent, represented yet another mode of America's involvement with the world beyond. So did the slave trade. Ships transporting slaves from Africa and the Caribbean entered American ports yearly (a significant proportion of their human cargo having died en route), and slavery was an essential part of the economies of the thirteen colonies, not merely of the South, where it would become a way of life.[2]

From the first days of the Republic, national security, commercial, and diplomatic considerations necessitated extensive American engagement with the European powers, even though the United States was founded by individuals who rejected the institutions and political doctrines of Europe. Consider American expansion to the Pacific Ocean. While the federal government was not the sole force behind this expansion, it played an important role, and was motivated in part by the belief that the new nation could face a mortal threat were Britain, France, Spain, and Russia to ensconce themselves in the expanse between Canada and Mexico. The same calculation underlay a variety of specific initiatives, including the purchase of Louisiana from France, the annexation of Florida from Spain, the agreements reached with Britain over the Oregon Territory and the Canadian-American border, the intermittent schemes to expand into the crown colony of Canada, and the decision to buy Alaska from Russia. Likewise, while President James K. Polk's 1846–1848 war against Mexico had complex origins, one was the fear (however unfounded) that Britain had designs on Mexico, and another was the conviction that a perch on the Pacific would position the United States to compete in the China market and prevent it from becoming an exclusive European preserve.[3] By then, America had already demonstrated that it would combine muscle and diplomacy to enter Far Eastern markets. Hard on Britain's heels, the United States secured trading rights from China under the 1844 Treaty of Wanghia. Its also gained immunity from Chinese law for Americans accused of crimes—other than opium trafficking—and their right to be tried under U.S. law. And in 1853, Commodore Matthew Perry's "Black Ships" pried Japan's markets open, paving the way for European access.[4]

Closer to home, in Central and South America, the United States showed its determination to thwart European designs. A milestone was the Monroe Doctrine of 1823, which declared that European interference in the Americas would be regarded as "the manifestation of an unfriendly disposition toward the United States."[5] While measured on account of American weakness, the Doctrine was an independent and ambitious initiative. Because of its opposition to entanglements abroad and its determination not to play second fiddle to European powers, the United States spurned Britain's proposal for a joint declaration. As an official memorandum written for the secretary of state a century after Monroe's proclamation put it, "this Government decided to make the declaration of high policy on its own responsibility and in its own behalf. The Doctrine is thus purely unilateral."[6]

The 1904 Roosevelt Corollary supplemented the Monroe Doctrine. It restated even more forcefully—the United States was by then a rising power—that the United States considered Central and South America a special sphere in which Europe's presence would be minimized. While pabulum about America's noble intentions, the natural harmony of interests between it and the states to its south, and the assurance that force would be used reluctantly and as a last resort were all present in the declaration, at its core, the Corollary reflected the realities of power. The governments of Central and Latin America were told that they must manage their internal affairs and foreign relations in ways consistent with American interests and that the United States would, when faced with "flagrant cases of . . . wrongdoing or impotence," use "international police power" to ensure compliance.[7] Left unsaid, but understood by all, was that the United States as the dominant power would decide whether these vaguely worded conditions were being met.

Successive administrations, including Woodrow Wilson's, which is typically associated with idealism and support for self-determination, acted in accordance with the Monroe Doctrine and the Roosevelt Corollary. They employed hard-nosed diplomacy and force to secure American supremacy in Central and Latin America, all the while invoking high-minded principles, as imperial powers have through the ages.[8] This stance was adopted not only toward the states of Latin and Central America but toward Europe as well. When Britain tried to adjust the boundaries of British Guyana and Venezuela to its colony's advantage in 1895, American muscle flexing forced it to retreat. So as to leave no doubt who was boss in the Western hemisphere, Secretary of State Richard Olney proclaimed that "the United States is practically sovereign on this continent, and its fiat is law upon the subjects to which it confines its interposition." America's "infinite resources," he added, "render it master of the situation and practically invulnerable as against any and all powers."[9]

Thus, robust policies toward European powers coexisted in easy harmony with the studious avoidance of alliances. This same approach was again evident as the United States, having extended its domain to the shores of the Pacific, set out to acquire its own overseas empire. This turn, which occurred in the final years of the nineteenth century, was a logical one despite the early Republic's anti-imperial ethos. Empire had long become the insignia of the great power, and the Europeans had carved up much of the world already. Why, American proponents of empire asked, should the United States stand aloof? Itself now a major power, as witness Olney's boastful words, the United States proceeded to create a colonial network of its own—and in a short span of time: Hawaii was annexed in 1897; Guam, Puerto Rico, the Philippines, and Cuba (for a time) following victory in the 1898 Spanish-American War.[10]

Tough-minded diplomacy and raw power were again employed to build and exercise exclusive control over the Panama Canal.[11] The path was simple and inexorable. The United States eroded Britain's influence in Colombia (of which Panama was part), using adept diplomacy fortified by the advantages conferred by propinquity and power. The provision for joint control of the Panamanian isthmus stipulated in the 1850 Clayton-Bulwer Treaty was undone by the 1901 Hay-Pauncefote Treaty, under the terms of which Britain accepted that there would be an American-built canal defended by the United States alone. Colombia received rougher treatment. When its parliament rejected an accord that gave the United States a one-hundred-year lease over the isthmus in exchange for $10 million up front and an additional $250,000 annually, Washington backed a Panamanian revolt, sending marines and warships to aid the secessionists. Independent Panama accepted the terms

Colombia had rejected, and the American-controlled Panama Canal was completed in 1906. Once again, no alliances, but fulsome engagement backed by power and confidence. That power and resolve were not, however, directed exclusively at Britain. By the last decades of the nineteenth century, the United States became increasingly perturbed by the rise of the German navy, which would surpass the size of America's fleet by the dawn of the twentieth century. American policies in Samoa, the Philippines, Hawaii, and Latin and Central American were shaped by concerns about German territorial designs. Indeed, American leaders, such as Admiral George Dewey and Theodore Roosevelt, spoke plainly of the possibility of war with Germany. Others, including Henry Cabot Lodge and Elihu Root, explained and justified American policies by pointing to the competition with Germany.[12] (The Germans, for their part, also considered the United States an archrival.)

The overall pattern is clear: as the twentieth century opened, the United States was embedded in the world—politically, economically, and militarily. Unlike during the cold war, however, America pursued its interests without creating or joining alliances, which were rejected as wasteful, even dangerous. And Britain, a pivotal ally after World War II, was seen—and treated—as a rival, even an adversary, for most of the era leading up to World War I, until the fear of Germany produced an alignment of interests. This distinctive, prolonged phase in the annals of American statecraft was disrupted by containment, which elevated alliances, once reviled, to unprecedented, indispensable status. Until then, the United States had engaged the world through a strategy that might be called engagement without alliances. Isolationism it certainly was not.

The same strategy was in play just prior to America's entry into the two world wars. The "isolationist" label is often attached to those individuals and groups who campaigned to keep the United States apart from these conflicts.[13] Some were certainly bigots or xenophobes. Most, however, were well informed, thoughtful individuals. They advocated neutrality for fear that embroilment in Europe's seemingly incessant wars would weaken the United States. They were not opposed to foreign trade and investment; nor did they advocate severing America's contact with other countries. They did not believe that the United States should abandon its aspirations to become a great power, or forgo the military means needed to protect itself in a dangerous world. And they were not against participation in multilateral efforts to limit armaments (the Washington and London Naval Treaties) or cooperation with other states to reach agreements designed to reduce the chances of war (such as the Kellogg-Briand Pact).[14] Most did not quarrel with the notion that the United States should, when possible, help alleviate humanitarian crises, or with the long-established precept that the United States should check European intrusions that challenged its preeminence in the Western Hemisphere.

They favored an energetic American role in the world, but wanted it to be played in a particular way. Alliances and an involvement in faraway wars (particularly in Europe) not self-evidently connected to American security would, they believed, inevitably reduce the nation's security, deplete its income, corrupt its politics, endanger its liberty, and damage its interests. To support this assessment they could—and often did—invoke those who led the fight for America's independence, designed its political institutions, and defined the tenets of its foreign policy. By appealing to first principles they could claim that it was the proponents of alliances and interventions in distant wars who were breaking faith with the nation's authentic principles and steering it into treacherous waters.

They were on solid ground in doing so.

First Principles

The original warnings against policies that would entrap America in the wars of others or assuming binding commitments to secure their safety came from the Founding Fathers, and flowed from the circumstances of America's birth. The Republic arose in a revolt against two institutions that had been fixtures on Europe's landscape for centuries: monarchy and empire. Not surprisingly, the writings of the American leaders most

closely associated with the struggle for independence reflect both revolutionary pride in rejecting monarchy and worry about the threats the
weak, newborn state still faced from Europe's imperial powers.

The first of these twin sentiments was natural for a new country
that saw itself as the embodiment of liberty and democracy (not for all
its people, to be sure, and certainly not for slaves). The second boiled
down to the practical, undeniable reality that the United States had re-
volted against the world's most powerful state in what Britain's rulers
considered an act of sedition. Quite naturally, those who led the infant
Republic worried that the British would try to recoup their loss or, failing that, pose threats to the security of the rebel state. The War of 1812
and the Civil War were reminders of this danger.[15] More generally, they
had no illusions about where their country stood on the scale of power.
By any conceivable measure, America wielded far less might than the
European powers, and the question of how best to remain secure amid
that reality was never far from the minds of those at the helm of the new
state.

The belief that America's independence represented a new chapter
in history, and that the rejection of monarchy and colonial subordination and the embrace of representative government would inspire others, is evident in all of the key documents associated with the struggle
against Britain and the consolidation of the Republic. The writings
of Thomas Paine (who, despite his fiery words and fluid pen, never
achieved the canonized status of George Washington, John Adams,
Alexander Hamilton, or James Madison) represent an excellent example
of this combination of disdain for Europe, national pride, and revolutionary idealism. The early pages of Paine's most celebrated work,
Common Sense, excoriated monarchy, the form of politics the United
States had just rejected, condemning it as illegitimate, inefficient, and
warlike.[16]

Paine proceeded to explain how America gained little, and lost
much, from British rule and why the best strategy for dealing with Europe in general was to keep it (at least) at arm's length in political and
military matters. Trade with Europe was, by contrast, desirable, and not

just for the wealth that it would bring but also for the security that it would provide: "Our plan is commerce, and that, well attended to, will secure us the peace and friendship of all of Europe; because it is in the interest of all of Europe to have America as a free port."[17] Paine presented the earliest formula for American statecraft, the essence of which was the importance of maintaining America's flexibility in foreign policy and its defense and solvency by determined efforts to avoid being dragged into the quarrels and wars of retrograde, monarchist Europe.

In contrast to the post–World War II paeans to the "special relationship" uniting the United States and Britain, Paine warned that "any submission to, or dependence on, Great Britain, tends directly to involve this continent in European wars and quarrels; and sets us at variance with those who would otherwise seek our friendship, and against whom we have neither anger nor complaint."[18] America's best course, he continued, was to "steer clear of European contentions." America's geographical separation from Europe, Paine concluded, was a providential boon. However, his emphasis on developing a strong navy for expanding overseas trade, protecting the coasts against invasion, and defending the sea-lanes shows that he was not presenting a formula to avoid the world.[19] Rather, he was formulating ideas on how best to engage it. The insistence of Paine and America's other earliest thinkers and leaders that the physical distance from Europe should be complemented by maintaining a political and military distance was, therefore, not a variant of isolationism. This is apparent from the "Plan of Treaties," which set forth the terms of the short-lived alliance with France. From the American standpoint, the pact not only strengthened the nation's security against Britain in the narrow sense, its provisions also made the seas more secure for American merchant vessels.[20]

Paine's was hardly a voice in the wilderness. His ideas are echoed in other key documents linked to the early years of the Republic, particularly *The Federalist Papers* and George Washington's Farewell Address. Alexander Hamilton's was by far the most eloquent voice on foreign and national security policy in the first of these treatises.[21] Like his collaborators, Hamilton's first order of business in this canonical collection of essays was to explain why the thirteen colonies, having broken free of Britain, could only be secure and prosperous if they took the next, and necessary, step of going beyond the Articles of Confederation and cohering into a unified nation governed by an effective central government, or as John Jay put it, "one good national government."[22]

Along the way, Hamilton expounded his conception of the best foreign policy strategy for America. Unlike Paine, Hamilton was well known for pro-British sentiments, but in other respects both men conveyed essentially the same message. Among Hamilton's rationales for a closer union superseding the decentralized Articles of Confederation was that without an effective central government, America's hard-won liberty would be jeopardized. Weak and disunited, the country risked becoming "gradually entangled in all the pernicious labyrinths of European politics and wars."[23]

America's proper course, Hamilton wrote, was to learn from the example of Britain, which used its separation from the European continent to avoid entwinement in its wars. Such a policy would allow the United States to be secure without maintaining a large army. Had Britain possessed a massive army, Hamilton argued, it would have incurred vast expenses. Worse, Britain would have undermined its liberty and come to resemble Europe's absolute monarchies. The lesson was clear: naval power was best and the United States should follow the British example and build a navy suited to expanding commerce and defending the nation. That would also prevent European states from setting one American political unit against the other, dragging one or more of them into the Continent's perennial, sordid struggles.[24] A strong navy would also enable America to define the terms under which European colonial powers could trade with it; that in turn would win it access to their protected overseas markets. This strategy would, in sum, protect liberty, increase prosperity, and ensure security.

Like Paine, Hamilton believed that the wisest way to secure America's defense was by acquiring the wherewithal to thwart European encroachments while not taking sides in the Continent's conflicts. He shared Paine's distrust of Europe's intentions and worried about its capabilities, as witness his observation that "the superiority [Europe] has long main-tained has tempted her to plume herself as the mistress of the world and to see the rest of mankind as created for her benefit."[25] America, in his view, not only had an obligation to protect itself against this drive for dominance; it had, in addition, a duty, indeed a calling, to defy "these arrogant pretensions of the European . . . [and] to vindicate the honor of the human race, and to teach that brother moderation."[26]

The themes found in Paine's writings and in *The Federalist Papers* reappeared, but were developed with even greater perspicacity in Wash-ington's *Farewell Address* of September 1796.[27] The continuity with the *Federalist Papers* is unsurprising: Madison drafted the first iteration of the *Address*, which was set aside when Washington decided to accept a second presidential term, and Hamilton—who was then busy opposing Jefferson's idea of favoring revolutionary France in its wars against its Eu-ropean enemies—played the pivotal part in the writing of the second.[28]

Washington's parting counsel is invoked mostly as an admonition against participating in "entangling alliances," but to reduce its richness to an aphorism is to short change it. The *Address* contains an eloquent and elaborate exposition of how American foreign policy—which occu-pied roughly two-thirds of his text—should be conceptualized and con-ducted. Like the portions of Paine's *Common Sense* and *The Federalist Papers* concerned with foreign policy, the *Address* radiates high-minded idealism. Washington's vision was that America must "give to mankind the magnanimous and all too novel example of a People always guided by an exalted justice & benevolence."[29] The heart of the text, however, is a clear-eyed realism—one that calls on Americans to maximize security and flexibility by avoiding permanent attachments and enmities of a permanent nature and hewing, instead, to neutrality.

Washington was well aware, of course, that the 1778 alliance that had been concluded with France to check Britain during the Revolu-tionary War remained in effect, and he took care to clarify that current "engagements" should be honored.[30] Yet even when "temporary al-liances for extraordinary emergencies" were unavoidable, he continued, "it is unnecessary and unwise to extend them."[31] The overarching maxim remained: "'Tis our true policy to steer clear of permanent Alliances with any part of the foreign World."[32]

When war broke out between revolutionary France and Britain, Washington listened to the debate between Hamilton and Jefferson on what the United States should do, given its alliance with France. Thomas Jefferson, then Britain's opponent and France's admirer, did not support military intervention in behalf of the French, but he opposed a precipitous rupturing of the alliance: France, after all, had provided critical support for America's war for independence from Britain, and there was a matter of gratitude, not to mention the 1778 alliance; moreover, the French Revolution embodied the same revolutionary, antimonarchical principles that had inspired America's own fight for independence. Alexander Hamilton, by contrast, made an impassioned case for ending the pact with France forthwith. France, he said, assisted the United States in its war to break free of Britain for its own practical reasons, above all animus toward Britain, its nemesis; likewise, the United States, Hamilton asserted, should stay clear of Europe's wars and be guided by its own national interests, for a foreign policy steered by sentiment was "hollow" and would turn Americans into "dupes."[33] Washington sided with Hamilton, convinced that the young and relatively weak republic would be swept into the continental conflict shaping up in Europe were it to remain true to France out of fealty.[34] His voice was decisive: the United States issued what later came to be known as the "Neutrality Proclamation."[35]

Washington offered a comprehensive explanation consisting of six interrelated points to demonstrate why alliances were bad practice—in effect a concise conceptualization of a grand strategy for America. The first point expressed Washington's conviction—shared by the other Founders—that the United States was a new and better sort of state, with a wider mission and an exalted duty. It could not remain true to its ideals if it were dragged back into the past that it had rejected, and alliances would do just that. In particular, Washington harked back to the physical and political separation between Europe and America that animated Paine's *Common Sense* as well as *The Federalist Papers.* "Europe," he remarked, "has a set of primary interests, which to us have none or a very remote relation," and our "detached & distant situation invites and enables us to pursue a different course."[36]

Washington also believed—and this was his second point—that alliances would lead to loss of independence and a transfer to allied states of "concessions" that "ought to have been retained" by America; hence the warning that "the Nation, which indulges toward another an habitual fondness, is in some degree a slave."[37] Alliances, he added, might dull Americans into believing that they can expect "disinterested favors" from allies; in reality, not only will there be no free lunch, the provision of resources and assistance to partners abroad will more often occasion complaints that more was not provided.[38]

Permanent alliances would not adjust to changing circumstances and interests and would provoke the enmity of states that were threatened by the alliance; as such, alliances would rest upon sentiment and not soberly calculated interests, which would be better served by retaining flexibility and bargaining power through neutrality.[39] This third point comported with the general principle that informed Lord Palmerston's dictum, proffered almost a century later, that England had no permanent friends, only permanent interests. But if his *Address* is any guide, Washington would most likely have gone further to assert that the best mode of statecraft is that which accommodates changing friendships and interests.

Washington's fourth observation was that alliances would enable special pleading by particular segments of the citizenry who are motivated less by a regard for American interests than those of the ally. Or, in Washington's words, an alliance "gives to ambitious, corrupted, or deluded citizens (who devote themselves to their favorite Nation) facility to betray or sacrifice the interests of their own country . . . sometimes even with popularity; gilding with the virtuous sense of obligation, a commendable deference for public opinion, or a laudable zeal for the public good, the base or foolish compliances of ambition, corruption, or infatuation."[40]

A related and fifth assessment offered by Washington was that alliances would afford allies privileged access to the institutions of government and to public opinion, enabling them "to tamper with domestic factions, to practice the arts of seduction, to mislead public opinion, to influence or awe the public Councils!"[41] It would have been both empirically accurate and logically consistent for him to add that a democracy's very openness offers multiple pathways for such inroads, though he did not say so explicitly.

Finally, the *Address* underscores that Washington's antagonism toward alliances did not rest solely on his belief that they would not strengthen America's diplomacy and defense; he also worried about the baleful effect they would have on American society itself. By allowing alliances to implicate it in the competitions and conflicts of other states, he believed the nation would be burdened by "those overgrown Military establishments, which under any form of Government are inauspicious to liberty, and which are to be regarded as particularly hostile to Republican Liberty."[42]

The essentials of Washington's foreign policy philosophy were reiterated in 1823 by Thomas Jefferson in a letter to President James Monroe. The issue at hand was whether the United States should accept Britain's proposal for a joint statement to prevent the Holy Alliance (the coalition created by the counterrevolutionary eastern monarchies in post-Napoleonic Europe) from intervening in the Americas. "Our first and fundamental maxim," Jefferson wrote, "should be to never to entangle ourselves in the broils of Europe. . . . America . . . has a set of interests distinct from those of Europe, and peculiarly her own. She should therefore have a system of her own, separate and apart from Europe. While the last is laboring to become the domicile, our endeavors should surely be, to make our hemisphere that of freedom."[43] Curiously, despite this recitation of the traditional line on the perils of entering Europe's quarrels, Jefferson, while not recommending an alliance per se, favored a bilateral statement, believing that an understanding with the world's premier power would strengthen American security. As it turned out, Monroe and Secretary of State John Quincy Adams did not heed Jefferson's counsel. They understood that part of Britain's motive was to prevent additional territorial acquisitions by the United States it-self and that accepting the British offer would have limited America's freedom of action. Monroe and Adams stuck to the traditional policy of neutrality, refusing, as John Quincy Adams put it, "to come in as a cock-boat in the wake of the British man-of-war."[44] The United States acted unilaterally to declare the Western hemisphere off limits to Europe. The result was the Monroe Doctrine, which, even though its enforcement depended on British seapower, was an assertion of American indepen-dence in foreign affairs—and, as such, was consistent with Washington's parting counsel.

The founders of the American Republic believed that the United States embodied timeless, noble principles, that its democratic order was the wave of the future, and that it was in this sense a revolutionary state, which would change the rest of the world; what they said makes that plain. But unlike the leaders of the later revolutions in France, Rus-sia, and China, they flinched from crusades conceived to remake the world and opposed intervention in other countries even in the name of liberty or democracy. They were, in this respect, also unlike those liberal internationalists of today who favor "humanitarian intervention" to counter such abuses as ethnic cleansing, or present-day neoconserva-tives who believe that, in a "unipolar" world, the United States should employ its power unapologetically and fulsomely to bring down odious regimes and "rogue states" and to remake entire societies in democratic form on their ruins.[45] Rather, their sentiments are in accord with the "realist" school of American foreign policy, whose watchword is pru-dence, defined as the alignment of means and ends. Like the Founders, realists believe that American interests abroad are best served by attend-ing to the balance of power among key states and resisting the tempta-tion to transform the balance of forces within them in the name of sweeping ideals, no matter how worthy.[46]

The classic statement of this prudent position appears in John Quincy Adams's 1821 Fourth of July address. Adams was no isolationist or denier of power politics. He believed strongly that America should expand across the continent, prevent Europe from establishing positions of strength, and establish a dominant position in its immediate environs, using war (even its preemptive form) when necessary; he also viewed the United States as an icon of liberty.[47] Yet in his 1821 speech, he stressed that American power should not be applied to bring to others the freedoms enjoyed by the United States. Whereas neoconservatives call upon the United States to remake the world on the grounds that it is both the world's most virtuous state as well as its most powerful, Adams, addressing the question of whether the United States should help the Greeks in their fight for independence from the Ottoman Empire, warned against crusades that sought "monsters to destroy." The United States, he said, must be the "well wisher to the freedom and independence of all. . . . She is the champion only of her own." Intervention to support noble causes would, he feared, plunge the country into conflicts "beyond the power of extraction."[48]

World War I: Abiding Fears of Alliances and Entanglement

America's commitment to avoiding alliances and maintaining neutrality toward Europe's wars was most strenuously tested during the two world wars. On both occasions, the American public (and very many foreign policy experts and opinion makers) overwhelmingly opposed a declaration of war. This opposition sprang from the unshakeable belief, present since the birth of the Republic, that choosing sides and joining alliances would drag Americans into a melee and consume their blood and treasure to no good end. A corollary proposition was that we could best safeguard vital interests—chief among them the safety of the homeland and unrestricted trade—without embroilment in this latest and most dramatic installment of European war. In the end, it was Germany's provocative policies, not the public's rejection of neutrality and alliances, that eventually drew the United States into both wars. As for Germany's foes, Britain and France in particular, they rebuffed President Woodrow Wilson's proffered good offices, calculating that America would be forced to join the war on their side and that they would then be able to force the Germans to accept their ambitious demands. In any event, they were not about to enter negotiations while Germany had the military advantage and would not have done so without an American pledge to enter the war if Germany did not accept their terms. That, however, was wishing for the impossible, particularly because Wilson was angered by the rebuff and by the restrictions Britain imposed on American shipping.

Neither the public at large nor Wilson was inclined to join the war, despite remarkable German provocations, and the president warned London and Paris that their refusal to consider his proposals for mediation would only strengthen the American determination to remain above the fray.[49] Ironically, Germany proved to be an asset, in this regard, to Britain and France by engaging in conduct that alienated the United States. On three occasions, German submarines attacked British passenger ships, taking American lives—128 of them when the *Lusitania* went down in May 1915. Despite the anger at home, however, Wilson refused to be drawn. He limited his response to dispatching diplomatic protests and demanding that Germany exempt neutral shipping and unarmed commercial ships and liners from U-boat attacks.

Wilson's determination to steer clear of war has often been attributed to his idealistic vision of using America's neutral position to mediate and to orchestrate a postwar settlement that would replace the Continent's traditional ruinous balance of power struggles and violent land grabbing with a new order based on cooperation, collective security, and democracy.[50] That is certainly true, but the president was also a shrewd politician, and he understood the risks of swimming against the strong current of public opinion, not least because an election was on the horizon. Americans, seeing the horrors of brutal trench warfare and of carnage without surcease, were determined to stay out.

This sentiment was another reason why Wilson tried, through his emissary, the trusted Colonel House, to convince the warring powers to commit to a diplomatic solution instead of their obstinate quest for victory on a blood-soaked battlefield.[51] Wilson was determined to prevent his opponent in the 1916 presidential campaign from outflanking him by posing as the candidate of peace. Wilson's numerous military interventions in Central America and the Caribbean, while presented as necessities driven by high-minded ideals, show that he was no stranger to power politics.[52] His recognized the political reality: Americans opposed joining the war. That, not solely his dreams for a new and more enlightened world order, let alone a squeamishness about using force, explain why he hewed to neutrality despite critics, among them Theodore Roosevelt, who savaged his position as morally obtuse and weak.[53]

The proponents of intervention were, like Britain and France, helped by Germany. In the spring of 1917 the Germans sank three American ships, abandoning their pledge to Wilson to exempt nonbelligerent shipping from attacks, and in an even more provocative move, which was designed to ensure their victory, declared that the U-boat offensive would be directed at all shipping. They then made a move that hit the United States closer to home and that proved decisive in bringing America into the war. Through the infamous "Zimmerman Telegram," Germany's leaders offered Mexico an alliance that would, among other benefits, return significant amounts of the territory it had lost to the United States in the mid-nineteenth century.[54] That step crossed the red line that America had drawn in the Western Hemisphere, starting with the Monroe Doctrine. Still, even in late 1916, "the prevailing conviction" among Americans was that the outcome of the war would not affect their fate, and "neutrality was the reigning passion."[55] As for Wilson himself, the eventual decision for war amounted to "agony."[56]

Ultimately, then, it was the Germans who foolishly, and needlessly, turned the United States against them. Still, while Wilson led the United States into war in April 1917, he did not jettison the traditional American aversion to alliances. To the contrary, just as he had before American participation, he blamed them, along with the other typical features of European great power rivalry, for having paved the road to war. Even when the United States fought alongside Germany's enemies, it did so as an "associated power," not as an ally—a distinction that, in its curious terminology, was telling.[57] The message that Wilson's words and deeds conveyed, to Americans and to the rest of the world, was unmistakable: in joining the war, the United States was not condoning alliances and becoming like the Europe that the Founders had warned against. It had taken this momentous step with great reluctance, and in order to turn the world, and, in particular, the retrograde Europeans, toward a better path—one defined by principles that were authentically American. Paine and Washington would have applauded this script.

Wilson's aim was a new international order—one in which peace would be preserved not by the deterrence created by rival alliances but by the comity created by an international organization. American entry into the war as an associated power was a means to forge a postwar settlement on such terms. That vision would not be realized. The United States would retreat from binding commitments abroad because too many senators saw Wilson's vision as entanglement clad in new clothing; and America's disengagement was among the reasons why the League of Nations, the organization that represented Wilson's attempt to supplant war with collective security, would fail.

FDR Battles Neutrality

Americans' fear of entangling alliances was revealed anew once Adolf Hitler came to power in 1933 and Europe heard the drumbeat of war again. By the late 1930s, President Franklin Roosevelt had realized that Nazi Germany posed a threat—to Europeans and to Americans—and that the United States could not stand aside and deny help to Britain and France. Yet Roosevelt could not run ahead of the American public, which was determined to avoid fighting in yet another of Europe's wars and believed that abandoning neutrality and assisting those fighting Hitler would inevitably lure the United States into the conflict. Even after Hitler's initial conquests in eastern Europe were well underway, Roosevelt took pains to assure Americans that he would not send their boys to war, even as he sought to persuade a reluctant Congress and citizenry that strict neutrality would favor Germany and that there were ways to assist Hitler's worthy opponents short of military intervention.

The president's own thinking was still evolving though, and it would be wrong say that he was eager to get involved in Europe's conflicts, even indirectly. Like all Americans, he had been shocked by the slaughter of World War I. Roosevelt refused to arm the Republican side when the Spanish Civil war broke out in 1936 and refused to be swayed by those who argued that the United States should act to prevent the rise of a fascist regime in Spain. Before Britain and France struck the now-infamous September 1938 Munich deal with Hitler, handing him Czechoslovakia's German-majority Sudetenland, the United States had conspicuously refrained from urging resistance to German demands. Indeed, when Prime Minister Neville Chamberlain agreed to meet Hitler in Munich, FDR cabled the British leader with terse but approving words: "Good man," said the president.[58] The response was not surprising, either in its tone or length. As talks aimed at resolving the crisis sparked by Hitler's claims were held earlier that year, FDR urged a peaceful solution, but made it plain that "the United States has no political involvements in Europe, and will assume no obligation in the conduct of the present negotiations."[59] The president adopted a similar tone when Hitler annexed the rest of Czechoslovakia the following year despite his promise that the Sudetenland would be his final claim.

Americans were reassured by Roosevelt's stance. They were determined to avoid Europe's quarrels for many reasons.[60] Although the advances in military technology had created weapons with a greater reach and destructive power, and modern ships and submarines had rendered the sea a conduit for attack and no longer an effective barrier, Americans continued to believe that distance still mattered: America's physical separation from Europe was, in their eyes, an asset that made neutrality still viable. Moreover, Americans feared that war would sabotage the "progressive reforms" of the New Deal, which were slowly extricating them from the abyss of poverty into which the Great Depression had plunged them.

Then there was the horrifying experience of World War I. Memories of its trench warfare and pitiless consumption of young lives had the same effect on Americans as it did on most Europeans: they dreaded another such round of carnage. Once war erupted in Europe again, the impulse of the overwhelming majority of Americans was not to intervene to save Europe once more, but to stay home. The Continent seemed to be reverting to its old ways and the hopes aroused at Versailles by the plans to create a new, pacific European order had failed. Inaction seemed the best course of action. That the rest of the world was not doing much to stop the aggressors only reinforced this inclination. From Japan's invasion of Manchuria in September 1931 until Hitler's assault on Poland in September 1939, Europe's major powers seemed all too willing to placate Japan, Italy, and Germany, who used war and cunning to overturn the status quo. The League of Nations for its part was virtually paralyzed.[61] Seeing this passivity, Americans were even more convinced that neutrality was best. Many of them believed by then that the United States had been dragged into World War I not to defend essential national interests, but to serve the parochial needs of financiers and arms merchants. This sentiment, disseminated and reinforced in the writings and speeches of prominent clergymen, journalists, professors, and politicians, served as the setting in which the Nye Committee (headed by arch-isolationist Senator Gerald P. Nye) investigated munitions makers.[62] It was in this milieu in which Congress passed the Neutrality Acts of 1935, 1936, and 1937, each with substantial majorities.[63]

From Hitler's remilitarization of the Rhineland in 1936 to his invasion of Poland in 1939, Americans' attitudes did change slowly. They moved away from a disinterested attitude toward the war in Europe, but were still firmly against military intervention. Nevertheless, with each of Hitler's conquests, a growing number began to hold Germany responsible. Once Britain stood alone against Germany, Americans began to question the view of hard-core isolationists that America's security and England's survival were separable. The proportion of Americans who favored sending arms and economic assistance to Britain and France began to increase. That, in turn, enabled Roosevelt to amend and eventually rescind the neutrality legislation and to press ahead with the 1940 Destroyers-for-Bases deal and to secure congressional approval of the 1941 Lend-Lease bill, both of which helped Britain to stay in the war. The fall of France in June 1940 made aid to Britain a matter of urgency to FDR and the "internationalists," but the political battles against dogged anti-interventionists in Congress and the America First Committee (which waged a fervent campaign to defend neutrality) summoned all of FDR's powers of persuasion. It was hardly a foregone conclusion at the time that he would succeed.[64] Churchill certainly did not think so. His frantic appeals for help elicited measured responses from Roosevelt. The president well understood the public's fear of plunging into another European war barely two decades after the last one and he chose his words carefully.[65]

Roosevelt was obliged to walk a careful line during this time. He did so by presenting his proposals for assisting Britain not as a prelude to embarking on war, but as an alternative. Following Japan's move in 1937 to conquer the rest of China beyond Manchuria, the president had come to the conclusion that neutrality was no longer tenable or wise. He took steps to increase American military aid and sought to persuade Congress that a modification of the 1937 Neutrality Act was in order. As late as the summer of 1939, however, his efforts were unsuccessful. But the fall brought some success. New congressional legislation authorized the sale of American weapons on a "cash-and-carry" basis, and perhaps more important, the public mood had changed. Americans remained staunchly opposed to war, but as they observed Hitler's rampage in Europe, they concluded, reluctantly, that Britain and France deserved help. Support for amending the neutrality legislation was growing in Congress as well.

The German assault on Poland in 1939 proved to be the catalyst for this change. Nevertheless, Roosevelt still had to tread carefully. The fear that lifting the arms embargo would inevitably take the United States into the war remained widespread among the citizenry and was being tapped by those who were determined to block the United States from taking sides. Roosevelt turned this liability into an asset. He argued that the best way to keep the United States at peace was by enabling Britain and France to purchase American arms, while denying that right to the Axis powers.[66]

Despite FDR's growing concerns about the aggressors' advances in Europe and Asia, he had to move delicately. Even before the amendment of the Neutrality Law, he had taken small steps to help Britain and France indirectly. But foreign policy promised to be a key issue in the 1940 election, and he did not want to be outflanked by opponents of intervention. Still, the 1940 political platform of his own party, which assured the public that the United States "will not participate in foreign wars . . . outside the Americas," went further than FDR would have liked. Yet the Democrats assayed the public's mood correctly. Polls showed that as late as May 1941, 79 percent opposed American intervention.[67] FDR, a canny politician ever mindful of electoral exigencies, continued to reassure a nervous public. In October 1940, for instance, he promised a Boston audience that "your boys are not going to be sent into a foreign war."[68]

The struggle between proponents and opponents of joining Britain's fight against Hitler still continued, even though the latter's appeal declined. That they seemed blind to the growing threat posed by Nazi Germany even after the fall of France in June 1940, and had within their ranks extremists, including reflexive Anglophobes, anti-Semites, fascists, and racists, hardly helped their case. Even allowing for the pitfalls of counterfactual history, however, one must wonder whether Americans' long-standing aversion to alliances and engagement in Europe's wars would have given way had Japan not attacked Pearl Harbor on December 7, 1941; had Germany not declared war on the United States a week later; and had both powers not convinced all except diehard anti-interventionists that their aims were limitless.[69]

Pax Americana as Paradigm Shift

Pearl Harbor was a turning point. It not only pulled the United States into the war but also set the stage for Pax Americana and for a paradigm shift in foreign policy. Following the defeat of the Axis powers in 1945, the United States adopted a new grand strategy—one without precedent and a drastic departure from the Founders' foreign policy playbook. It was not conceived and applied immediately, but by the mid-1950s the essentials were in place: permanent peacetime alliances, an international circuit of military bases, the deployment of tens of thousands of American troops abroad, and guarantees to defend an array of countries across Eurasia. This shift was stark and it emerged in short order. For more than 160 years American strategy had been guided by the axiom that long-term alliances were dangerous because they would enmesh the United States in conflicts beyond the Western Hemisphere and endanger, deplete, and corrupt the country in the process.

That was about to change.

The premise of the new strategy, containment, as it came to be known, was that America's power and military presence abroad were indispensable to ensure stability in Europe and Asia and to foil the expansionist drives of the wartime-ally-turned-peacetime-adversary, the Soviet Union. After the Korean War, a network of American-led (or American-blessed) alliances arose and the defense expenditures of the United States reached levels unimaginable prior to World War II. Maximalism supplanted minimalism as the "domino theory" and its latter-day variants became embedded in the nation's strategic discourse. The conceptions and organizations supporting containment rested, ultimately, on the proposition that the security of the United States did, in fact, depend on what happened beyond the Americas and that, therefore, in contrast to what had occurred after World War I, there could be no withdrawal to the homeland if a Soviet-dominated world order were to be prevented. Such certainly was the logic of American national security planners.

This assessment marked a change of direction from FDR's strategy for dealing with the Soviet Union. Although he is sometimes portrayed as a naive figure who failed to understand the true nature and aims of the Soviet regime, Roosevelt knew, even as the war against Germany was being fought, that Stalin would emerge in a strong position after victory and would pursue his agenda, which would inevitably include retaining the territory gained following the 1939 Nazi-Soviet pact and establishing a sphere of influence in eastern Europe. The president believed that the appropriate strategy to moderate Soviet conduct and to ensure a stable postwar world was to include the Soviet Union in a great power club whose members would cooperate to oversee a new, peaceful order and lead a new global organization, the United Nations.

Yet even before FDR's death, many in the American government and military were skeptical of this plan. Containment arose from this dissenting perspective. The bedrock presumption of this doctrine was that the Soviets were adversaries bent on expansion, not allies susceptible to neo-Wilsonian solutions. The corollary to this premise was that the Soviet Union could only be dealt with through deterrence, which in turn required the creation of effective counterweights created by the power of the United States and its allies.[70] The Kremlin held a similar conception, and the result was a decades-long competition driven by many forces, waged at several levels and in numerous regions, and pursued through various means by different administrations. There were crises (over Berlin and Cuba), regional wars in which the United States and Soviet Union armed opposing sides (in Africa, South Asia, and the Middle East), and, during the 1970s—the decade of détente—and the latter part of the 1980s, periods of limited cooperation.[71] Like its analogue, the Peloponnesian War, the cold war has been subjected to microscopic analysis in a trove of books and articles, and I will do no more than sketch its essential historical context so as to show how it was a new American grand strategy—one that embraced, in what was certainly a paradigm shift, alliances as an essential means.

The place to start is by considering some canonical assessments that launched this new strategy.[72] Foremost among them are George Kennan's 1946 "Long Telegram" and his pseudonymous "X" article of 1947. Kennan would later complain—with some justification—that his ideas had been misunderstood and misapplied, but these two analyses did provide a systematic rationale and plan for confining the Soviet Union within the boundaries and spheres of influence that it possessed as a result of the Nazi-Soviet deal and the Soviet victory in World War II.[73] The objective was to deny it the Eurasian regions critical to the global balance of power and to discredit the Kremlin's ideologically based confidence in the inevitable victory of socialism.

The Truman Doctrine and Marshall Plan were consistent with Kennan's emphasis on selectivity and the importance of nonmilitary instruments of policy, but the construction of an extensive system of military alliances at various points around the Soviet Union's perimeter was, as he claimed, a mutation of his ideas, not a logical extension.[74] Kennan did not see the struggle against the Soviet Union as principally a military one and believed that building long-term alliances at points adjacent to the Soviet Union's borders was therefore a mistake. To his mind, such an approach wrongly stressed military means over economic assistance. As he saw it, promoting recovery and stability in Eurasia's strategically most consequential areas was the best response to the challenge of the Soviet Union in particular and communism in general.

Two momentous developments in 1949 displaced Kennan's subtle conception of containment in favor of one based on fixed alliances and military power. The first was the Soviet Union's acquisition of atomic weapons; the second, the communists' triumph in China. The change in official thinking produced by these shocks is reflected in NSC-68, an assessment of Soviet motivations that was written in February-March 1950.[75] This document was a clarion call for a military buildup that would provide the United States with the might it needed to counter Soviet challenges across the world. It presented—at least implicitly—the raison d'être for creating a chain of alliances that would serve as platforms to position American military forces across a geographic expanse that far exceeded Kennan's narrower demarcation of critical regions. NSC-68 advocated the very universalism that Kennan had warned against, and it committed America to the defense of countries located far beyond its historic spheres of influence. But it was not entirely divorced from the strategy he had advocated earlier.

NATO came to be the linchpin of the capacious conception of containment presented in NSC-68. Created in 1949, soon after the Soviet blockade of West Berlin, NATO remained more a concept rather than a full-blown military alliance until the Korean War. Thereafter, it evolved into a vigorous organization headquartered in and designed for the defense of Western Europe, but commanded by an American general. The real muscle of the alliance derived from the permanent presence of tens of thousands of American troops, who supplemented the much more limited military resources of its European members. Once the People's Republic of China emerged and the Korean War began, American leaders concluded that the threat of communist subversion and expansion extended far beyond Western Europe. These two developments and the U.S. response—the formation of U.S.-led alliances with Japan and South Korea—extended the ambit of the cold war into Asia and interrupted a trend. The United States had planned to remove its forces from Korea and to end the occupation of Japan; now it positioned substantial military forces in both countries, supplementing NATO by establishing bastions of power on the Soviet Union's eastern flank. These three alliances still remain in place.

Although the alliances in Europe and Northeast Asia were the critical hubs of containment, they were soon complemented by CENTO, SEATO, and ANZUS, the U.S. pact with Australia and New Zealand.[76] Even these additions did not depict the universality of containment, its "pactomania." By the end of the cold war the United States operated or used some 1,700 military installations (including bases, listening posts, facilities for storing weapons and supplies, and training centers) in a hundred countries, of which some 725 were bases.[77]

In 2001, ten years after the definitive end of the cold war, this enormous complex hosted many thousands of troops from the different branches of the military, with NATO, Japan, and Korea accounting for the overwhelming majority. The deployments in these pivotal triadic alliances have been reduced following the war against Iraq (which began in March 2003), but as late as December 2002, they remained substantial, with the European members of NATO accounting for 106,898 troops, Japan for 41,626, and South Korea for 38,725.[78]

To some, the era of containment was not a disjuncture. American foreign policy after World War II, this argument has it, was consistent with past conduct: internal colonization, purchases and annexations that expanded American territory at a furious pace for a century after independence, the Monroe Doctrine, the Roosevelt Corollary, the serial interventions in Central America and the Caribbean, and the empire gained at the end of the nineteenth century—these were in effect a warm-up act for an imperial role on a global scale.[79] This teleological thesis is not convincing. No doubt, the United States was created through a brutal, violent process (state creation invariably is) that is comparable to that which produced other continental empires, whether Ottoman, Hapsburg, or Romanov. But the conquest of North America that was completed by the end of the nineteenth century and the annexations that followed the Spanish-American War are hardly comparable to containment's universalism, which amounted to a true paradigm shift. (Moreover, conquest was not the motif of containment.) The various permanent alliances, the magnitude of defense spending, the size and scale of the overseas military presence, the global scope of U.S. strategy, and the forces configured to allow the rapid projection of American power—these attributes of containment were not variations on an existing theme. They represented a revolution, not an evolution, in grand strategy and were both expansive and (as figure 2.1 shows) expensive. Throughout the cold war Americans debated the wisdom of burdensome alliances, strategic overextension, partnerships with repressive regimes, and the harmful domestic effects of this grand strategy,

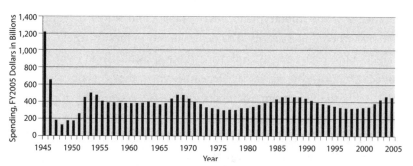

Figure 2.1 U.S. National Defense Spending, 1945–2005, in Constant FY2005 Dollars
Source: Congressional Research Service Report, Department of Defense Data
http://www.fas.org/sgp/crs/natsec/98-756.pdf.
Note: Does not include spending on Desert Shield/Desert Storm. FY2005 based on February 2004 administration request.

which was global in scope and militarized in nature. That debate continues today, but its influence is as limited now as it was then. Whether it is the Democrats or the Republicans, neoconservatives, liberal internationalists, or realists, a remarkable consensus prevails. The essential axioms of containment remain. The differences among these schools are of degree—tactical, not strategic—despite the disintegration of the Soviet empire. There have been many twists and turns and modifications in American foreign and national security policy since the expanded variant of containment was articulated and implemented in the 1950s. But the constant elements have been commitments to permanent alliances, to the defense of allies, and to the forward deployment of forces in Europe and the North Pacific. The cold war formally ended with the dissolution of the Soviet Union in December 1991, but these commitments remain nevertheless.

But how relevant are the assumptions, theories, military forces, deployment venues, and alliances that grew out of the doctrine of containment now that the strategic milieu has been transformed? This is the central question underlying this book, and it can now be addressed directly by examining America's alliances in Europe (NATO), Japan, and South Korea.

Whither the Atlantic Alliance? **3**

The march of the Industrial Revolution was both good and bad for the United States. On the one hand, by diffusing technology and capital, it helped transform the United States into a major economic power—one that by the turn of the twentieth century was eclipsing Britain, paving the way for Pax Britannica to be supplanted by Pax Americana. Yet by generating weapons and modes of transportation that extended the reach and lethality of threats and eroded the effectiveness of oceanic barriers, it linked the security of the United States to that of faraway places to an unprecedented degree; this was particularly true of Europe, from whose seemingly incessant wars geography had shielded the United States. It was in this new context that Americans reluctantly reconsidered their attachment to neutrality and entered World War I, even if as an "associated power" and not an ally. Once the Great War was over, however, Americans discarded alliances as if they were strange, ill-fitting clothes and hurried home, only to be drawn back into conflict in 1941 despite the best efforts of the anti-interventionists and the ambivalence of the public in general.

The retreat of 1918 was not possible after World War II. The world had changed utterly. Britain was now a declining power; the Soviet Union, while battered by the war, a rising one. Europe could not once again be left to its own devices, not for altruistic reasons but for ones rooted in Realpolitik. American strategists feared that an abrupt departure by the United States would produce disorder in Europe and tilt the balance of power sharply against America—this supposition was reinforced by British refrains, which, while cast in Wilsonian language, were born of old-fashioned realism. The worry was not necessarily that the Soviet Union would expand through war but that demoralization among Europeans and an increase in the strength of pro-Soviet communist parties would gradually work to Moscow's advantage.[1] This was the logic behind the 1947 Marshall Plan. Western Europe—like Japan— would, it was believed in Washington, eventually recover from the damage sustained during war and reemerge as a center of economic power. Moreover, it was too big a strategic prize to be conceded to Moscow. Eastern Europe was already falling under Moscow's control, and the risks that would follow if the Kremlin made further gains westward were deemed unacceptable. Eventually, Washington would conclude that an American military presence on the Continent—permanent, substantial, visible, and codified by treaty—would reassure Europe, while also serving American interests, by preventing any one power from dominating the Continent and controlling its riches. Such a military guarantee would complement the Marshall Plan by supplementing economic recovery with military security and political reassurance. For its part, Western Europe, weakened by war and overtaken by feelings of vulnerability, welcomed American protection—and not just against Russia. World War II had offered yet another sobering lesson about the perils of runaway German power.

Yet despite the concerns about a power vacuum in Europe and the temptations that circumstance would provide to the Kremlin, the

United States did not proceed blithely to form an alliance that would commit its troops permanently to Europe's defense; and, given the American attitudes toward alliances that I discussed in the last chapter, it would have been surprising had such a precipitous change in policy been undertaken. While a retreat to the homeland was ruled out, other choices were not. Among them was the so-called "dumbbell" strategy suggested by George Kennan, which envisaged a partnership between the United States and an independent European coalition that possessed its own capacity for self-defense. But Kennan's strategy was abandoned, even though the formation of the Brussels Pact and the Western European Union suggested that European unity was gaining momentum; in the end, American policymakers concluded that Europe remained too weak and divided to operate as a separate partner. In the event, the Brussels Pact and the WEU proved precursors to the North Atlantic Treaty Organization (NATO).[2]

These were the circumstances that produced the Atlantic alliance in 1949. Its purpose, as Lord Ismay, NATO's first secretary general, put it memorably, was "keeping the Russians out, the Germans down, and the Americans in." After the Korean War the alliance acquired teeth, but not its own: American military forces were deployed to defend European allies on a permanent basis. George Washington's admonition to eschew entangling alliances and to stay removed from Europe's battles was cast aside. The onset of the cold war, the term coined by journalist Walter Lippmann, slowly displaced popular misgivings about embroilment in Europe that had marked American history since the founding of the Republic. The forces supporting neutrality, which had been so influential in U.S. history for so long, were cast to the sidelines. The stage had been set for a signal change in American politics and grand strategy.

The March of Time

Because the cold war lasted for nearly half a century, most Americans cannot remember a time when the Atlantic alliance was not an essential item in our strategic toolkit or a staple of our foreign policy lexicon. The demise of this familiar institution will hence necessitate major changes in how we think about, and act in, the world. The changes will not be welcomed—or perhaps even acknowledged, until the evidence becomes undeniable—by the experts and bureaucracies specializing in national security and foreign relations. Moreover, the extent to which NATO came to rest on a complex institutional structure merely adds to the inertia inasmuch as the will for persistence intrinsic to bureaucracies and the power of vested interests are built into the system. The theories, prescriptions, reputations, influence, and rewards of the transAtlantic foreign policy mandarins have for decades been based on the earlier, more familiar world. Not surprisingly, ideas for redesigning and reorienting—rather than dismantling—NATO are omnipresent.[3] It's not just the foreign policy establishment that will feel the discomfort of change. The American public will also find it hard to apprehend a world that lacks the familiar signposts, the customary cluster of partners, and even the standard threats. Together, these realities were what made NATO central to American strategy.

Alliances have, however, always been contextual and contingent. Pageantry and proclamations accompany their creation, and permanent interests and eternal principles are invoked with solemnity. Nevertheless, the changes wrought by time's march inevitably corrode institutions, which are ultimately rooted in historical circumstances that are never static. Alliances are no exception: think of the great number that, signed with pomp and splendor, now lie on history's junk pile. Consider, more recently, SEATO and CENTO, which few young Americans have probably heard of—or, if they have, know little about. Recall the American alliance with the Philippines, which gave the United States access to the massive Subic Bay Naval Base, deemed by strategists as pivotal for the U.S. Navy's operations in the Pacific. With the birth of Filipino democracy after the end of Ferdinand Marcos's dictatorship, though, demands for American withdrawal from Subic Bay, regarded by many Filipinos as a colonial holdover, grew and the base was closed. Many think that NATO is immune from such obsolescence. But little in the history of alliances warrants such optimism. NATO may not be on the brink of dissolution, but Kenneth Waltz's quip that while the alliance's days are not numbered, its years are, is on target, and very much in keeping with my argument.[4]

This is a point to keep in mind as the debate about the utility of our cold war partnerships unfolds, as it inevitably will. The process of reevaluation is still at an early stage, indeed barely perceptible, and those who question the logic behind our traditional military commitments and doubt their endurance remain a minority. Some are dismissed as Cassandras who do not appreciate the lofty ideals cementing these partnerships; others as isolationists who cannot understand that the world is too complex for the United States to go it alone; and still others as wooly-headed idealists oblivious to the fact that the world remains a dangerous place and that the American alliance network remains indispensable. The prevailing assessment, confidently voiced, is that NATO and our other pacts, far from withering, will adapt and evolve and acquire new reasons for being. This Pollyannaish view rests principally on faith and is mistaken. When the circumstances that created an alliance vanish, shared practical objectives, far more vital to the health and lifespan of alliances than ethereal sentiments, begin to dissolve slowly, but surely.

Iraq: The Tie That Did Not Bind

The American foreign policy community accepts the obvious, namely, that the strategic context that anchored our system of alliances has changed. What it does not, in the main, concede—because intellectual habits and bureaucratic routines are fertilized by familiarity—is that the new world threatens to make those alliances superfluous. This shift does not stem from the failings of political leadership within these alliances. Rather, it is the product of deeper changes that transcend the comings and goings of presidents, prime ministers, and foreign ministers. Among them are the disappearance of the Soviet Union, the danger that served as NATO's rationale; changes in the balance of power created by the revival of Europe and Japan; the transformation of Europe into a community of comity; and the rise of new threats to the United States (such as terrorism from al-Qaeda or similar groups) that do not emanate from Eurasia and that cannot be thwarted by some latter-day variant of containment.

And yet the propensity to reduce international politics to the virtues and vices of individuals remains strong. Consider, for example, the prevailing explanation for the spat within NATO in the months preceding the 2003 war against Saddam Hussein.[5] American commentaries typically—and American leaders relentlessly—explained it by invoking French contrarianism, personified by President Jacques Chirac, or electoral opportunism, represented by German Chancellor Gerhard Schroeder. Former Defense Secretary Donald Rumsfeld contrasted the spinelessness of France and Germany to the gritty loyalty of NATO's new East European members. President Bush praised the leaders of England, Italy, and Spain for their unflinching support of his Iraq policy and for remaining resolute during the war itself. But in virtually all of these countries, in "new" and "old" Europe, a significant segment of public opinion solidly opposed using war to topple the Iraqi regime. Even in Britain, Tony Blair's shoulder-to-shoulder-with-the-Americans stance did not reflect the sentiments of most Britons, and as the war dragged on it would become his biggest political liability.

The most graphic illustration of this was the outcome of the 2005 British elections. Iraq proved to be a major issue even though the rival Conservative Party had backed Britain's decision to help the United States demolish Saddam Hussein's regime. Blair's Labour Party won the vote, but its decisive advantage in Parliament was cut dramatically—down from a 167-seat majority in the House of Commons after the 2001 election to 66. Labour's share of the popular vote fell to 35.2 percent, the smallest proportion ever.[6] It is impossible to isolate the specific role that Britain's role in Iraq played in shaping the outcome, but Blair himself conceded that it had been a "deeply divisive issue" in the election. Blair's was a historic victory. No other Labour prime minister had won three consecutive terms. The only other leader to have achieved this distinction since the end of World War II was Margaret Thatcher. Yet the theme that dominated post-election analyses in Britain was that Tony Blair had suffered a personal defeat, in large part because of the war in Iraq.

Immediately following the July 2005 terrorist bombings of London's Underground and bus systems, Blair vowed that Britain would not be deflected from its mission in Iraq, and he dismissed claims that the attacks were motivated by Britain's role as chief American deputy in the Iraq campaign. The real question for the future is whether British public opinion, in light of the Iraq experience, will, instead of showing the resolve Blair represented, conclude that the price of participating in American military interventions is simply too high. Certainly Downing Street's claim that the terrorist strikes and the war in Iraq were entirely separate was not shared by Britons, two-thirds of whom believed otherwise.[7]

The Iraq war continued to take a toll on Blair's political standing, and in September 2006, amidst a revolt within the Labour Party, the prime minister announced that he would step down the following summer. Few doubted that the decision had been forced principally by growing opposition to his backing of the Bush administration's war in Iraq, and by then, even Conservative Party leaders were seizing on that issue as a political weapon, much to the consternation of Labour.

Support for the war was weaker still in Spain and Italy. Like Tony Blair, prime ministers José María Aznar and Silvio Berlusconi were swimming against the current of public opinion once the insurgency in Iraq began exacting its toll, defying predictions from Washington that it was crumbling, or in its "last throes" as Vice President Cheney put it in June 2005. The overwhelming majority of Spaniards and Italians soon turned against their countries' participation in the postwar occupation, joining the ranks of their fellow citizens who had condemned the preceding invasion. The strength of this opposition was documented in public opinion polls and demonstrated by protest rallies, but its practical significance became evident when the dangers of maintaining troops in Iraq hit home in graphic ways.

The first to feel the pain was Spain. A string of coordinated bombings targeted Madrid's commuter rail system on March 11, 2004—3/11, as

Spaniards referred to them—killing 192 people and injuring another 1,800. It was the worst terrorist attack in Spanish history. The bombers wanted to show Spaniards that Aznar's fervent support of Bush's invasion and occupation of Iraq and his decision to send Spanish soldiers to help secure that country after the war were endangering their lives; and they did so with cold-eyed opportunism.

Spanish parliamentary elections were set to begin when the attacks occurred. Aznar's conservative Popular Party (PP) and the Socialist Workers' Party (PSOE), a staunch critic of the government's participation in nation building in Iraq, were locked in close competition. The bombers struck three days before the vote, and in all likelihood determined its outcome. The Socialists' victory had hardly been a forgone conclusion; indeed it was not expected. They had (barely) edged out the PP in the 2003 regional and municipal elections, but they then failed to ride the wave of opposition to Spain's role in Iraq and did not garner the votes needed to gain control of major towns and regions. Moreover, prior to the 2004 parliamentary election, Aznar, who had benefited from Spain's impressive economic growth, was in a strong position. But the bombings redefined the political situation. They lodged the Iraq war, and the different positions the two leading parties had adopted toward it, squarely in the minds of Spaniards just as they prepared to vote. Aznar's initial efforts to control the damage by blaming the bombings on the Basque separatist group ETA backfired by making it seem as if he were seeking to deflect attention from Iraq, especially once an official investigation produced a string of evidence tying the attack to radical Islamists with international ties.

The Socialists wasted no time responding to the voters' message. No sooner had they won than the new prime minister, José Luis Zapatero, fulfilled his preelection pledge and announced that the 1,300 Spanish troops stationed in Iraq would be summoned home within a fortnight. Thus Spain, a key member of NATO, and one of only five European NATO members to contribute over a thousand troops to Iraq (the others were Britain, Italy, the Netherlands, and Poland), abruptly exited the allied coalition. The lesson Spaniards took from the bombings was not that George Bush was right in proclaiming that Western democracies must stand together in the war against the common scourge of terrorism, but that it was dangerous to be an American ally. Conservative political commentators in the United States accused Spain of spinelessness and warned that it would only encourage further attacks on itself by caving into terrorism. These warnings cut no ice among Spaniards. They applauded the departure from Iraq.

Like Aznar, Italian Prime Minister Berlusconi had lent unqualified support to the Bush administration's war against and occupation of Iraq. Berlusconi basked in the glow of Bush's approval and expressions of gratitude. In Italy as in Spain, however, the Iraq war had created a large divide between the leader and the led. Most Italians opposed the war from the outset and were not persuaded by Berlusconi's logic that Italy's national interests required deploying its troops in an increasingly unstable, perilous postwar Iraq. The brittleness of Italians' support for their government's policy toward Iraq was shown by a single incident which, while unquestionably tragic, was far less gruesome than the Madrid bombings.

Given Italians' opposition to the Iraq war, the fate of one man was enough to reverse their government's policy. On March 4, 2005, Italian secret service agent Nicola Calipari, who was escorting journalist Giuliana Sgrena out of Iraq after she had been released by her kidnappers, was shot to death by American troops at a checkpoint on the road to Baghdad airport. That Calipari had been the victim of an accident (an American investigation concluded that the troops fired after the car carrying Calipari and Sgrena failed to respond to signals to stop) failed to stanch the outcry in Italy, where the American version of the episode was hotly disputed. Nevertheless, Berlusconi struck a defiant note immediately after the shooting, telling the Italian Senate that the larger context of Calipari's death was Sgrena's kidnapping, itself part of a rash of hostage-takings. Italy, he said, would not succumb to intimidation and blackmail: it would remain in Iraq.[8] Barely two weeks after Calipari's death, however—following street demonstrations and interviews by Sgrena that challenged American accounts of the incident—the prime minister changed course. During a television interview he announced unexpectedly that Italy would withdraw its 3,000 troops in Iraq (the fourth largest contingent after those of the United States, Britain, and South Korea) in stages, starting in September.[9]

Blindsided, the Bush and Blair administrations downplayed the connection between Berlusconi's announcement and Calipari's death, emphasizing the Italian prime minister's caveat that the Italian troop drawdown would be conducted with an eye on the progress being made in training Iraqi forces. That rendition strained credulity. Few believed that Berlusconi's volte-face would have occurred had Calipari not been killed and had Italians not been so opposed to the war. In explaining his decision, Berlusconi himself specifically mentioned public opposition to Italy's military presence in Iraq.[10] Nor could he have forgotten that local elections in Italy were two weeks away and that national elections (which he would lose) were scheduled for 2006. Berlusconi felt compelled to distance himself from the war the more it became clear that success in Iraq was elusive. In October 2005, he claimed that he had tried repeatedly to persuade Bush not to pursue "regime change" by force of arms and that he had never believed that war was the right policy.[11] The withdrawal of Italian troops began on a limited basis at the end of 2005, and in the following January Berlusconi pledged a full withdrawal by year's end.[12] He did not have a chance to fulfill the commitment: Romano Prodi's coalition of parties defeated Berlusconi's in the April 2006 parliamentary elections, and soon after his victory, the new prime minister, a staunch critic of the war, stated that the invasion of Iraq had been unjustified and that all Italian forces would be out of Iraq before the year was up.

It was not just the withdrawals of Spain and Italy that showed that Iraq-like "out-of-area" interventions will not provide a reliable rationale for NATO's continued existence.[13] As the insurgency in Iraq intensified and successive predictions of its imminent demise by senior American officials were undercut by relentless suicide bombings, ambushes, assassinations, kidnappings, and sectarian slayings, other NATO members began leaving Iraq. Norway sent its units home in July 2004, leaving only fifteen troops behind to help train Iraqi personnel. The Dutch withdrew their 1,300 troops in March 2005, following Portugal, which had removed its 127 police units the previous month.

NATO's newest members from East Central Europe ("new Europe," in Defense Secretary Donald Rumsfeld's parlance) proved no more steadfast in the end. Hungary brought its 320 troops home by the end of 2004. Poland wavered as well. Arguably the most pro-American country in Europe, Poland had contributed 1,700 troops to postwar operations in southern Iraq, assuming responsibility for one of the four sectors into which the country had been divided; but Poles became disenchanted with the war. In October 2004, the Polish authorities announced that they would start drawing down forces in January 2005 and complete the process by the end of the year. Unlike what occurred in Spain and Italy, however, the United States received a temporary reprieve following the defeat in the September 2005 election of the ruling leftist Democratic Left Alliance (SLD) and the emergence of a new government formed by the conservative Law and Justice Party (PiS). Yet even Poland's new leaders could not ignore realities, for Poles were by then overwhelmingly opposed to their country's participation in the war. Although Polish troops were not withdrawn on the timetable set by the SLD, it was announced that 900 of them would depart in the spring of 2006 and that the rest would return home by the end of that year.[14] And Bulgaria, another new NATO member, whose force of nearly 500 had operated under Polish command, started pulling out after gaining parliamentary approval in May 2005. (Quite apart from the lack of steadfastness, the troops provided by Central European and Baltic States were few and the number of providers relatively large; this made it impossible to meld them with U.S. forces or to assemble them to create a larger and separate European force. Only Poland's forces were large enough to accomplish much on their own, but they too relied on American support.)

Other European states that had sent troops to Iraq, in part to help turn their aspirations for NATO membership into reality, broke ranks as well.[15] Moldova evacuated its forces in February 2005, but the consequences were minimal inasmuch as they were among the smallest contingents in Iraq. That was not true of Ukraine, whose 1,650 troops served under Polish command. Ironically, Ukraine's decision to leave Iraq was taken after the "Orange Revolution" of late 2004 segued into the election as president of the pro-Western, reform-minded Viktor Yushchenko. American support for the Ukrainian democratic movement that produced Yushchenko's victory made no difference to Ukrainians; nor did the desire to join NATO (which a majority of the Ukrainian public opposes in any event). What mattered was political opposition at home. As 2005 came to a close the defense ministry announced "not a single Ukrainian soldier remains on Iraqi soil."[16]

By the summer of 2005, aside from 8,000 British troops, there remained no substantial NATO contribution to America's nation-building venture in Iraq. Only some 858 continental European troops, from Denmark (which alone accounted for 496), Latvia, the Czech Republic, and Lithuania, stayed on. At its peak the international coalition in Iraq consisted of some thirty-eight countries, and together with the United States, this partnership yielded 300,000 troops. By the spring of 2005, 170,000 soldiers remained, 150,000 of them American. About two-dozen partners remained in the coalition. But Britain aside, the principal ones had left, or were heading for the door.[17] Italy's decision to withdraw its forces basically ended whatever there was by way of a NATO military partnership in Iraq: once the Italians departed, the United States aside, Britain would be the sole NATO member with more than 1,000 troops in Iraq.

The Bush administration stressed time and again that the participation of troops from the NATO allies and various other countries demonstrated that there was an allied "coalition" in Iraq—and that the war was therefore not, contrary to critics' complaints, an act of American unilateralism. But the blunt reality was that the combat capability of a small number of forces from a gaggle of NATO members added precious little to the military might of what had always been, and within three years of the fall of Saddam Hussein had become even more of, an American operation, with Britain serving as a junior partner. Several NATO members did not provide forces for war fighting; for example, the Czech contribution, slightly more than one hundred, consisted largely of medical personnel, while most of the 150-person Norwegian contingent consisted of engineers. Above all, NATO's most significant members either opposed the war from the start (France and Germany) or withdrew when the political costs of staying were seen as excessive. Most people in the world regarded the war as essentially an American campaign attired in a thin veil of multilateralism. The accuracy of this view is evident whether one considers the numbers of troops deployed, lives lost, money spent, or political influence exercised. What the war showed was not NATO's centrality for American policy, but its marginality and disunity.

One Instance, but a Telling One

The split over Iraq is a landmark in the strategic divergence occurring between the United States and some of NATO's essential members. It is also a particular manifestation of a deeper process, not an anomaly stemming from French President Jacques Chirac's craving to emulate Charles de Gaulle, the parochial priorities of former German Chancellor Gerhard Schroeder's pollsters, or a flare-up of Europe's supposed chronic animus toward America. As I have already shown, even in NATO countries that contributed troops to police Iraq, Europeans' commitment to staying in Iraq once the going got rough proved skin deep—a sure sign that they did not believe that their critical interests were at stake. It is not clear that the problem was the process—that the war was essentially decided upon in Washington with NATO being consulted after the fact in a pro forma manner. Consultation is the life-blood of alliances, but it can never ensure joint action and tenacity in the field if allies are divided over the key issues: whether an operation is indeed part of the original mission and whether the dangers invoked to justify it are in fact central to their security. This was the nub of the problem in Iraq and will remain so for other large, distant military interventions that the United States considers necessary but its European allies do not.

NATO's waywardness will not, therefore, cease once Iraq no longer dominates the headlines and airwaves. Nor, contrary to Robert Kagan's claim, does it stem from the incompatibility between European pacifism and American realism and the disparity of power between Europe and the United States (although both conditions do exist), which allegedly breed an amalgam of resentment and envy on the Continent.[18] How could a divergence of planetary proportions ("Americans are from Mars, Europeans are from Venus," in Kagan's catchy phrase) have occurred suddenly, hard on the heels of the Soviet Union's demise, particularly if, as per Kagan, it flows from complex social and cultural trends in Europe? And if Europe's malaise has been long in the making, why did the Atlantic alliance work so well during the cold war—despite periodic discord—for nearly half a century?

If the American campaign that destroyed Saddam Hussein's tyranny reveals anything about the Atlantic alliance, it is this: the disagreements between the United States, NATO's leader, and two of the alliance's principal members, France and Germany, were caused by substantive and substantial differences on how best to address the threats posed by weapons of mass destruction, on the wisdom of preventive war, and on the likely effect of Iraq's occupation on the (already delicate) equilibrium of the Middle East. Furthermore, in much of Western Europe—not just in France and Germany—neither the governments nor the public believed that Saddam's WMD (weapons of mass destruction) program was the clear and present danger the Bush administration insisted it was, or that the links between al-Qaeda and the Iraqi tyrant were as strong and unambiguous. NATO's divisiveness revealed the deep distrust of America's power and motives. Most people on the Continent saw the Bush administration's dire warnings about Saddam's WMD and support of terrorism as a cover for its real goal: regime change. It was not a matter of differing "perceptions" or poor "communication." NATO's dissidents and most European citizens understood the Bush administration's position perfectly. They simply rejected it.

This was no ordinary squabble comparable to the transient tiffs of the cold war over, say, Ostpolitik (West Germany's decision under

Chancellor Willy Brandt to increase cooperation with East Germany) or the function of nuclear arms in NATO's defense. What was remarkable about Iraq, and without precedent in NATO's history, was the public and acrimonious nature of the quarrel. What enabled the brazen challenge to Washington mounted by France, Germany, and others in NATO was a signal change: the end of the Soviet Union and, with it, the cold war. The new world contains a paradox. America's power stands unrivaled, but in the absence of the Soviet Union, Europe is freer than ever before to defy the United States, and will remain so. Risks to Europe's security have seemingly been reduced; so has the indispensability of American protection. Moreover, U.S. efforts to push NATO's European members to acquire additional military power so that they can contribute real muscle will exacerbate disunity within the alliance because any substantial reduction of the gap between America's military power and that of its NATO allies would increase their capacity to resist U.S. leadership.[19]

That Russia and China broke with the United States on Iraq was unsurprising. What was surprising, though, was that key members of NATO did not just break ranks with Washington, they worked hard to derail American policy. Consider some examples. As the momentum for war increased, France, Germany, and Belgium tried to block the transfer to Turkey—a fellow NATO member—of military equipment intended to strengthen its defenses against Iraq and to coax the Turkish parliament into permitting the U.S. Fourth Infantry Division to open a northern front against Saddam from Turkish soil. The bid by American allies to thwart this plan amounted to mutiny given the Bush administration's all-out efforts to win Turkish approval. (And the alliance's inability to agree that an Iraqi attack on Turkey should trigger a collective defense of its fellow NATO member under the terms of Article V of the founding treaty was a testament to the alliance's waywardness.) Once Washington began drafting a second United Nations resolution—later shelved for lack of support in the Security Council—to build international backing for the war against Saddam, there was much speculation about what France and Germany would do. Tellingly, few American observers believed that France would shirk from using its veto, or that Germany, then serving as a nonpermanent member in the Council, would automatically support Washington. Some seasoned observers were convinced that the French would eventually fall in line, realizing that, in Henry Kissinger's words, their obduracy would be "catastrophic" for the alliance. They were proven wrong.[20]

Counterfactual claims are tricky, but France would most likely have opposed the resolution had it been put to a vote and its revolt would have been widely applauded in Germany. A dramatic example of discord that did actually occur was France's warning to NATO's East Central European members, the Baltic states, and Romania and Bulgaria that they were behaving like delinquent children, and Chirac's veiled threat that they might suffer for having backed the United States. This was more than a matter of Chirac's arrogance and ham-handedness (a theme prevalent in American press reports at time). France was in effect fomenting rebellion and challenging Washington's leadership of the Atlantic alliance. True, successive French governments have considered NATO an instrument for achieving American ascendancy in Europe, but Chirac's campaign had few equivalents. So serious was the split over supplying arms to Turkey that a leading French foreign policy expert, and a supporter of American leadership, exclaimed: "Welcome to the end of the Atlantic alliance."[21]

Evidence of a rupture in NATO mounted even after the end of Saddam's regime. Germany and France joined Russia to reaffirm openly their opposition to the war and made no effort to disguise their differences with the United States. France, Germany, and Belgium convened to discuss the creation of a command structure for an independent European force. The triumvirate did state that it was not trying to undermine, let alone supplant, NATO. Moreover, absent British participation and sharp and sustained increases in European defense spending, any continental military force will prove hollow. What such comforting caveats miss, however, is that these acts of dissidence would have been unimaginable during the cold war when the Russian bear was at the door.

The bickering over Iraq was really only one, albeit critically important, episode in what amounts to NATO's slow demise. Key continental European members of NATO had years earlier begun to see the world differently from the way the United States did. In 1998, France's foreign minister, Hubert Vedrine, warned about a world in which the United States acted as a "hyperpower." The assessment was extreme, even by Gaullist standards, but it was not an eccentricity. Other European leaders, including former German Chancellor Helmut Schmidt, a longtime and stolid supporter of the alliance, voiced this same concern in one form or the other. Such views highlight a big change: during the cold war the magnitude of American power reassured Europeans—though hardly all of them, as witness the antinuclear protests—but it now makes them resentful, and they are beginning to bridle under what they see as its unrestrained character. This discomfort about a unipolar world—one in which American power is peerless—runs wide and deep in Europe, and is shared by Russia and China. Hence a striking role reversal: Moscow, long the principal threat to Europe's security, is now a kindred spirit.

Perceptions and Politics

Now, it could be said that the divisions created within NATO by the war in Iraq are transient and that like past instances of discord within the alliance during the cold war—for example, French President Charles De Gaulle's ambivalence toward NATO, American concerns over Germany's Ostpolitik, or public protests against the deployment of American intermediate-range nuclear weapons (despite strong support for this move by the leaders of European NATO) in the 1980s—they will pass, creating no lasting damage and enabling the alliance to persist and to adapt to new challenges by agreeing on new missions.

One line of reasoning that reflects such optimism has it that the resistance to the war against Saddam Hussein within NATO was whipped up by France and Germany and did not, therefore, reflect Europeans' general sentiment. An example is former Defense Secretary Donald

Rumsfeld's disdainful comment that NATO's newest members are un-encumbered by the supposedly reflexive anti-Americanism of Germany and France that surfaced yet again during the Iraq war. The newcomers, in this account, will prevent NATO from succumbing to malaise and will reinvigorate the trans-Atlantic alliance, particularly by insisting on American leadership. Their efforts, furthermore, will be fortified by Britain, Italy, and Spain, all of whom at one point backed the invasion of Iraq and showed their fealty by putting combat troops on the ground.

This is wishful thinking—and not merely because of what the Iraq war has shown about the frailty of NATO's cohesion in a post-Soviet world. The new NATO members from the Baltic states and East Central Europe will never possess the bargaining power within the alliance's European contingent that the major European states wield and will certainly be unable to offset the influence of France and Germany, even in conjunction with Britain. These new members of NATO also belong to the European Union (EU) and, by becoming ever more deeply involved with the workaday issues of the latter organization, will eventually be shaped by European perspectives on international politics which, when it comes to using military power in distant locales, contrast sharply with American attitudes. (European NATO's role in the Balkans and Afghanistan is, as I shall show later, a special case, not a window on the future.) The true motive of the Baltic and East Central states for joining NATO was not to sign up for expeditionary missions involving peacekeeping and nation building beyond Europe, but to safeguard themselves against the possibility of a revived, predatory Russia and a nationalistic Germany, and to ease their passage to the EU.[22] Their contribution to the postwar efforts in Iraq and Afghanistan were in the main minor, and one would be mistaken to assume that it indicates a strong consensus in their societies in favor of joining extra-European military campaigns undertaken by NATO.[23] The goodwill born of gratitude for American moral support during the decades of Soviet domination and the desire to please Washington will, particularly as the perils become evident and unpopular at home, eventually yield to Realpolitik, the true currency of states. NATO's East Central European members are also apt to become disappointed—as Poland was when it expected major concessions on immigration policy from the United States in return for its military contributions in Iraq—if they expect to make large gains by acquiring Washington's goodwill for their military role in Iraq and Afghanistan.

Will the clouds hovering over the EU's political future preserve NATO solidarity by blocking the rise of a Europe solidified by a common foreign and defense policy? Unlikely. True, following the decisive rejection by Dutch and French voters of the proposed EU constitution in the summer 2005 referendums, and opposition to the EU constitution in Britain, Luxembourg, and Sweden, skepticism abounds about whether the EU's plans to move from economic integration toward a unified foreign and defense policy—which are not to the liking of all members in any event—will ever succeed.[24] This pessimism is warranted, but even if Europe remains a collection of states bound together chiefly by economic transactions, it hardly follows that solidarity with the United States or support for the trans-Atlantic military alliance that follows the American lead will result in NATO's acquiescence to an enduring post-cold war mission that extends beyond Europe. Europeans will not be persuaded that this is needed to invigorate the alliance with a new purpose that fortifies its staying power. Quite apart from differences related to the use of force, the social and cultural divide between America and Europe is likely to widen. Consider, for example, the issues of allocating resources between guns and butter or the role of the state in the economy. European expenditure on defense as a proportion of GDP contrasts starkly with American practice. That stems from deep and persistent differences in priorities and in demographic realities and will inevitably produce quarrels over free-riding and will worsen as Europe's population grows even older and creates added pressures to give priority to social programs over military spending.

Strong evidence for the proposition that Europeans' future misgivings about the EU constitution will not translate into benefits for NATO or even greater goodwill toward the United States appears in a survey released in June 2005 by the Pew Research Center. The report, based on

extensive public opinion polling, begins optimistically. Anti-Americanism in Europe, Asia, and the Middle East, it observes, "shows modest
signs of abating" when tracked over the previous five years. On balance,
though, the study found that "the United States remains broadly dis-
liked in most countries surveyed, and opinion of the American people is
not as positive as it once was. The magnitude of America's image problem is such that even popular U.S. policies [such as aid to the 2005
tsunami victims] have done little to repair it."[25]

Particularly relevant for my reading of the future of the trans-
Atlantic alliance is the Pew project's finding that virtually all of America's
NATO allies shared this outlook and that on questions pertinent to
NATO's future and the global role of the United States the negativity runs
across the alliance. Consider popular attitudes toward the United States,
for example. Supporters of Rumsfeld's dichotomy will not be surprised
that only 43 percent of French and 41 percent of German respondents
were positive about the United States, although the notion that anti-
Americanism is simply a part of political life in these two countries is not
supported by the data. A majority of those surveyed in France and Germany had favorable views of the United States. More surprising is that
only 55 percent of those polled in Britain, a country widely seen in
America as a special friend, responded favorably. A similar trend was apparent in NATO states that sent troops to Iraq. The percentages showing
goodwill toward the United States were 45 for the Netherlands, 41 for
Spain, and 62 for Poland, a country that, according to the Rumsfeld
thesis, would be Exhibit A for "new Europe." Moreover, in all European
countries included in the Pew survey, there was a sharp and steady
decline in favorable rating in the years between 1999/2000 and 2005.[26]

The Pew report does suggest that dislike of George Bush and opposition to the American military intervention in Iraq has much to do
with these attitudes; however, there is more to it than that. The evidence
also reveals broader changes—ones that augur ill for NATO. Although
the rejection of the EU constitution in France and the Netherlands has
effectively killed the prospects for a United States of Europe emerging as
a counterweight to the United States, it hardly follows that a by-product

will be perennial European enthusiasm for the trans-Atlantic alliance. As the Pew survey concludes, "there are no signs . . . that Euroskepticism about the EU has fueled a desire for a close trans-Atlantic partnership. On the contrary, most Europeans surveyed want a more independent approach from the U.S. on security and diplomatic affairs. Indeed, opinion of the U.S. continues to be mostly unfavorable among the publics of America's traditional allies."[27] Furthermore, France and Germany, condemned by Washington for their lack of loyalty in the lead-up to the Iraq war, are more popular among Europeans (including Britons and Poles) and Canadians, and in another NATO country, Turkey.

Not only do the NATO states surveyed want reduced political and military cooperation with the United States, they believe it would be a good thing if a counterpoise emerged, ending the unipolar order celebrated by American neoconservatives. The percentage supporting this outcome was as follows: Britain (58), Canada (51), Germany (73), the Netherlands (71), Poland (68), Spain (69), and Turkey (81).[28] On this critical question, then, there is no split between old Europe and new Europe (assuming that Poland can be considered a stand-in for East Central Europe generally) or between states that dispatched troops to Iraq and those that did not. It won't do to blame this enthusiasm for a check on the United States to French anti-Americanism, particularly because the Pew figures show that, in contrast to most countries' numbers, America's standing among the French has actually shown a modest improvement since 2004.

The Pew survey's results also give ground for skepticism about some of the most commonly suggested rationales for NATO, even though the study itself does not explore this question explicitly. The sine qua non for NATO's survival is the conviction of Europeans that an American-led alliance still serves their interests. Yet only a minority from the NATO countries covered by the Pew project opined that the United States took account of their national interests. The nation with the largest proportion that said the United States took account of its national interests was, surprisingly, Germany (38 percent) and the lowest, equally surprisingly given the Rumsfeld hypothesis, was Poland (13 percent).[29] In at least one important instance this assessment translates into diminishing support for NATO: the *New York Times* reported in its September 10, 2006, issue that "Though Turkey has been a staunch NATO member since 1952, only 44 percent of Turks in this year's survey [by the German Marshall Fund of the United States] agreed that NATO was essential for Turkey's security, versus 52 percent in 2005."

Another requirement for NATO's future viability—indeed for that of any alliance—is that its members must agree that they face a common, clear, and present danger. One scenario, already prominent in American discussions on foreign policy, that could engender the requisite solidarity is an ascendant China, particularly if it looks poised to flex its muscles to refashion the world to comport with its status and aspirations as a great power. If China narrows the gap in power between itself and the United States, a coalition may be needed to offset it. In theory, NATO could fill that role. Yet the public in most NATO countries surveyed by Pew responded that it was the United States that required a counterweight. Remarkably, in all NATO countries save Poland, China was also more popular than the United States—and by a large margin. This despite the anxiety Europeans expressed about the threat China's booming economy poses to their standard of living.[30] What is more, the place where the United States will require help if indeed it is faced with a need to check China is Northeast Asia, and it is hard to see how NATO (particularly if it excludes Russia) will make a difference in this part of the world.[31]

An additional common purpose for the alliance invoked frequently by NATO boosters is the war on terrorism. More on this later. What is significant for now is the Pew project's finding that support for the American war on terrorism fell steeply between 2002 and 2005 in most European states.[32] (There was also a universal and sharp fall in the percentage of those who believe that the world is safer with Saddam Hussein out of circulation.[33]) Far from being a unifying force, the amalgam of militant Islam and terrorism, represented by 9/11 and the bomb attacks on the Madrid rail network and London's transportation system, could divide the alliance, particularly if the proffered American remedy for terrorism is military unilateralism and "regime change." It is of course possible, even likely, that the Iraq campaign is not a guide to the future of American strategy but an exception, but that raises the question of what other objectives—ones that require a military alliance as opposed to like-mindedness on various global issues—will unite NATO around a clear mission so that it does not become a forum resembling the Organization for Security and Cooperation in Europe (OSCE), the functions of which are overwhelmingly political.

From Anti-Communism to Anti-Terrorism?

Like harried architects, NATO's champions are hard at work crafting new missions to steady the alliance. These include participation in the war against terrorism, peacekeeping in war-ravaged countries, and the promotion of democracy. Yet not one of these will prove to be NATO's salvation; they will neither evoke the passion nor build the consensus needed to carry the alliance forward. Worse, some of the putative purposes could actually increase discord because Europe will see them as decreasing its security—precisely the opposite of what any alliance is supposed to do. Each of these new job descriptions will also extend NATO beyond Europe. Such ventures—"out-of-area operations"—have typically produced friction, not fellowship, in the alliance. Furthermore, it is not obvious that NATO will have a comparative advantage over other states with which the United States has convergent interests, but not a formal alliance, when it comes to acquiring partners for such missions. Nor is it clear why these missions require a military alliance that commits the United States to defending Europe and stationing thousands of American troops on the Continent when there is no conceivable military threat to Europe.

Still, so that the alternative futures imagined for NATO are not dismissed without fair consideration—as serious proposals by people in the know, they deserve nothing less—I want to consider each in turn.

Let's start with the most common candidate: the war on terrorism. At first blush, this would seem to be the most compelling post-Soviet unifier for NATO. That terrorist attacks launched by militant Islamist groups now pose a grave, perhaps even the primary, threat to the United States and Europe is obvious. The 9/11 attack and the subsequent bombings in Madrid in 2003 and London in 2005 are proof of this terrible truism. Yet terrorism could prove to be the great divider, not the supreme unifier, especially if there is a difference on the critical question of what its roots are, as there is between Europeans and Americans. Americans, in the main, are persuaded by President Bush's view that the terrorist tactics used by extremist Muslim groups have nothing to do with particular American policies, but rather with the American way of life. Seen thus, terrorists target Americans because the United States represents a beacon for secularism, individualism, capitalism, and equality between men and women; terrorism is a war against what America is, not what it does. Bush and other proponents of this interpretation, such as Tony Blair, would extend it to the West generally, in effect validating Samuel Huntington's "clash of civilizations" thesis and its variants.[34]

Europeans are much less persuaded by this account of Islamic terrorism's etiology than Americans are.[35] Certainly, very few Europeans would support the proposition that the killing and maiming of innocents is acceptable, or deny that terrorism threatens democracy's fabric. Nevertheless, there is a difference of perspective about the underlying causes of terrorism. To many Europeans terrorism stems from socioeconomic conditions in the Islamic world and the sense of powerlessness and humiliation and cannot, therefore, be overcome through a "war on terror," which, to them, casts the problem chiefly as a military one.[36] Likewise, Europeans, far more than Americans, are sympathetic to the view that terrorism is a reaction to what the West, the United States in particular, has done, failed to do, or let be done. The idea that the West, by its sheer existence, provokes militant Muslims to blow up subways and buses and to slam airplanes into buildings has less purchase among Europeans than among Americans. Interestingly, many Europeans appear to accept, as if by default, much of what Muslim militants like bin Laden say, although none of what they do, of course. In bin Laden's reading, of course, terrorism, although he would not call it that—for him, the attacks on the West constitute a defense of Islam—is a reaction to specific American policies, some of which Europe has aided.

One of these policies is what many in the Muslim world consider America's near-unconditional support for Israel's policies in the West Bank and Gaza, including its use of force and collective punishment and its continued construction or expansion of settlements, even when peace negotiations, such as the Oslo process of the 1990s, have been in progress. Few Europeans would support bin Laden's one-sided portrayal of Israeli policies, not to mention his true aim, which is not the modification of Israel's policies but the eradication of the Jewish state. That said, the view that American support for Israeli policies is an important source of terrorism is far more prevalent in Europe—and not just among European Muslims—than in the United States, no matter how debatable that contention may be. Europeans would also agree that the maintenance of American military forces in the Arabian Peninsula, home of the holy cities of Mecca and Medina, after the 1990 Gulf War and the invasion and occupation of Iraq stoked terrorism's fires. In this reading, then, policies matter.

These differences are not mere academic ones; they have practical significance. If Europe signs on to a muscular American-led military offensive it will seek cover by pushing for changes in Israeli policies—and not just because Europeans tend to have a different view of the sources of the Arab-Israeli dispute. Muslims in Europe are bitterly critical of Israeli policies and what they see as America's blanket support of them, and access to instant television news has made their outrage even more visceral. This, in turn, means that for European governments there is no separation between policy abroad and politics within.[37] But the United States, not to mention Israel, will not be receptive to European entreaties. The prevailing American appraisal of the sources of terrorism is quite different from that of most Europeans. Moreover, organizations—and not merely those assembled by American Jews—that advocate strong support of Israel are much more influential in America than in Europe. The United States will also continue to hold a virtual monopoly when it comes to arranging future peace negotiations between Palestinians and Israelis because the latter consider European views on Israel to be unfriendly. The upshot is that Europe will have little say on the Israeli-Palestinian problem, certainly not when it comes to the hard choices that both sides will have to make in effecting a political settlement based on swapping land for peace.

Will Europe's continued exposure to terrorism weaken NATO or infuse it with new purpose? One possibility is that terrorism will brace the alliance because its European members conclude that their safety lies in embracing the United States. A second is that they will conclude that their best bet is to get out of harm's way by dissociating themselves from American policies that, in their view, strengthen the variants of Muslim militancy that employ terrorism as the weapon of choice. The latter reaction will not necessarily be confined to continental Europe and could take root in Britain as well. Days after the 2005 London bombings, for example, one British commentator wondered whether the carnage would have occurred had it not been for "Blair's co-dependent love affair and our repellant involvement in Iraq."[38] Another stated that the United States needed to broaden its war against terrorism beyond the current strategy that rests chiefly on the implements of war if Washington hopes "to retain the ability—and moral right—to ask British citizens to die for that strategy."[39] A report that the Royal Institute of International Affairs (RIIA) released soon after the London attacks concluded that Britain's participation in the American war against Iraq and its willingness to become a "pillion passenger" of the United States had exposed it to terrorist attacks by Islamist radicals. Former Foreign Secretary Robin Cook charged shortly before his death that the invasion of Iraq was launched despite intelligence assessments that it would increase terrorism.[40] This assessment was shared by ordinary citizens. One-third of respondents in a poll taken soon after the London bombings said that the war in Iraq had contributed "a lot" to the London bombings, nearly an equal proportion said that it had contributed "a little," and only 28 percent denied any connection.[41] The attacks did not spawn mass demonstrations demanding a withdrawal from Iraq and in this respect the effect was different from what occurred in Spain. Still, it was striking that many Britons were inclined to connect the attack to Britain's participation in the war against Iraq and to observe that they had never faced a massive terrorist strike by radical Islamists prior to enlisting in the American campaign.[42]

A third possibility when it comes to European NATO members' reaction to any upsurge in homegrown terrorism is that some of them will pull away from the United States while others keep the faith. The relevant question for here is who will defect and who will stay. If some or all of the alliance's major powers disengage, the remaining partners will, apart from loyalty, have little to offer by way of military forces suited to supplement American wars in faraway lands. More fundamentally, what is the future of an alliance that repeatedly divides on missions that its leader considers indispensable? An alliance begins to live on borrowed time when its most powerful state asks: "What am I getting out of this arrangement?"

The second and third outcomes are hardly implausible (the attacks against Madrid and the fraying of the coalition in Iraq prove that terrorism can make states change course), and they would doom NATO's prospects for reinventing itself as an antiterrorist alliance, particularly if the United States expects its allies' contribution but engages in consultation that they regard as no more than pro forma and avoids the thoroughgoing sharing of intelligence—something the United States has traditionally been reluctant to do for fear of leaks—needed to foster unity.

But it's not just fear of a terrorist tide from without that could make European members of NATO unwilling to join the United States in using military power to combat terrorism. There is also the risk of a terrorist tide from within. Islamic radicalism and terrorism appeal to certain constituencies within Europe's own Muslim communities. European Muslims are, it must be stressed at the outset, varied in ethnicity and national origin, hailing as they do from the Maghreb, Turkey, South Asia, Africa, and the Balkans. They do not constitute a monolithic bloc. Some are immigrants; others were born in Europe and have assimilated to local culture and feel more bound to their birthplace than that of their parents. Some consider Islam central to their identity and are believers; others do not and are agnostics. Interpretations of Islam vary. There are divisions rooted in class and the degree of education and professional advancement. Nevertheless, there is no denying that militant return-to-roots variants of Islam that condone attacks on civilians have gained adherents in Europe's Muslim communities. That the extremists do not represent mainstream attitudes is irrelevant. The oxygen of terrorist cells is secrecy: infiltration and surveillance are constant dangers, trust and allegiance all important. Terrorism, for these reasons, has never been a mass movement. Fewer is better.

Three facts are germane to assaying the nature and magnitude of Islamic extremism in Europe.[43] The first is that Europe's Muslim population is large in absolute terms. There are barriers and uncertainties that make compiling accurate data difficult. For instance, France does not permit the compilation of official statistics of citizens' religious affiliation; some Muslims live in Europe illegally; many are citizens, others are not. But estimates are that between fifteen and twenty million Muslims live in Europe. They constitute a significant proportion of the population in some NATO countries, but not in others. At the high end are France (between 5 and 10 percent), the Netherlands (4.4 percent), Belgium (4 percent), and Germany (3.7 percent); at the low end are Britain (2.5 percent) and Denmark (2 percent).

The second point is that the population growth rates of European Muslims far exceed those of the rest of the population of the countries in which they live, not a startling fact given that the fertility rate in most European countries is either below or barely above net replacement. The upshot of this second point is that the proportion of Muslims in Europe's population will rise substantially in the next twenty years. Even if many forecasts are wildly implausible, there is no denying that the continent's political, cultural, and social landscape will be vastly different in the decades ahead because of a growing Muslim population. This will be true despite rising opposition to immigration, if the population growth rates of non-Muslim Europeans remain roughly what they are now and the shortage of labor created by their aging brings continued immigration, both legal and illegal. Differences in age structure between Muslim and non-Muslim populations also matter here. In each of the European countries just mentioned, the proportion of Muslims below the age of eighteen far exceeds the corresponding share for non-Muslims; in Belgium, according to one study, "almost thirty-five percent of the Moroccans and Turks, who constitute the largest Muslim groups in the country, are below 18 years old, compared for 18 percent for native Belgians."[44]

Muslims in Europe tend to be concentrated in some of the largest cities—and this is my third point—that are by virtue of sheer size the political and economic nerve centers. Most, moreover, are also poorly integrated into local culture and society, and economically are markedly worse off than the Europeans in whose midst they live. Far from having embraced secularism, many European Muslims (even those who are well-educated and economically successful) remain attached to Islamic religious and cultural values. They are also critical of Western policies in the Muslim world. Moreover, radical Islamist ideologies appeal to the young, whether or not they are citizens of the countries they inhabit.[45] Militant, millenarian renditions of Islam offer them an escape from anomie and underdog status by inculcating pride and identity. Such doctrines also provide an explanation for the barriers that block their own advancement and that account for the unenviable position of a once-glorious Islamic civilization. The 1993 attack on the World Trade Center in New York, 9/11, the 2003 Madrid bombings, and the 2005 terrorist strike against the London Underground reveal a particularly disturbing fact: Muslims who have lived in Europe for many years, or who are citizens of their countries of residence by virtue of naturalization and even birth, were participants in the atrocities, whether as planners or perpetrators.

The point here is assuredly not that most of Europe's Muslims are drawn to violence unleashed in the name of Islam, let alone that they carry out or even condone terrorism. They do not and indeed they stand to lose much from xenophobic backlashes fueled by outrage over terrorist attacks. The fact remains, though, that a minority of Europe's Muslims has served as a recruiting ground for transnational organizations like al-Qaeda, which see terrorism as a legitimate weapon against what they believe is a Western, American-led campaign against Islam.

Given these realities, if NATO joins or aids American military operations in the Islamic world, Europe's own Muslim population could be radicalized, creating the specter of homegrown terrorism, which will prove even harder to suppress than its foreign counterpart. The evident danger is a partnership between radical Islamists based in Muslim countries and their counterparts within Europe dedicated to unleashing terrorist strikes in major European cities. A less evident danger is that Europe's multicultural societies could begin to fray as religious conflict and xenophobic and quasi-fascist groups gain sustenance from an edgy public. That, in turn, would radicalize Muslims by underscoring their vulnerability, the more so if nativist anti-immigrant movements and parties (the British National Front, and others, such as those led by Jorg Haider, Jean-Marie Le Pen, or the late Pim Fortuyn) move from the political fringe into the mainstream.

The bottom line: the American war on terrorism, insofar as it comes to have a sharp military edge, will not unite the trans-Atlantic alliance by serving as the new post-Soviet glue. Its principal effect may be to promote discord instead of concord. Iraq, even insofar as Britain is concerned, may prove to be an exception, not a harbinger.

None of this changes a basic fact: terrorism presents a substantial threat to America and Europe (but to many other parts of the world as well). Ironically, the danger has been made more potent by globalization, in the spread of which the West has played a signal part. Globalization offers terrorists multiple pathways that they use to recruit operatives, disseminate their ideology, send coded message, make demands, distribute money, and penetrate increasingly porous borders.[46] The irony is that the democracy and capitalism that are the sources of Europe's and America's liberty and prosperity and the essential preconditions of globalization bring vulnerabilities too.

The members of NATO can do much under these conditions to reduce their exposure, including sharing and coordinating intelligence, monitoring the worldwide flow of money and banking transactions, and creating forums and procedures to deepen collaboration between European and American immigration and police agencies. These measures must not be ad hoc and momentary, but rather long-term, purposeful, and based on institutions. But while such cooperation is essential, there is no reason to confine it to NATO and many sound reasons to extend it to encompass countries outside North America and Europe that also face the scourge of terrorism: to limit the geographic scope of antiterrorism operations would be to hobble them. Terrorism, courtesy of globalization, is a global enterprise. Combating it requires a capacious and many-sided multilateralism that, while using military power, employs many other means besides that are more important than raw force.

NATO's institutions and capabilities and its long-standing and well-honed practices of intelligence sharing and policy coordination will be essential to a wider effort, but to be truly effective they must be supplemented with the cooperation and expertise of countries outside Europe and North America who have learned to fight terrorism, having long experienced its ravages. But the creation of an antiterrorist organization with a wider membership will transcend NATO, not reshape and reorient it. What is more, the United States will also benefit from forging bilateral relationships with states that are vital for monitoring and disrupting terrorist networks and apprehending their members, and that may prove more important in the fight against terrorism than NATO. The 2005 joint framework on defense cooperation signed between India and the United States, which lists cooperation against terrorism as a central goal, is an example of what could become a typical practice.

Good Global Citizen?

NATO could also remake itself by rethinking its traditional military conception of security and its focus on Europe by concentrating on combating problems that contribute to instability and violence in other parts of the world. Three examples come to mind. First, the alliance could devise a comprehensive and long-term agenda to alleviate poverty, focusing on countries in which the basic necessities for any semblance of a normal life are absent. A second possible future mission is intervention to stop gross violation of human rights, such as genocide or large-scale and systematic ethnic cleansing (Rwanda and Darfur come to mind). This would be of obvious relevance to a world where the death toll from violence within states far exceeds the tally from violence among them. A third example is peacekeeping, possibly even counterinsurgency operations, in non-European countries, such as Afghanistan and Iraq.

Variants of the first of these missions—tackling poverty—have been suggested by some advocates of NATO's reorientation, and the alliance certainly has much to offer in this realm.[47] Together, its members account for the largest concentration of wealth and technological resources in the history of humanity. This gives NATO states plentiful resources—and not merely financial—to help control the HIV/AIDS epidemic in the world's poorest regions and to assist in providing basic human needs (clean water, medicines and primary healthcare, electricity, nutrition, shelter, and elementary schooling) to the planet's poorest places. NATO countries now individually devote less (and several, much less) than 1 percent of the value of their annual economic output to developmental assistance; and, for the most part, what they provide is not targeted on providing prosaic necessities to the world's most destitute. NATO's members can do much more, and with minimal sacrifice, guided by an intelligent division of labor and a clear underlying principle. In addition to providing financial resources, NATO could also deploy its expertise to launch and sustain programs on the ground that promote education, nutrition, and health. A plan for helping the one-third of humanity who survive (barely) on less than a dollar a day has been already been proposed by Columbia University economist Jeffrey Sachs and former UN Secretary General Kofi Annan. It combines morality and self-interest; the logic is that the planet's poor will receive much-needed help, while wealthy countries will gain from a more stable world and the emergence of additional markets for their exports.[48] To succeed, such efforts must be sustained, incorporate a sensible division of labor among the participants, and receive adequate funding; NATO's members have what it takes to create each of these preconditions.

This would be a worthy project, and one that would present security in a refreshingly different light. Yet there is no reason to limit it to NATO or to make the alliance the prime mover and financier. There are other pockets of substantial wealth in the world, such as South Korea, Taiwan, oil-producing states, and Japan. A concerted effort to help the wretched of the earth must mobilize resources on a massive scale by creating as large a coalition as possible. In addition to states, it should include international organizations (the World Bank, the International Monetary Fund, the World Health Organization, the World Food Program, and the United Nations Development Program); nongovernmental organizations; and private charities. European participation is crucial, but it is best organized through the European Union, not NATO, which brings with it too much political baggage and also has fewer members than the EU and therefore fewer resources as well. The EU is also better suited to take on economic and social missions than NATO, a military alliance that has no particular strengths in this field that make it a superior mechanism. But even if NATO were to make economic and social advancement its chief mission, it will, while doing much good, also have ceased to be a military alliance.

The second and third missions that NATO could undertake to ensure its relevance in the twenty-first century—humanitarian intervention and peacekeeping and counterinsurgency missions—can be considered in tandem because both require military capabilities. Alas, the problems that will prevent NATO from embracing these missions are readily apparent. Leave aside the thorny problem of whether it is desirable to have a world in which a small collection of states that are unrepresentative of the rest of humanity should decide whether and when the concept of state sovereignty should be set aside. Ignore, as well, the question of whether a defensible, consistent standard for intervention can be devised, even though it is sorely needed given the selectivity with which the world has responded to mass killings.[49] While NATO provided help in transporting troops from African Union states to Darfur, what is striking is that it showed no appetite beyond that to deploy forces that would defend innocents from the killings and unspeakable atrocities committed by the Sudanese government and its murderous proxy, the Janjaweed. Bypass, as well, the vexing question of why only some postconflict states deserve NATO forces to create stability (Afghanistan, Iraq, and Bosnia) but not others (Darfur, Liberia, or Sierra Leone).

Even with these difficult questions set aside, other problems will prevent NATO from taking on humanitarian intervention and peacekeeping and counterinsurgency as its future missions. Aside from the United States, Britain, and France, NATO's other members have but a rudimentary capacity to project power over vast distances and to sustain large forces in the field. The peacekeeping assignments that NATO has accepted so far have spotlighted these weaknesses. They are hardly insurmountable from a technological and financial standpoint: European NATO states have the means to create the air, naval, and logistical capabilities needed to mount protracted missions far from the Continent.

The real problem is that there is little reason to believe that they will do so. The proportion of GNP that most NATO members devote to defense spending is tiny and in all cases substantially smaller than the American effort. Consider some representative examples.[50] Six members of NATO were in the 1.1 percent to 1.4 percent of GNP range (in ascending order, Canada, Spain, Latvia, Germany, Denmark, and Belgium); four were in the 1.5 to 1.9 percent range (the Netherlands, Poland, Hungary, and Lithuania); two devoted between 2 percent and 2.6 percent (the United Kingdom and France). Only Greece and Turkey exceeded 4.5 percent, but their military forces are directed to a significant degree toward each other. The United States' proportion has indeed declined from the cold war range—6 to 10 percent—but the fact that the American economy is about the size of all of Europe's combined makes it a special case: on a ranking of military spending in dollars, the United States allocates more to defense than the next ten countries combined.

Any serious attempt by the European members of NATO to acquire the air- and sealift capabilities, the airborne units, and the light combat divisions to support interventions far afield will require virtually all of them to make substantial changes in their military expenditures.[51] The chances of that happening are slim given that the pattern of defense expenditure has not changed during the sixteen years since the cold war ended. The reality is that building robust military forces remains a low priority for Europeans. One reason for this is their fear of war. This sentiment is often derided by American neoconservatives, but it's worth remembering that the United States has not experienced war on its mainland since 1812 if one counts only foreign invasions, or the mid-nineteenth century if the Civil War is included. Europe, by contrast, was shattered relatively recently (by historical standards), and during the span of a single generation, by two world wars that killed tens of millions of people. And for two hundred years before that it was trapped in a cycle of war as various would-be empire builders (the Hapsburgs, Louis XIV, and Napoleon) sought to subjugate the Continent. Understandably, this violent pattern created a visceral fear of war and a wariness of military might, even though this perspective was enabled by the protection provided by United States during the cold war. This dread of war remains deeply rooted in Europe, and the support for according a greater role to military power is, as a result, shallow at best.

True, steps have been taken in recent years to develop a joint European armed force, starting with the creation of the Franco-German Eurocorps in 1992. Once this project was joined in the following year by Belgium, Spain, and Luxembourg, the force grew to 50,000. After the 1991 Maastricht Treaty, which included among its goals the development of an EU foreign and defense policy, the Eurocorps mutated into the European Rapid Reaction Force (EURRF). It is slated to field a force of 60,000 by 2007 (from an overall pool of 100,000) capable of mobilizing within sixty days and conducting humanitarian, peacekeeping, and peace-making missions for up to one year. Germany, France, and Britain will provide the largest component of the force, but many other NATO members will pitch in as well. So far, so good.

But several uncertainties surround the EURRF—and all of them bear on the future of NATO. It is unclear whether the EU will muster the political unity needed to make the EURRF effective. The French and Dutch rejection in 2005 of the EU's proposed constitution has cast doubt on the prospects for European political integration robust enough to allow the EU to act as one on matters of security, and on the basis of having a separate, effective military arm. There is, in addition, significant disagreement within the EU about the goals of EURRF. The French see it as a means to make Europe more independent of the United States and NATO. Britain envisions it as a supplement to NATO that will reduce the imbalance between American and European capabilities within the alliance and create greater equity. Finally, based on past practice there is little reason to expect that the members of the new force will invest the resources required to provide it with truly effective air- and sealift capabilities.

The jury remains out on whether America's NATO allies are truly serious about creating an effective military force that rests on a sensible division of labor, minimizes duplication, and maximizes the "interoperability" of armaments. Even an optimist must concede that there is a long road ahead. Moreover, the armies of European NATO were configured and trained to fight an armored war against the Warsaw Pact nations. Although that goal is no longer relevant, there is precious little evidence that European forces are being revamped for a different mission. Nor are large increases in Europe's military spending probable given its aging population (which will reduce the tax base while also requiring added expenditures for pensions and medical care) and the political pressure its governments already face to preserve as much of the traditional social welfare state as possible.[52]

The United States, joined by Britain and France, will continue bearing the burden of maintaining forces suited to projecting military power, and the American military will exceed the capabilities of even the British and the French by a massive margin. Under the best of conditions, then, what will emerge is a European force that depends heavily on American military power and that is ill-suited to independent missions beyond the Continent. This is the critical point missed by those who, in an effort to argue for NATO's continuing relevance, claim that by the end of 2006 it will possess "25,000 rapid reaction forces capable of intervening anywhere in the world within five days."[53] There is little sign that the alliance is acquiring the means to do anything of the sort.

But as America's population ages, the claims on its own budget will mount. At that point, what amounts to a one-sided arrangement will be unsustainable politically, if not economically, given that Europe has long since become prosperous and secure. Americans will start to wonder what NATO adds to their security and why its members can do more but will not. Europe's leaders may proclaim NATO's continuing relevance, but some, such a former Spanish Prime Minister José María Aznar, who referred to it as "a zombie organization," and British Defense Minister John Reid, who warned the alliance's European members that they would have to invest the resources needed to increase their military capabilities and not confine themselves to political discussions within the alliance, are certainly aware of the danger and realize that denying it amounts to whistling in the dark.[54]

Despite the role NATO forces have played in Bosnia, Kosovo, Iraq, and Afghanistan, such missions will not become an integral part of the alliance's post–cold war strategy. To begin with, NATO's first ventures into war and peacekeeping, which occurred in Bosnia, demonstrated the weakness of European NATO's power projection capacity and its political disunity. Furthermore, Britain and France, the most important non-U.S. members of the alliance from the military standpoint, dragged their feet on intervention even after the scale of the slaughter was evident to all.[55] (In fairness, it should be said that the United States was hardly keen on intervention, but when it did intervene, it made all the difference.) While most European NATO members strongly supported the intervention to stop the Serbian military offensive in Kosovo, here, too, there was no disguising European NATO's military weakness. One European defense expert noted that "the U.S. mounted roughly 60% of the 38,000 sorties flown and provided two-thirds of the aircraft. . . . European forces could not match American capabilities in surveillance, all-weather precision munitions, and stealth technology, and European units . . . moved slowly and with great difficulty."[56] The result, in the words of a leading expert on contemporary Europe, was that "the Alliance suffered further in the course of the Yugoslav wars, when U.S. generals resented sharing decision-making with European counterparts who were reluctant to take the initiative and could offer little practical support in the field."[57] Or as the American scholar David Calleo put it: "The Europeans were lucky to have their American hegemon, since they themselves were still woefully unprepared for collective military action."[58] This observation remains valid: Europeans have yet to prove that they can conduct a joint military campaign without American involvement.

Political constraints will also limit European NATO's inclination to wage war and keep the peace far from home. The civil wars that shredded Yugoslavia occurred in Europe, and most Europeans believed therefore that the fallout presented a near and real threat. By contrast, the failure of France and Germany to participate in the 2003 Iraq campaign and the serial disengagement of most of the NATO states that did take part in the postwar occupation showed that an American military operation conducted outside Europe was seen very differently. In addition, while the European intervention in Bosnia was authorized by the United Nations, Kosovo was undertaken by the alliance acting on its own, and it was widely criticized, particularly by Russia and China, for precisely this reason. The question for the future is this: will NATO's European members agree to reengineer NATO from an alliance conceived to defend Europe into one that assumes self-anointed responsibilities of military intervention, peacekeeping, and peacemaking beyond the Continent, even as the rest of the world registers its disapproval of an American-led Western posse?[59] Even in the case of the 1991 Gulf War—a clear-cut case of aggression by one state against another—the campaign to evict Iraqi forces from Kuwait was not restricted to NATO; it was a collective security operation sanctioned by the United Nations and included countries outside the Atlantic alliance. Two major Arab states, Egypt and Syria, took part in the fighting; a third, Saudi Arabia, provided vital infrastructure; and several others contributed money.[60] Kosovo and Bosnia, then, were special cases, not previews of NATO's future agenda.

Does Afghanistan prove that NATO can, in fact, act outside Europe in the future and create a new rationale for itself? At first blush, the answer seems to be that it can. In post-Taliban Afghanistan, some 10,000 troops from thirty-five countries constituted an International Security Assistance Force (ISAF), with over 7,000 of them provided by the twenty-six non-U.S. members of NATO.[61] From its initial deployment in December 2001 until August 2003, ISAF was responsible for keeping the tenuous peace and helping the reconstruction effort, and the early ISAF deployments were restricted to Kabul and its environs. But in October 2003 the UN Security Council authorized operations with a wider reach, and ISAF units, which by then had been placed under NATO command, were sent to Afghanistan's northern provinces, and in 2005 to the western regions of Herat and Farah.[62] Despite the enlarged radius of ISAF's operations, however, strictly speaking, the mission's UN mandate was to help stabilize Afghanistan so that economic reconstruction could proceed. ISAF's Provincial Reconstruction Teams (PRTs) were deployed to fulfill this specific function, not to fight a war, and they remained far removed from the thick of the battles against Taliban remnants in the south and east of Afghanistan. There, some 19,000 American forces did the heavy lifting. Nor, even in its safer regions of responsibility, did ISAF attempt to take down Afghan warlords and their independent armies. As an Italian officer based in the western city of Herat commented, "Our military component is just for self-protection—it's a very, very, very light presence."[63]

This pattern started to change during the fall of 2005. ISAF's numbers had already been increased to provide security during the September 2005 central and local parliamentary elections in Afghanistan. Then NATO's secretary general announced that its strength would be increased even further and that its units would start operating in the southern regions, the focal points of the Taliban's insurgency.[64] By the fall of 2006, the ISAF contained some 20,000 troops; more important, some were deployed for counterinsurgency missions in the southern provinces (the focal point of attacks by the Taliban) and were placed under NATO command, some American units included. This shift enabled U.S. forces in Afghanistan to be cut by some 3,000 and for those that remained to focus principally on search-and-destroy operations against al–Qaeda remnants and Taliban fighters in the east of the country.

But the importance of this change must not be exaggerated. It was possible only after overcoming dogged resistance from France and Germany, who were adamant that ISAF limit itself to the original mission and avoid any counterinsurgency responsibilities.[65] Moreover, the combat troops deployed to the south came principally from three NATO countries: Britain, Canada, and the Netherlands. Furthermore, although this would change, at least in the initial stages even they seemed to hold differing views of their mission: Canadian officers saw it as a counterinsurgency mission; the British and Dutch, for their part, defined it as providing security to help economic reconstruction and training Afghan soldiers—not fighting insurgents.[66]

European NATO's military weaknesses, the unevenness of enthusiasm within the alliance for assuming tough combat missions in Afghanistan, and the variation in ISAF armies' rules of engagement, threaten to become serious obstacles to fighting an effective war should a full-blown insurgency similar to Iraq's emerge. This is particularly true given that, Britain aside, the allies able to contribute the most to the extended mission—France, Germany, Italy, and Spain—are precisely the ones holding back. As the *Economist* observed tartly: "In theory, ISAF's advance south should lead to the merging of the two forces [U.S. and NATO] in Afghanistan. But with most European NATO members still unwilling to fight, America will keep charge of the rough stuff even if its troops are melded into ISAF. Whether the merger happens . . . may depend on how many NATO troops in the south the Taliban manage to kill in the interim."[67] The risks of that happening seemed considerable by 2006, as the Taliban's insurgency became more potent and lethal and

NATO's death toll mounted. By then the insurgents were demonstrating increasing prowess, moving beyond sporadic hit-and-run tactics to sustained operations, suicide bombings, and, most impressively, the capture of entire towns, such as Lashkar Gah, capital of the southern province of Helmand. With his troops under severe strain from the frequent operations, the British general commanding NATO forces in the south appealed to the alliance for additional troops in September and was joined by NATO's supreme commander in voicing frustration over the tepid response. Quite apart from their militaries' lack of capabilities to fight a fearsome foe in a hazardous environment, the leaders of the Atlantic alliance understood the deep public opposition in their countries to sending troops to fight the Taliban in its southern stronghold and the risk that full-blooded support for the American war in Afghanistan would expose their countries to terrorist attacks. In all, Afghanistan, the first major ground campaign in NATO's history, revealed more about its members' military weakness and political disunity that their resolve, power, and cohesion.

NATO's presence in Afghanistan does not foreshadow the future. ISAF was enabled by special conditions. To begin with, it was not solely a NATO operation; although the alliance has supplied the bulk of the troops, the forces of thirty-seven states participated—a point that itself raises the question of whether NATO per se offers special advantages for such missions. The ISAF deployment was carried out under Article VII of the UN Charter and was authorized by four separate UN Security Council resolutions (1386, 1413, 1444, and 1510). It was, in this respect, fundamentally different from Kosovo and the 2003 war against, and subsequent occupation of, Iraq. The legitimacy conferred by the UN mandate (which, incidentally, cannot be assumed for future missions, not least because Russia and China are unlikely to support such operations) was critical for gaining political support in Europe for ISAF's Afghan venture. Even then, the increase from the initial deployment of 5,300 ISAF troops in 2001 to almost four times as many by the fall of 2006 did not come easily. Pressure from Washington was necessary to overcome the reluctance of America's European NATO allies, whose citizens were fearful of wading into a quagmire.[68] A protracted war that involves mounting NATO casualties and comes to resemble the quagmire in Iraq could generate public opposition within Europe and make the alliance's extra-European peacekeeping career short lived. It should also be kept in mind that NATO forces entered Afghanistan after al-Qaeda, which had ensconced itself there, directed a major assault on the United States. These extraordinary circumstances made it much easier for the leaders of the alliance to win public support for participating in ISAF's mission. Seen thus, NATO's deployment in Afghanistan may be the exception, not the norm.

The alliance has certainly played a significant part in peacekeeping operations in the Balkans and Afghanistan. European NATO has provided the majority of the troops attached to the thirty-four-nation peacekeeping force in Kosovo, thus allowing a substantial reduction in the American military presence there. And K-FOR, the multilateral force deployed in Kosovo in 1999, was placed under the command of Eurocorps in 2000. In Bosnia, EUFOR, or European Union Force, took over responsibility for peacekeeping from NATO-led SFOR (Stabilization Force) in 2004. Even before that, European troops (including those from non-NATO states) substantially exceeded American forces in Bosnia, although an American-dominated war set the stage for peacekeeping. America's NATO partners have also deployed about as many soldiers in Afghanistan as the United States has, and they have contributed more money to the country's reconstruction. Still, as Robert Cooper has observed, very little has changed; in each of these regions, the result of Europe's military weaknesses is that "the key decisions are taken in Washington and the real muscle when it comes to security is American."[69]

Moreover, apart from Afghanistan, these military missions have been in Europe, and all of them, ISAF's included, have been conducted with the United Nations' blessing. They do not, therefore, tell us much about whether NATO's European states will agree to military missions that are undertaken outside Europe and without the United Nations' authorization. Indeed, the alliance's record after the cold war leaves no doubt, as even believers in NATO's adaptability and continuing importance concede, that its European members are loath to move from continental missions to more ambitious ones elsewhere.[70] Europeans regard the latter as beyond the purview of Article V of NATO's charter, which defines the alliance's self-defense mission as a continental one; and they refuse to accept wider obligations on an automatic basis. To the contrary, they insist on the right to say yea or nay based on individual calculations of national interests and, in sharp contrast to the United States, require that military missions outside NATO's traditional geographic domain (Western Europe) gain UN authorization beforehand. They are, in short, determined that the alliance's 1999 military campaign to halt the Serbian military's assault on Kosovo not be a precedent. When it comes to assuming grander responsibilities, then, NATO is less an alliance than a disparate, disunited assemblage.

Peacekeeping missions in the Balkans and Afghanistan do not provide a model for NATO's reinvention for still other reasons. Peacekeeping is inherently a pallid, uninspiring replacement for the old mission of protecting home and hearth against the mighty military machine of the Warsaw Pact. Moreover, the formula offered by some American strategists, according to which the United States fights the wars while its NATO allies keep the ensuing peace, will not appeal to Europeans, for it allots them the longer, messier, and inglorious part of a deal in which "America does the cooking; Europe does the washing up."[71] As a European defense expert has put it, employing a similar metaphor: "To be cast in the role of sweeper up after America is not an enticing prospect." He goes on to add that "without addressing the shortfall in military capability, EU members will find themselves less and less able to operate individually or collectively to support their common interests. Nor will they have a strong voice in where and how future operations are conducted."[72] Stated differently, short of defying expectations and transforming its military capabilities, NATO will become tangential to American national security interests.

What Have You Done for Me Lately?

A continuing imbalance in military spending between the United States and its NATO allies is bound to make Americans particularly impatient about what many already consider ungrateful European moralizing. The argument that Europe could not spend much on guns because of its serious need for butter was persuasive in the years immediately following World War II; but it has long since ceased to be. European NATO's defense spending policies are a matter of politics, not economics; they reflect the lack of will, not the lack of capacity. Europe's population exceeds America's, as does its combined GNP. The European Union is now a robust rival of the United States in global markets. American tolerance for Europe's unwillingness to spend more on defense will accordingly wear thin, not least because important missions undertaken by the American military, such as ensuring the unhampered flow of oil from the Persian Gulf, are no less consequential for Europe—and arguably more so given Europeans' greater reliance on Middle Eastern petroleum—than for the United States. If the United States continues spending more than the rest of its NATO allies put together while European NATO members devote a substantially smaller fraction of their resources to defense and, worse, insist on maintaining or even reducing the proportion, Americans will balk at the free riding. And they will not be mollified by the argument that European states contribute to security in other ways, such as by allocating a larger share of their national wealth for assistance to the world's poor.

Europeans, for their part, will resent what they see as an American habit of defining solidarity as reflexive agreement. And if the United States decides, as a matter of policy, to threaten and punish allies who have the temerity to dissent, NATO will be less an alliance than a bad marriage. Changes in the leadership of European NATO members (the departure of a Chirac or a Schroeder), redefinitions of NATO's objectives, and the fear of America's wrath will not banish the basic problem, which is that an alliance that succeeded so magnificently cannot long survive the disappearance of the strategic conditions that enabled its magnificent success. NATO may remain in form for a number of years, but long before that it will, slowly but surely, cease to matter in substance.

This may seem an odd verdict when NATO has been expanding—apparently proving its continuing relevance. Once an alliance of sixteen states in 1991, NATO added the Czech Republic, Hungary, and Poland in 1997, and, pursuant to a decision taken in November 2002, admitted seven other states: the three Baltic republics (Estonia, Latvia, and Lithuania), and Slovakia, Slovenia, Romania, and Bulgaria. Furthermore, more than two dozen states have joined the alliance's Partnership for Peace (PfP) program, which they see—perhaps with undue optimism—as a segue to full membership. Yet expansion—from sixteen members at its peak during the cold war to twenty-six by 2005—promises to make NATO less coherent without making it much more powerful.[73] The admission of so many new members with such diverse backgrounds will make decision making, which NATO's unanimity rule already makes cumbersome, even more complicated. Nor will the states of East Central Europe, the Baltic region, and the Balkans appreciably increase European NATO's general military might, or reduce its specific deficiencies, such as an anemic power projection capability. And as I argued earlier, the admission of "new Europe" will not be the magic potion that ensures NATO's future enthusiasm for American-inspired missions beyond the Continent.

What does NATO do for American security now that the cold war is over? The question does not have a clear answer any longer. Despite the demise of the Soviet Union, the alliance still ties down tens of thousands of American troops even though the major threats now confronting the United States lie beyond Europe. Yet missions outside the Continent will occupy most of America's attention and power in the twenty-first century and will turn on sea power, long-range aircraft, and light forces—precisely the capabilities NATO lacks. These limitations were revealed not just in the Balkans, but also after 9/11. While America's NATO allies invoked Article V of the alliance's charter—and for the first time—in a display of solidarity, the reality was that this amounted to symbolism.

NATO had little to offer by way of firepower in support of the American war against the Taliban regime.[74] As a leading authority on Europe notes, what occurred was a "snubbing of his NATO allies' offer to help" by President Bush, who politely told them that their services were not required.[75] They did assist in less critical ways, for example, by conducting naval surveillance in the Mediterranean to foil terrorist attacks on ships and ports; but even that task involved only a handful of NATO navies, given the pallid capabilities of the others.

The conflicts in Afghanistan and Iraq have put extreme pressure on regular American forces and necessitated an increased reliance on reserve and National Guard units, which soon accounted for one-third of the deployment in Iraq. What sense does it make to maintain large, long-term deployments of armored units in Europe, when there is no identifiable threat there and when European NATO is more than capable of dealing with any threat that could arise?[76] Persisting with the previous (cold war) pattern merely perpetuates Europe's strategic infantilization and misallocates U.S. resources. So long as American power can be relied on to defend them, Europeans will have no reason to develop the forces, to engage in the strategic thinking, or to devote the funds necessary for their own defense, particularly now that Europe has become a community of peace and that war within it is virtually unimaginable, as is war against it.

In NATO's early years, American leaders assured the public that the stationing of American troops in Europe was a temporary measure that was necessary because Europe's means were so meager and the Soviet threat so massive. Over time, they said, Europe should and would develop its own military might so as to reduce its dependence on the United States.[77] That time has long since arrived.

The corollary of my claim that NATO has become irrelevant is not that the United States can (or should) act alone as the all-powerful lord of a unipolar world. Even if it could, such hubris is a surefire recipe for overextension, the loss of legitimacy, and, if history is a guide, the emergence of a countervailing coalition. Nor am I suggesting that Europe and the United States, once allies, will now become antagonists, or will even be estranged from each other. Both will continue to share many common values and interests, among them democracy, thwarting terrorism and nuclear proliferation, arresting environmental degradation, and managing the global economy. Leaders on both sides of the Atlantic will have to identify and build on such convergent interests and contain the damage created by divergent ones so that trans-Atlantic cooperation is sustained. That will necessitate a robust trans-Atlantic partnership based on sound diplomacy, imagination, and wisdom. But it does not require a military pact.

A Japan That Can—and Will—Do More   **4**

If the fate of the North Atlantic Treaty Organization (NATO) is uncertain despite efforts to reshape it for the post–cold war era, this is also true of Japan's military pact with the United States, albeit to a lesser degree. Europeans are comfortable debating what strategies are appropriate in a new world where their dependence on the United States has diminished. Not so the Japanese, who are reticent to contemplate that prospect and seem to believe that by not discussing it, they will keep it at bay. Small wonder, for the American alliance has been the bedrock of their foreign and national security policy and a precondition for their economic triumphs. The alliance has also enabled Japan to play an extensive political and economic role in East Asia because, by containing Japan in the course of protecting it, the United States allays fears in the region—especially in China and Korea—that an activist Japan could metamorphose into an assertive one.

The military pacts that Europe and Japan concluded with the United States differ in other respects as well. Many Europeans were fearful that military decisions taken by NATO under Washington's leadership during the cold war—such as those that led to the American deployment of Intermediate Nuclear Forces (INF) on the Continent in the 1980s—could provoke the Soviet Union and imperil their security by sparking a war they had no part in initiating and little ability to control but that would be fought on their territory. European peace movements were not reassured by the reality that the Atlantic alliance acting in concert, and not the United States acting via fiat, made major military decisions, such as those related to the INF emplacement. Among rank-and-file Europeans, anti-American sentiments manifested themselves in a variety of ways, ranging from cultural condescension to protest marches. Furthermore, European leaders such as Charles de Gaulle, Willy Brandt, and Helmut Schmidt were not shy about questioning American policies, acting independently, or offering the occasional, or in de Gaulle's case intermittent, lecture.

Japan was different—for the most part the docile, grateful ally, its leaders and ordinary citizens much less ambivalent about, let alone critical of, American protection and the ways in which it was provided. De Gaulle-like public critiques of American policies did not fall from the lips of Japan's leaders. (As for the public, there were mass antinuclear protests and rallies against the renewal of the U.S.-Japan security treaty in 1959 and 1960, but overall the attitude toward the United States has remained favorable, and with considerable consistency.) This attitude became so prevalent, ingrained, and institutionalized that the idea that Japan should depend less on the United States never entered mainstream public discourse in Japan, even as the country's capacity to do more to defend itself increased substantially. Japan has seen dependence on the United States as a good deal, economically and strategically, and for the United States, Japan's docility and its willingness to take its cues from Washington were both flattering and convenient. Japan's true worries have centered on the possibility of American disengagement (a case in point is Tokyo's stunned reaction to President Jimmy Carter's announcement that he planned to remove American troops from South Korea), not, in contrast to Europe, with entrapment on account of American recklessness. Public opinion polls and the commentary emanating from Japanese intellectual circles show that America remains popular, a marked contrast from Europe, as we have seen, and from South Korea, as we shall see. Japan has the world's second-largest economy and is a leading producer of cutting-edge technology. But it is content to entrust its security to the United States—and why not? It has been a long, inexpensive, and comfortable ride.

Strange Bedfellows

That there would be such comity and endurance in the partnership between the two countries was hardly obvious in the aftermath of World War II, not least because they had just concluded a pitiless war, one that had ended with the demolition of two Japanese cities by nuclear weapons. When, following the 1951 San Francisco Peace Treaty, they signed the 1954 U.S.-Japan Security Treaty (it was revised to yield the 1960 Mutual Security Treaty, which gave Japan somewhat more control over how U.S. forces would be used, while retaining the substantial extraterritorial rights of the U.S. military), the alliance seemed incongruous, so different were the partners.

The United States had been a democracy for more than one and a half centuries by then, but while Japan had a democratic interlude in the 1920s, it had been a monarchy for most of its history and a society in which obedience trumped accountability, and in which the state evoked reverence, not caution. There were other differences. Civilian control of the military was a bedrock principle of American politics, one consistently applied in practice; by contrast, Japan's armed forces were a formidable and overt political force, particularly in the 1930s and early 1940s. Americans and Europeans have had their spats and instances of mutual suspicion, but the members of NATO were united by multiple historical and cultural bonds as well. Like Europe, America is a cultural and ethnic mosaic and a land of immigrants, the earliest of whom hailed from Europe. Japan was, and remains, very ethnically homogeneous, and immigration is considered a carrier of cultural contamination. The storyline of a melting point was absent in Japanese national discourse when the alliance was formed, and that is no less true today. In addition, there were (and are) divergent views of duty and obligation; in Japan, unlike in America, individualism yields to social obligation.

When the U.S.-Japan alliance was forged, the legacy of rivalry and suspicion, and eventually full-blown war in the Pacific, between both countries was still powerful. It was Commodore Perry's "Black Ships" that (in 1853) pried Japan open to Western influence, and the asymmetry in power that enabled this intrusion was as evident to the Japanese then as it was unwelcome, even though the event spurred Japan's modernizing reforms. Despite interludes of cooperation thereafter, competition and mistrust marked the dealings between the two countries. For instance, Japan resented the failure of the Versailles Peace Treaty—itself emblematic of America's emergence as a major power—to include the principle of racial equality in its text and a U.S. immigration policy that discriminated against Japanese.

The tensions between Japan and the United States were also revealed by the (brief and inept) American intervention in the Russian Far East, which was motivated less by a desire to topple the infant Bolshevik regime in Soviet Russia than by the fear that Japan would use the civil war between the communists and their "White" foes to carve a sphere of influence in the Russian Far East. Likewise, the Japanese understood full well that among the American goals in the negotiations on the Washington Naval Treaty of 1922 was to constrain Japan's sea power by gaining its consent for a ceiling on warships that would lock its navy into an inferior position. That was precisely why Japan withdrew from the agreement in 1934 as it pursued its quest for primacy in East Asia. Less than a decade later came the attack on Pearl Harbor, seen then and now in the American historical narrative as a supreme act of perfidy.

This was not, to say the least, an auspicious backdrop for a military alliance. Yet the passage from animosity to alliance—itself a paradigm shift—is not hard to explain. Japan was a vanquished nation, and the

United States was the victor. That reality gave Washington extraordinary leeway to shape Japan's postwar politics. The American occupation reflected this asymmetry of power and allowed Washington to craft the institutions and agreements that transformed the erstwhile enemy into a dependent, even subservient ally. While the occupation nurtured democracy in Japan, it also guaranteed Japanese dependency. The 1947 constitution designed by General Douglas MacArthur barred Japan's rearmament, thereby placing the country in a vulnerable position. The Soviet ideological and military threat was made worse by the rise of a pro-Soviet (or so it seemed at the time) regime on the Chinese mainland and another on the Korean peninsula, and Japan had few options but to delegate its safety to the very state that had not long ago been its most fearsome foe. In any event, an attempt to close the gap independently would have spooked its neighbors, most of whom had been part of the Japanese empire. In view of these constraints, relying on the United States seemed not just the safe choice, but, realistically, the only practical one.

Given these various differences, it is remarkable that Japan and the United States became allies and have remained partners for over fifty years—and with few significant open disputes, barring the tiffs over trade in the 1980s and 1990s.[1] Indeed, despite the cultural kinship of Europe and the United States, NATO's future is more uncertain than that of the U.S.-Japan alliance (and, as we shall see in the next chapter, of the alliance between the United States and South Korea); while there are cracks beneath the surface, they are fewer and less deep. Nevertheless, the conditions that have supported this mutually suitable arrangement are changing faster than either side is prepared to admit and are chipping away at its foundations.

Export Goods, Import Security

Under the postwar deal with the United States, Japan renounced old-fashioned power politics, the habitual mode of state behavior, and transformed itself into a "trading state" that pursued prosperity pacifically by subcontracting its security to a superpower.[2] The alliance with the United States was a good deal in terms of the guns versus butter equation. Japan was able to brave the hazards of the cold war in a dangerous region while spending on average barely 1 percent of its GNP for military ends. American guardianship had the added advantage of being one-sided: the United States promised to defend the Japanese homeland without any equivalent obligation from its ally, not even in Japan's immediate environs. While Napoleon once scoffed that the British were a nation of shopkeepers, in the main, postwar Japan reconciled itself to this status even though it was at odds with the martial values and samurai spirit that had marked its history. In a rare convergence of views, Japan's leftists and conservatives saw dependence on the United States as a stain on sovereignty; yet few Japanese were troubled by this, except those on the political fringe, such as the ultranationalist writer Yukio Mishima, who took his life in despair over the erosion of Japan's independence.[3]

Fewer than five years after having stripped Japan of its armed forces, American leaders, and especially U.S. commanders in the Pacific, decided that a controlled buildup of Japanese military forces was essential, notwithstanding the fact that Article IX of the 1947 constitution explicitly denied Japan the implements of war. From their standpoint, there were sound reasons for this change in policy. By 1950 the onetime Soviet ally had turned antagonist, and its ambitions seemed to stretch beyond Europe; the Communist Party had taken power in China; and North Korea had launched a war, with Beijing and Moscow's support, to unify the Korean peninsula. American leaders took these realities to mean that the cold war now encompassed Asia, where they faced a nefarious tripartite alignment, and because the United States was by then assuming commitments to protect Europe, they reassessed their policy of demilitarizing Japan.

At first, Japan's leaders were opposed to demilitarization, and this was reflected in the 1946 draft of what, a year later, would become the U.S.-designed constitution, but they eventually submitted to MacArthur's will and a national consensus formed in support of the peace constitution. Once U.S. policy changed in light of cold war exigencies, the Japanese adjusted accordingly. Even before the San Francisco Treaty was signed, and the U.S.-Japan alliance was formalized, the Japanese followed MacArthur's directive to establish a National Police Reserve and to increase the size of the Maritime Safety Agency. They agreed, as well, to permit the continuation of American military bases on Japanese soil and accepted American military contracts that helped revive and boost Japan's industrial and technological capabilities, enabling it as well to produce weaponry that fit U.S. specifications.[4] By 1954, the Japanese Self-Defense Force (JSDF)—with air, naval, and ground units—had emerged, under the direction of the Japanese Defense Agency (JDA).[5] But Shigeru Yoshida—who served as prime minister several times between 1946 and 1954—was reluctant to do more, convinced that an expansion of Japan's military capabilities was ill-advised both from the standpoint of prosperity and security, and invoked Article IX to parry American pressure. This amounted to a curious role reversal: the United States, which not long ago had been engaged in dismantling Japan's military power, was now seeking to increase it; Japan, which had initially been resistant to give that power up completely, was now resisting American entreaties to rearm.

This push-and-resist pattern was not limited to the early postwar years. It would mark the alliance throughout the decades of the cold war and continues to do so today: the United States insisting that Japan assume a larger military role within the context of the alliance; Japan resisting, citing limitations imposed by the constitution and self-imposed policies, and seeking to placate Washington as much as possible by making payouts in cash, whether to reduce the burden of stationing U.S. troops in Japan or to contribute to the costs of waging the 1991 Gulf War.

For the most part this approach has been successful: Japan has relied on American protection, and that, in turn, has limited its military expenditures, enabling it to focus on developing what has long since become a successful export-driven economy. Indeed, by protecting Japan the alliance helped produce what would come to be known as the Japanese economic miracle; so impressive was it that a leading American expert on Japan paid homage with a 1980 book titled (misguidedly as it turned out) *Japan as Number One: Lessons for the United States.* The American security guarantee offered Japan the supreme luxury of inhabiting a rough neighborhood while spending little to defend itself.

The numbers tell the story. In 1982, by which time American awe over Japan's economic advance had been supplanted by anxiety, Japan's military expenditure was a mere .93 percent of its GNP and, on a per capita basis, $91. The equivalents for the United States were 7.2 percent and $938. True, the United States had a worldwide military presence at the time, and Japan did not, but other American allies also devoted substantially greater resources to national defense than Japan did. Canada, for example, allocated 2 percent of its GNP and spent $247 per capita; for France, the corresponding figures were 4.1 percent and $408; for Germany, 4.3 percent and $461; for South Korea, 7.6 percent and $132.[6] More than twenty years later, the basic picture had not changed. A U.S. Defense Department report assessing allied contribution to the combined defense placed Japan's defense spending at barely 1 percent of GNP, placing it next to last in rank.[7] Defenders of Japan downplay this statistic on the grounds that its defense budget is the third or fourth (the order varies by year) largest in the world. That is true, but what counts is the degree of effort, which is an index of priority, and the below-one-percent reality is revealing in that respect.

While America's military policies helped Japan's economic revival indirectly by reducing the burden of defense, U.S. economic policies did so directly. This was not a matter of American altruism: it stemmed from Washington's assessment during the cold war that a strong Japanese economy would supplement America's wider effort to ensure a favorable balance of power in the North Pacific, and that an economically weak Japan would burden the United States by raising the costs of defending it. This was why the initial plans to break up the *zaibatsu,* Japan's industrial conglomerates, soon after World War II, and to exact reparations were abandoned and why Japanese goods were given access to the American market on a favorable and nonreciprocal basis. (This did not, however, prevent the United States from running a positive trade balance with Japan until the 1970s.)

Even Japan's contribution to the security partnership, tendered in the currency of what has come to be known as "soft power," provided it economic advantages. A case in point is the Japanese strategy of "comprehensive security."[8] This was a formula under which Japan took responsibility for promoting security in Southeast Asia by fostering trade and extending economic aid on the assumption—shared by Washington—that this would promote regional stability and prosperity, thereby countering the appeal of communist movements. As it worked out, this strategy helped diminish the suspicions toward Japan, while also helping it to cultivate what eventually would become a lucrative market for its exports. Japan's trade with, and aid to, Southeast Asia also enabled it to cultivate an economic zone where its companies could establish factories and use cheap Southeast Asian labor to help keep their goods competitive in international markets. The economic value of this approach became particularly evident in the 1980s, once American complaints about the undervalued yen began and protectionist sentiment against "unfair" Japanese exports pervaded the U.S. Congress. "Comprehensive security" reflected Japanese leaders' sincere belief that their country's imperial past precluded Realpolitik in East Asia and that an alternative and unobtrusive way had to be found to supplement America's cold war strategy of containing communism and to advance Japanese interests. No matter. In practice, the policy furthered Japan's export-driven economic growth and offered a hedge against the threat of Western protectionism, while also serving as proof that Japan was doing its part as an ally.

This was hardly a case of Japan snookering Washington. The relationship was—and still remains—what psychologists call a "codependent" one. Japan gained security, to be sure, but benefits accrued to the United States as well, chiefly the access to a network of Japanese military bases, which enabled a massive deployment of American power on the Soviet Union's eastern flank, forcing Moscow to contend with a second front that supplemented NATO and stretched Soviet power. The alliance also codified Japan's subordinate status and averted the rise of what might otherwise, given Japan's immense financial and technological resources, have become an independent and unpredictable center of power in the world, one that might not have been aligned with the United States down the line. Japan's dependence on the United States for so basic a necessity as safety also gave Washington leverage in the economic realm. For instance, it is hard to imagine Japan succumbing to American arm-twisting in the 1980s and agreeing to increase the value of the yen (during the Plaza Accords), to boost domestic demand for American exports by stimulating the economy, and to accept "voluntary" restraints on Japanese automobile exports, had it not been utterly dependent on American power for security.[9] That same dependence, along with threats by the U.S. Congress to impose trade restrictions, prompted Japan in 1991 to increase the contribution it had agreed to make in 1978 to the costs of stationing U.S. forces on its territory. This payment, "host nation support" in Washington's delicate parlance, now amounts to almost $5 billion per year, the largest contribution of any U.S. ally. (That Japanese call this arrangement "omoiyari yosan," or "sympathy budget," makes it clear that from their perspective, the payment is intended to placate Washington.)[10]

One Japan or Many?

The sentiment shared by most Japanese after World War II was that Japan's imperial ambitions had led to a catastrophe and should be abandoned once and for all. So heavy was the price that the Japanese people paid that the prevalence and persistence of this belief are all too understandable. This assessment was shared by Japan's neighbors as well, for they had been on the receiving end of Japanese imperialism. The determination to change course and to embrace a near-pacifist policy was reflected in Japan's 1947 constitution, particularly Article IX, which proscribed the creation of a national military. That accounts for why Japan's military is called Self-Defense Forces and why there is no ministry of defense or a minister of defense, but rather a defense agency led by a director general.[11] (In 2006, legislation was introduced in the Diet to elevate the JDA to ministerial status, itself a telling move.)

The creation of the JSDF was itself undertaken gingerly. While Article IX, read literally, seems to prohibit a military of any sort, the San Francisco Treaty and the UN Charter (Japan joined the UN in 1955) both treat self-defense as an inherent right and also recognize the right to participate in collective defense. This was the basis for reconciling the formation of the JSDF in 1954 and the strictures set forth in Article IX. Under the 1954 formula, Japan asserted the right to have the means to protect itself, but it renounced offensive war and took the position that it would be unconstitutional to send the JSDF on missions beyond the homeland. Though Japan has not renounced the right of collective defense as a matter of legal principle, in 1972 the Cabinet Legislative Office, an arm of the prime minister's office, stated that Japan could not exercise it as a matter of policy inasmuch as Article IX prohibits the use of force to settle international disputes.[12] Japan stressed its rejection of *Machtpolitik* in other ways as well. In 1967, it proclaimed the three non-nuclear principles, pledging not to produce or procure nuclear weapons or to allow third parties to station them on its territory; in 1976, it adopted the policy of placing a ceiling of 1 percent of its GDP for defense spending; and in 1967 and 1976, it instituted a ban on the export of weaponry and military technologies.

Policymakers, pundits, and the public within Japan and in countries that have a stake in its foreign policy are happy with these limitations and are united in the belief that the best Japan is a militarily weak Japan that pursues its ends through economic and political means. This consensus and the curbs, whether rooted in the constitution or enunciated as policy, that Japan has placed on its national security policy explain why the overwhelming majority of American and Japanese foreign policy specialists believe that Japan has irrevocably decided on a low-profile national security policy that it will never abandon. Accompanying this assessment is the view that a Japan that is cut adrift from, or that abandons, the U.S. alliance would destabilize Northeast Asia, a region pivotal to the world's prosperity and stability. Even Japan's traditional adversaries—China, North Korea, and Russia—prefer a Japan tethered to the United States and see the alliance as protection against an unconstrained, and therefore potentially militant, Japan. When it comes to wielding military power, then, Japan does not trust itself, and the world does not trust Japan.

Yet the widespread tendency to see Japan as a country so committed to a culture of military minimalism that a change of course is well-nigh impossible is flawed.[13] A deterministic assessment, it neither accounts for what Japan has done, or helps foresee what it might do.

To begin with, there is no historical basis to claim that what Japan is now doing (or not doing) on the military front must necessarily be what it continues to do (or not do) indefinitely. At least since Toyotomi Hideyoshi's invasion of Korea in 1592, there have been sharp twists and turns—or paradigm shifts—in the means and ends of Japan's policy toward the outside world. These changes, often dramatic and not always predictable from preceding patterns, resulted from a synergy between changes in its internal order and its external environment.

During the Tokugawa era (1615–1867), Japan—hermitlike—shunned foreign influences. But following the jolt delivered by Perry's armada it switched course. During the Meiji period (1868–1912) it switched gears and opened itself to the world, casting aside exceptionalism and emulating the West in order to become a front-rank economic and military power. Its success not only enabled it to avoid the fate of the rest of Asia, which had been subjugated or colonized, but to embark on its own quest for empire, starting with the colonization of Korea in 1905. The success of the Meiji strategy made Japan powerful, and when the democratic interlude of the 1920s failed, that power was married to overweening nationalism. The result was yet another change of course: imperialism, a phase that would end in disaster, but began with the creation of the puppet state of Manchukuo in northeastern China. The calamitous consequences of the imperial years set Japan on yet another, and radically different, course, this one marked by the pursuit of commerce and the abandonment of militarism, war, and conquest. This much should be clear from even so brief a survey: the notion that what Japan is today is necessarily a guide to what it will be tomorrow is an ahistorical and essentialist fallacy.

What Paper Tiger?

Japan's military power is already substantial and it has the capacity to make it even more so. While Japan has indeed kept a low military profile in the postwar period, it has not been as quiescent as is commonly believed; nor, contrary to a prevalent perspective, is it militarily a paper tiger. As table 4.1 shows, it is true that Japan's defense expenditure is barely 1 percent of GDP, but because its GDP is the world's second largest, and almost twice the value of France's (which is the fifth largest), its defense budget is surpassed only by the United States and Britain. It allocates a considerably smaller fraction of its GDP to military spending and, given its $4.5 trillion economy, can increase expenditures on defense with barely any sacrifice—an advantage that the other top military spenders do not have anywhere near that degree. Moreover, while the size of the JSDF is small compared with the armed forces of the United States and Russia, it is larger than Britain's forces and not that much smaller than those of France and Germany. By global standards, then, Japan is anything but a military pygmy, and it has the wealth and technological resources to ramp up its military power. It is also considerably better placed in this respect than China—the state Tokyo considers the greatest long-term threat to Japan's security. China's 2005 GDP was $1.7 trillion, considerably smaller than Japan's, and given a population almost ten times larger than Japan, its GDP per capita was a mere $1,293, compared with $36,598 for Japan.[14] The comparative potential of the two putative adversaries when it comes to mobilizing military power weighs heavily in favor of Japan in all key indices, save population size.

In addition to the military capacity it currently has and the options available for the future, Japan has taken important steps that are not easily reconcilable with the peace constitution, showing that its military policy and thinking have not been static.[15] Article IX of the constitution stipulates unequivocally that "land, sea, and air forces, as well as other war potential, will never be maintained,"[16] but no sooner was this blanket renunciation of military power proclaimed than it was circumvented as a result of U.S. pressure and justified—as we have seen—on

Table 4.1 Defense Spending and Size of Armed Forces

Country	GDP (trillion 2004$)	Defense Spending (billion 2005$)	Defense Spending (% GDP)	Active Duty Forces (thousands)
Japan	4.5	44.7	0.98	239,900
Britain	2.1	51.1	2.39	205,890
France	2.0	41.6	2.60	254,895
Germany	2.6	30.2	1.45	284,500
Russia	1.4	18.8	2.60	1,030,000
U.S.	11.7	485.0	3.51	1,400,000

Sources: U.S. Department of Defense, *2004 Statistical Compendium on Allied Contributions to the Common Defense*, http://www.defenselink.mil/pubs/allied_contrib2004/allied2004.pdf; International Institute for Strategic Studies (IISS), *Military Balance*, 2005–2006 (London: Routledge, 2006); GlobalSecurity.org, *Russian Military Spending*, http://www.globalsecurity.org/military/world/russia/mo-budget.htm.

Note: The figure available for Russian military spending as a percentage of GDP is provided as a range (2.6–2.7), of which I have chosen the lower end.

the grounds that all countries possess an inherent right to self-defense and that Japan's was specified in the San Francisco Treaty. This paved the way for the creation, in 1954, of the JSDF, a force that is larger and more powerful than Japan's pacific reputation would suggest. Not only is the Japanese military sizeable by global standards (as I have noted already), it has been modernized over the years and is now an advanced force with certain robust capabilities, many acquired from the United States. Always eager to keep the American alliance healthy by soothing chronic American irritation over Japanese trade surpluses, Japan's governments have sought to mollify the U.S. Congress by purchasing significant amounts of U.S.-made weaponry, which has increased the JSDF's power and reach.

A quick survey of the naval and air components of the JSDF (the JSDF is weak when it comes to land warfare) makes this apparent.

Despite its limitations for waging offensive operations far from home, Japan's navy is among the world's best. It features forty-four destroyers (a number of them equipped with the U.S.-built AEGIS defense system that is capable of tracking multiple threats), nine frigates, sixteen submarines, four amphibious ships, thirty-one vessels designed for mine warfare and countermeasures, 100 American P-3C *Orion* antisubmarine (ASW) aircraft, eighty combat aircraft, and 155 helicopters (including 88 Sea King and Sea Hawk models configured for ASW). It is a modern, technologically advanced fleet, and steps have been taken to make it even more effective.

For instance, while Japan does not have aircraft carriers, and despite occasional discussions (obsessively catalogued by the Chinese who are exquisitely sensitive to signs of a Japanese military buildup) is unlikely to build them, its fleet has acquired, and relatively recently, considerable capabilities for distant operations. The three *Osumi*-class amphibious support ships exemplify this point: although they are small vessels, their decks can accommodate helicopters, and perhaps even vertical takeoff and landing (VSTOL) jets. Additional ships of this class are being built and plans are also afoot to build a new and bigger class. These acquisitions will address one of the navy's major, long-standing weaknesses problems: the inability to undertake naval missions that require effective sea-based air support. Similarly, Japan's submarine fleet (which, incidentally, was one of the world's largest and most capable during World War II[17]) is also being expanded, and future models will incorporate technologies such as "air-independent propulsion (AIP)," which increases the time that diesel-electric submarines can stay submerged and on station.[18]

The Japanese air force (which has, among other assets, three hundred modern fighter jets, thirty long-range transport planes, and ten airborne early warning aircraft) is also formidable, and its capabilities and repertoire of missions have been expanded significantly and steadily.[19] The F-15 jets, purchased from the United States and also built locally under license, are a case in point. Plans to equip them with aerial refueling capabilities have gone forward and were launched by the 2002 fiscal year budget, which appropriated funds for the first of four aerial refueling tankers that will extend their reach. This is more than a technical change: it crosses a sensitive political threshold by giving Japan a capability that East Asian states, particularly China, have long regarded as a marker of its military ambitions and intentions.

Japan not only has a significant military machine already, thanks to its cutting-edge technological network, it can also field new weapons far more advanced than those of its rivals, China and North Korea, whose economy is a byword for failure. With deliberate and long-standing encouragement from the government, Japan's industrial conglomerates and advanced complex of defense industries devote considerable resources to military-relevant research and development (R&D), and the R&D of Japan's other industries also routinely yield military applications.[20] This capacity to harness science and technology to military power is supplemented by a bureaucratic-political commitment. Groups within the Japanese Defense Agency (JDA), the JSDF, the powerful Ministry of Economy Trade and Industry (METI), and the Liberal Democratic Party (which has ruled for virtually the entire postwar era) have long served as powerful advocates for expanding defense production.[21] No doubt, the policy banning the freewheeling sale of arms abroad has made the development of weapons expensive and inefficient by denying defense industries the benefits of "economies of scale." Yet that prohibition resulted from a policy decision, which is by definition subject to change, and the production of new defense technologies and homebuilt armaments could increase significantly were the necessary political decisions made to remove the ban and, more generally, to make military R&D and the manufacture of Japanese weapons a high priority.

Pushing the Envelope

Apart from improvements in military hardware and technology there have been indications of a shift in military discourse. An important one occurred when Japan was forced to confront the possibility that North Korea could acquire nuclear weapons and use its Nodong ballistic missiles—the weapon was test launched in 1993—to deliver them to

Japanese targets in fewer than fifteen minutes. When North Korea tested the even more advanced and longer range *Taepodong* 1 in 1998, the missile flew over Japanese territory, creating a wave of anxiety that coursed through Japan's body politic. In 1999, JDA head Hosei Norota declared that Japan might be forced to resort to preemptive attacks against the new threat. In 2002, Japan's vulnerability increased when North Korea, which was already suspected of trying to build nuclear weapons, intimated that it already had some. Japan reacted by discarding its traditional passivity; on two occasions in 2003, another JDA chief, Shigeru Ishiba, an outspoken advocate for boosting Japan's military prowess, reiterated Norota's position on preemption, adding that Japan should consider purchasing American Tomahawk cruise missiles to acquire the requisite capability.[22] These statements went well beyond anything that had been said publicly by Japan's top defense official. Although Japan did not in fact formally integrate preemption into its military doctrine, or acquire the Tomahawks, the government sought to downplay Ishiba's remarks. Yet when North Korea tested—unsuccessfully as it turned out—a still more advanced version, the Taepodong 2, in July 2006, the possibility of a preemptive attack to protect Japan was raised again, this time by Cabinet Secretary Shinzo Abe, who added that such a response would be consistent with the constitutional right to self-defense.[23]

In fact, Japan's Cabinet Legislation Bureau had decided as far back as the 1950s that preemption was a legal response to a dire and imminent threat.[24] But public pronouncements made by two directors general of the JDA suggesting—in rapid succession—that preemption might have to be integrated into Japan's national security were a different matter altogether. Norota's and Ishiba's words illustrate the distance Japan has traveled since the days of the peace constitution.[25]

Other changes in policy do so as well. For example, despite its nonnuclear principles, Japan essentially ignored the American navy's practice of docking vessels laden with nuclear weapons at Japanese ports during the cold war and also permitted the storage of U.S. nuclear weapons minus their "fissile cores" at bases on the mainland, steadfastly denying all the while reports that it had been fudging the hallowed principles.[26] The 1983 U.S.-Japan accord on sharing Japanese defense technology represented yet another instance of adaptation inasmuch as it set aside the 1976 decision to extend the 1967 ban on arms sales to exports of military technology. That move cleared the way for joint R&D programs. Even though they have resulted in only a dozen or so instances of technology transfer, as a political matter, the shift in policy was significant.[27] Even the ceiling on defense spending was breached in 1987 by Prime Minister Yasuhiro Nakasone, who justified his decision in terms of national security needs, proving the point that attitudes and actions change when the context in which they arose changes. The limit on defense spending represented a policy decision and did not have legal status, but it had acquired a symbolic status, and abandonment was significant for that reason.

More important, Japan has used flexible interpretations of Article IX to allow the JSDF to skirt the prohibition on collective defense and to undertake operations that supplement American military efforts or that enable Japan itself to parry new threats. The JSDF provided maintenance and logistical assistance—but not combat support—to American forces during the Korean and Vietnam wars. Likewise, the Japanese government set aside its policy forswearing collective defense in 1982 when it yielded to pressure from Washington and allowed the JSDF to start defending sea-lanes up to a distance of one thousand miles from its coastlines to supplement the efforts of the U.S. Navy. And in 1992, the Diet authorized JSDF participation in UN peacekeeping operations (in Cambodia), providing that no more than two thousand troops were sent and they were limited to noncombat roles. In 1996, Japan agreed to provide American Pacific forces spare parts and fuel in peacetime and to review the constitutional prohibition against involving Japanese forces in conflicts beyond the homeland. Soon after 9/11, Japan's parliament enacted "anti-terror" legislation allowing the JSDF to provide transportation, supplies, and repair and maintenance services to Indian Ocean–based American naval forces, providing that such support was not extended into combat zones or required the use of military power, or entailed threats to do so. This enabled the Japanese naval vessels to refuel and supply American warships and to provide them with additional air defense by deploying frigates equipped with the AEGIS tracking system. While Japan did not send forces to post-Taliban Afghanistan, it did transport a Thai military construction battalion to the scene.[28] A new threshold was crossed in December 2003 when 550 Japanese troops were dispatched to Iraq and Kuwait for noncombat missions (humanitarian and construction services and delivering supplies by air) once UN Security Council Resolution 1511 authorized a multinational peacekeeping force.[29] This is the context in which the steady stream of discussions about amending Article IX of the constitution—a development that would have been hard to imagine not long ago—should be viewed. Japan is also deploying American-made defenses—the AEGIS system and the SM-3 and Patriot-3 missiles (having already acquired the older Patriot-2)—against ballistic missiles. It is also participating in joint research and development with the United States on regional missile defense, sharing relevant technologies and coordinating command and control networks in the process.

Planning documents, such as the March 2004 report of the Liberal Democratic Party's Defense Policy Subcommittee, the 2005 National Defense Program Outline, and the recommendations of the Council on Security and Defense Capability (a nonofficial group also known as the Araki Commission), show that despite the inevitable political and financial hurdles, military policy will be revised to give the JSDF the means and the mandate, operationally and geographically, to undertake more expansive missions.[30] Americans critical of Japan's slowness in changing its defense policy often dismiss discussions and documents indicating a rethinking of Japanese military policy as NATO ("No action, talk only").[31] This narrow, materialist conception of politics misses an important point. Language does matter in politics. It challenges existing beliefs and practices and often clears the way for new modes of thought and action (hence the significance of the Norota and Ishiba statements), which can become consequential if the strategic environment changes.

Catalysts at Home and Abroad

The changes in Japan's national security policy that I have discussed tend to be explained away in most Western analyses as reluctant Japanese acquiescence to American demands, or as proof that the U.S.-Japan alliance has evolved and strengthened following the cold war, driven by the apprehension that Tokyo and Washington share about China and North Korea. While valid, these interpretations miss another, and for my purposes more important, dynamic at play, which is that Japan's attitude toward national defense, the role of military power, and the alliance is shifting because of changes within Japanese society.

An important change is the slow emergence of a more confident nationalism. Nationalist leaders within Japan have artfully used American demands to do more as a means to weaken traditional political and constitutional strictures that, in their eyes, have limited Japan's freedom of action and prevented it from having a "normal" military. Their long-term aim is to redefine what it is permissible to say and do in the sphere of national security policy so as to prepare the political ground for abandoning Japan's passive defense posture, which they dislike for two reasons. First, they believe that Japan has become so reliant on American protection and so influenced by its neighbors' incessant reminders of its militarist past that it has lost the capacity and confidence to think and act independently on matters of national security. Second, they believe that Japan will become less secure if its safety is contingent on how much the United States is prepared to spend on the American armed forces, where and in what quantity it is prepared to deploy them, and the range of risks it is prepared to run for Japan's sake. The former critique reflects a rising nationalism, which will eventually bring forth a more powerful Japanese military guided by an independent national security strategy that rejects the established arrangement of subcontracting security to another state. While the latter critique reinforces the former, it rests on a more specific, cold-eyed assessment that the American guarantee will erode as the balance of power shifts in China's direction. Discussions about the inevitable change in Japan's strategic circumstances proceed gingerly, but in time they will become commonplace and enter the mainstream because of the realities of power and the emergence of a new breed of Japanese leader.

The calendar guarantees that a young, bolder, more nationalistic generation will move to positions of power in Japan's national security and foreign policy institutions; indeed, that process is already in progress. The passing of the torch is symbolized by the hard-line threesome of JDA chief Shigeru Ishiba, who was born in 1957; Chief Cabinet Secretary Shinzo Abe, three years younger than Ishiba; and Foreign Minister Taro Aso, who was barely five years old when Japan surrendered to the United States following the bombings of Hiroshima and Nagasaki, and is the most hawkish of the three. They represent a cohort that came to adulthood when Japan was already an economic superpower, or was on its way to becoming one; they have either no memory of a weak and vulnerable Japan or barely one. The new generation is entering the political scene at a time when Japan's environment is also being reshaped by China's emergence as a global economic and military power. (North Korea's nuclear and ballistic missile programs represent another threat, but China's rise is far more consequential in the long run.) This confluence between generational change in Japan and the change in the strategic milieu will produce new and bolder thinking relating to military strategy because those steering the ship of state will be less reticent about being nationalistic and more assertive than were their elders. It is in this light that the succession of the 52-year-old Shinzo Abe in September 2006 as Prime Minister over his predecessor Junichiro Koizumi should be seen. Notably, Abe retained the hawkish Taro Aso as his foreign minister.

Japan's future leaders will also find that the new strategic environment affects the alliance. For half a century, Japan has been in the fortunate position of being able to devote a minimal proportion of its wealth to defense spending because America's guarantee of protection was rock solid. That old shield remains in place, but things could change so that it becomes less reliable in Japanese eyes. Consider two possibilities: a narrowing of the gap in military power between China and the United States that increases the risks America would have to run to fulfill its commitment to defend Japan; and a sharp, prolonged deterioration in the U.S.-Japan relationship. Both developments would shatter Japan's long-standing national security strategy; but unlike most countries facing such a predicament, Japan possesses the resources needed to respond by amassing significantly more military power of a high technological caliber. The missing ingredients are the political will and the lack of public support for developing a larger, independent military force, but they could become available if it appears evident that the old policy of relying on Washington has run its course.

The new balance of power in the North Pacific that could result from China's breakneck transformation does not make conflict between Japan and China unavoidable. Yet the Japanese would be foolish—given the troubled history between China and Japan—not to prepare for the possibility that it could. As states typically do when facing a new threat, Japan will have to confront the fact that possessing palpable countervailing power is essential, not just to deter but to secure the bargaining power necessary to deal effectively with an ascendant power on political and economic disputes. The real danger for Japan is that the advances in Chinese military power could reach the point where the United States will be unable to protect it at an acceptable level of risk. But Japan no doubt understands the logic underlying China's Prime Minister Zhou Enlai's remark, made to the Albanian leadership when it asked about the steadfastness of China's support. Zhou responded that "distant water does not quench fire." As China's shadow extends over the North Pacific, Japan's declining confidence in the alliance will force it to develop a Plan B.

But Japan is not waiting; it has begun, albeit slowly, to develop an alternative defense strategy. There are two manifestations of this change. At one level, Japan is expanding defense cooperation with the United States, moving away from military minimalism in the process, but incrementally, given sensitivities at home and abroad. This may be a subtle strategy, but Japan's neighbors—China and Korea in particular—are not oblivious, as witness their shrill reactions. At another level, Japan, as I have shown, is taking steps to strengthen its military capabilities. Its motives for doing so are easily understood: it wants to avoid the predicament of its protector being able to do less precisely when Japan's security requires that it do more. Seen thus, Japan is behaving as states normally have, disproving in the process notions about its uniqueness. For now, both policies are proceeding within the confines of the alliance. Nevertheless, in my estimation, we are observing a paradoxical trend: Japanese policies that suggest the strengthening of the alliance are, in fact, laying the groundwork for its demise.

Crossing the Rubicon

Japan's declining confidence in American protection will also become increasingly evident when it comes to nuclear weapons. The traditional formula that it has relied on for over fifty years—"extended deterrence," courtesy of the American nuclear umbrella—will cease to be reliable once the United States cannot credibly deter nuclear attacks against Japan because the United States is itself vulnerable to Chinese nuclear weapons. Japanese confidence in the United States will be eroded even more if persistent trade disputes—a pattern in U.S.–Japanese relations since at least the 1970s—poison the political atmosphere of the alliance, creating resentment in Japan over American bullying aimed at forcing trade concessions, and evoking charges of Japanese free riding and ingratitude from the United States. To paraphrase Charles de Gaulle, Japanese leaders will then wonder whether Americans will risk Los Angeles to save Tokyo.

The prevailing view is that the horrific legacy of Hiroshima and Nagasaki has created a permanent opposition to nuclear weapons among Japanese so strong that a nuclear-armed Japan is impossible. No doubt, support for developing nuclear weapons is minimal among Japanese. Nor does the Japanese government have a covert nuclear weapons program. To the contrary, Tokyo's antinuclear credentials are impeccable. Japan remains a preeminent proponent of nuclear disarmament; it remains faithful to the Nuclear Non-Proliferation Treaty (NPT), and it allows the International Atomic Energy Commission (IAEA) to conduct stringent inspection of its reactors.[32]

At the same time, since at least 1957, successive Japanese governments have been careful not to rule out the nuclear option. While stipulating that Japan had no plans to go nuclear, several prime ministers— Nobosuke Kishi in 1958, Eisaku Sato in 1967, Masyoshi Ohira in 1979, and Yasuhiro Nakasone in 1984—made the fine but telling, albeit meaningless, distinction that defensive nuclear weapons would not violate the peace constitution. Japanese governments have also commissioned studies to explore the nuclear option, and the Foreign Ministry, the Defense Agency, and various prime ministers have observed that Japan has the capabilities for, and retains the choice of, acquiring nuclear weapons should the need arise. Some Japanese prime ministers and senior officials have even remarked that the Japanese people's aversion to nuclear weapons stems from memories of Hiroshima and Nagasaki that could be dissipated by the passage of time and in the event that hostile nuclear-armed states arise.[33]

In 1967, Prime Minister Eisaku Sato pledged famously that Japan would not make or possess nuclear weapons or allow them into the country, and a parliamentary declaration later that year reaffirmed his promise. The three antinuclear principles are, however, not a commitment codified by legislation or treaty, but a policy more easily subject to change.[34] It's important to be aware of the distinction because senior Japanese officials have suggested quite recently that the policy itself could be reconsidered in light of changing circumstances that expose Japan to nuclear attack. For instance, in May 2002, as concern mounted in Japan over the North Korean nuclear program and the increase in Chinese military capabilities, Shinzo Abe (then deputy chief cabinet secretary) stated that Japan had the right to acquire nuclear weapons providing they were of limited range. Not only was Abe—who is often touted as a likely future prime minister, a post his grandfather once held—not fired, he was promoted to chief cabinet secretary three years later. A month after Abe's statement, his boss, Yasuo Fukuda, followed up, observing that Japan's constitution and the three nonnuclear principles could be amended if needed. These statements were duly applauded by the hawkish governor of Tokyo, Shintaro Ishihara, and Liberal Party leader Ichiro Ozawa.[35] Ozawa repeated himself in the same year. Commenting on the threat posed by China's nuclear weapons, he claimed that "it would be so easy for us to produce nuclear warheads—we have plutonium at nuclear power plants in Japan, enough to make several thousand warheads."[36]

Abe's and Fukuda's statements stirred controversy, and true to form the government issued statements of clarification and reassurance meant to calm Japan's citizens and neighbors. Yet Abe and Fukuda were hardly heretics breaking fresh ground.[37] Other senior officials have made similar remarks, either advocating that Japan acquire nuclear weapons or specifying hypothetical circumstances in which it might do so. They did so with full awareness that a domestic and regional outcry would result and that they might lose their jobs, as one JDA chief, Shingo Nishimura, did for daring to say the unsayable. Japanese specialists on foreign policy and national security have also broached the once-proscribed nuclear option, which is now discussed in Japan with greater frequency than ever before. While open discussions are hardly a routine or frequent practice, and while a nuclear Japan is certainly not around the corner, a taboo has been broken and national security discourse has moved to a terrain once out of bounds.

What is one to make of these episodes? One explanation is that Japan's top officials and senior politicians are unusually prone to slips on so highly charged a topic, but there is no evidence that they are any more careless with words than their counterparts in the other major powers; if anything, they are more careful and professional. Another, and more plausible, answer is that Japan's national security establishment wants wiggle room to preserve the nuclear option should extreme contingencies arise and that these statements reflect that intent. This would mean, however, that Japan's nuclear weapons policy is in fact not inalterable and that the nuclear option is not dead and buried.

Japan's attitude toward the Nuclear Non-Proliferation Treaty (NPT) is also less clear-cut than the country's pacifist ethos would suggest. Although Japan did sign the NPT in 1970, it was among the last states to do so and it delayed the Treaty's ratification for six years. Japan tarried to ensure that adherence to the treaty would not prevent it from developing an autonomous fuel cycle for its nuclear reactors, which are configured for research and the generation of energy (nuclear power accounts for one-third of Japan's energy consumption). While there are technical difficulties in using reactor-grade fuel to manufacture nuclear weapons, the claim that they are insurmountable is false; having an independent fuel cycle would be a major advantage should Japan change course and decide to exercise the nuclear option.[38]

Japan's plutonium policy provides additional evidence that it wants to retain freedom of action. The Japanese plutonium stockpile amounted to 40.6 metric tons at the end of 2003, up from 9 metric tons in 1991 and 23 metric tons in 1997. Roughly 10 percent of it is held within the country and the rest in reprocessing plants in France and Britain. Despite this large accumulation, Japan has proceeded to build the large plutonium reprocessing plant at Rokassho-mura in northern Honshu—and at a time when most states with nuclear weapons are getting out of the plutonium separation business. More than a decade in the making, Rokassho-mura will provide Japan its own plutonium separation capability and is expected to produce a stockpile of 100 metric tons of nationally held plutonium by 2020. The Federation of American Scientists reckons that a small fraction of the plant's annual output will suffice to make one thousand nuclear bombs. Nuclear physicist Frank Barnaby, who refers to Japan as a "de facto nuclear weapons state," estimates that "a good nuclear-weapons designer could construct a nuclear weapon from three to four kilograms of the plutonium produced by the Rokassho-mura reprocessing plant," which he says gives Japan far more plutonium than it could conceivably need for generating energy.[39]

Japan would never cross the nuclear threshold lightly or quickly, but its leaders' statements and its plutonium program show that it has not shut the door.

In addition to having the wherewithal to make nuclear weapons, Japan can also develop missiles to deliver them. The space program at the Japan Aerospace Exploration Agency (JAXA) has built various solid-fueled rockets (the M-5, J-1, and follow-on versions of the H-2A), which show that a long-range ballistic missile capability is well within Japan's technical reach, even though systems with the accuracy needed to destroy an adversary's missile sites will take more time to develop.[40] No matter. Japan has the capability to deter nuclear-armed adversaries by retaining a limited second-strike capability.

The real question—and one being discussed in Japan—is how Japan will react if it must contend with a nuclear North Korea or a China with a much larger and technically advanced nuclear arsenal, and if the United States no longer serves as a reliable shield because of its own vulnerability.[41] It would seem that Japan's decision to build a joint regional ballistic missile defense system with the United States is proof that Tokyo sees reliance on the United States as the best solution. But the U.S. decision to proceed with a missile defense program in East Asia is itself seen by some Japanese as a warning about the undependability of extended deterrence.[42] One could of course claim that Japan's nuclear allergy is so severe and incurable that it would forgo nuclear weapons even if it faced an unprecedented risk of being attacked with nuclear weapons, or was being subjected to coercion as a result of that threat. That, however, would scarcely be persuasive, for it amounts to asserting that Japan would not reevaluate policies forged in a different, more benign environment, no matter how drastic the transformation of its strategic situation, and that official and public attitudes would remain immobile despite stark changes that increase the country's vulnerability.[43] How many states in the annals of history have refused to change their national security in the face of new circumstances that threaten their existence?

If Japan proceeds to build nuclear weapons plus a substantially more powerful conventional force, it will no longer need the American alliance in its present form; nor would it make sense for the United States to continue its role as guardian. To argue that Tokyo will never make these choices is betting that the balance of power in the North Pacific will remain roughly what it is now and that the American guarantee will remain solid for decades to come. Japan does not seem to be banking on so benign a future.

Asymmetrical Gains

The question I raised earlier with respect to Europe also applies to Japan: what is the logic for deploying troops and retaining a network of bases in countries that are now wealthy enough to protect themselves and that face no threat comparable to the Soviet Union? The continued positioning of 46,000 troops and substantial air, ground, and naval assets on and around the Japanese archipelago will become infeasible, imprudent, and unnecessary—not only because the challenges we face are new but also because of the imbalance of obligations within the U.S.–Japan alliance. Article V of the U.S.-Japan "Treaty of Mutual Cooperation and Security" obligates the United States to defend Japan, but it does not obligate Japan to defend even U.S. forces in the Pacific—let alone the United States, for which, in any event we would not need Japanese assistance—unless they are attacked "in the territories under the administration of Japan."[44] Whatever the original justification, this inequity will cease to wear well on Americans, not least because it is evident that Japan now has ample resources to defend itself.

The contention that Japan cannot do so unless American forces remain on its soil is simply unsupportable. As with Europe, so with Japan, the problem is not the lack of capacity but of resolve. The typical response of alliance boosters is that while Japan is certainly capable of building a more robust military force in the abstract, its efforts to do so in reality will, given the legacy of the 1930s, provoke its neighbors and set off reactions that destabilize East Asia. The notion that any changes in Japan's defense policy spell doom is popular. It is invoked by American experts who are wedded to the alliance, by China and Japan, and by much of the Japanese foreign policy establishment. Each wants to maintain the status quo—although for very different reasons. But as I have argued earlier, the "minimalism or militarism" dichotomy so often applied to Japan is both a caricature and a convenient rationalization for the United States and Japan to persist in the lazy practice of reenacting habits and routines that are increasingly becoming indefensible. The alternative to a Japan with its present military profile is not an imperial

Japan that menaces its neighbors or becomes the Asia-Pacific's loose cannon. The choice is not between a Japan that spends barely 1 percent of its trillion dollar GDP on defense or one that embarks on an intemperate military spending spree. To defend itself against missile and air attack and to ensure that vital sea-lanes remain open, Japan does not need an army the likes of which conquered most of East Asia. It could keep its ground forces—the only component of military power that can conquer and occupy territory—at their present minimal size, while building surface ships, submarines, tactical aircraft, missile defenses, and missiles sufficient in number to deter putative adversaries so as to configure a force effective for defense but useless for conquest.

The wars in Afghanistan, and particularly Iraq, have exposed another problem with continuing the cold war deployment patterns represented by the U.S.-Japan alliance (but also, as evident from this book, NATO and the alliance with South Korea as well): the strain placed on an American military that is required to keep old commitments while being ordered to meet new ones, and in nontraditional venues, particularly since 9/11. This is evident in the latest (2006) Quadrennial Defense Review (QDR), which, despite its self-proclaimed goal of transforming the military, has U.S. armed forces fulfilling customary missions, while undertaking an assortment of new ones.[45] America's armed forces are already badly overstretched and struggling to find sufficient troops by resorting to extraordinary measures: "stop loss," the extension of rotation periods, and drawing deeply from reserve and National Guard units.[46] These are band-aid solutions, not lasting remedies, and the problem will persist unless the volunteer force is enlarged or the draft reinstituted. The first fix will cost money; the second will tax politicians' political capital.

Not only does Japan offer no way out of this quandary; it is part of the problem. To be fair, the Japanese government has taken steps that appear to lend a helping hand. It wrote a multibillion-dollar check to help defray the costs of the 1991 Gulf War (which was even more in Japan's interest than ours given that Japan is far more reliant on Persian Gulf oil than we are). The Diet passed legislation in 1992 permitting the

JSDF to participate in peacekeeping missions—a historic shift that enabled Japan's military to operate far from home. After 9/11, the JSDF provided noncombat assistance to U.S. missions in Afghanistan and Iraq. But the conditions governing these missions were narrowly framed and prohibited the Japanese military from participating in hostilities, or even firing its weapons, except in response to attacks. Even then, the legislation enabling such circumscribed peacekeeping and supply-and-support missions produced political outcries at home.

Most Japanese oppose the American campaign in Iraq. Anniversaries of the war have sparked protest rallies driven by pacifist and left-wing sentiment, but also by general anxieties that, despite contributing to the war only by sending the barely battalion-sized JSDF contingent, Japan could be targeted by terrorists for assisting the U.S. occupation, as Britain and Spain were.[46] On top of that, the JSDF contingent based in Samawah (in southern Iraq) relies on Western (chiefly Dutch) combat forces to defend it and is so focused on self-defense (or "force protection" as it is called) that it can barely fulfill its humanitarian and reconstruction assignment, let alone defend Dutch troops under assault.[48] Not surprisingly, in June 2006, a little over a year after the Netherlands withdrew its troops from Iraq, Japan announced that its contingent would be returning home. These prohibitions, which show no signs of being modified, suggest that Japan will be of scant value for future U.S. military interventions outside its own territory.

The same reticence is evident even when it comes to the Asia-Pacific, which is of decisive importance for Japan's security. Washington has tried to recalibrate the alliance so that Japan does more in that region, but Tokyo has adamantly resisted any thoroughgoing change in the original narrow limits. The much-heralded October 2005 agreement reached at the annual sessions of U.S.-Japan Security Consultative Committee—also known as the 2+2 meetings of the foreign and defense ministers of both allies, which have been held since 2003—did contain provisions that modified the alliance. These included more joint exercises, better joint training and intelligence sharing, more Japanese logistical support for American missions outside Japan's immediate environs, and the establishment of joint command centers at Yokota Air Base and Camp Zama. The 2005 decision to relocate 8,000 U.S. Marines from Okinawa to Guam was also clearly part of the same effort to devolve more responsibility to Japan (and to address long-standing Okinawan complaints about the American military presence).[49] But these changes, while widely touted as evidence of the continued relevance of the alliance, are less significant than advertised, for Japan left no doubt that the accord would not result in JSDF units being sent into combat in ways that represented a radical departure from established, treaty-based obligations. So while the U.S. commitment to defend Japan remains intact as per the 1960 defense treaty, the Japanese government has stuck to its position, which is consistent with the terms of the defense treaty, that the JSDF has no obligation to fight alongside U.S. forces should war erupt in, say, the Taiwan Strait or the Korean peninsula.[50] This guarantees the perpetuation of a pact that fails to provide the United States commensurate and reciprocal benefits.[51]

This imbalance threatens to make the alliance hard to defend, strategically and financially, in America. Critics have long complained that defending Japan amounts to a subsidy paid by American taxpayers, despite the $4.4 billion per year that Japan pays in direct and indirect "host nation support," which covers 74.5 percent of the costs of stationing U.S. forces in Japan. These critics have been voices in the wilderness so far, given the consensus within our foreign policy establishment about the centrality of the alliance. That could change as Americans come to see the alliance, as currently configured, as the codification of an anachronistic and iniquitous allocation of burdens, benefits, and hazards.[52]

Japan also claims that it covers most of the costs of stationing U.S. forces on its soil. But the asymmetry is not a matter of money alone and has a more visceral side. Japan can count on American troops to fight for its defense, but the United States cannot call on Japanese forces to fight alongside it when conflicts arise in parts of the Asia-Pacific that lie beyond Japan but affect Japan's security. Even in terms of the financial ledger, Japan's host-nation support excludes covering major American expenditures—among them the salaries and benefits of service personnel and the costs of maintaining military forces in the region—that are needed to support those troops based in Japan. Japan's contribution, which comes to roughly 10 percent of its 2005 defense budget, must be weighed against what it saves (and has saved) by relying on America to defend it.[53] Were it responsible for it own defense, Japan would have to spend much more than an additional $4 billion. In light of this skewed distribution of burdens and benefits, consider that already nearly 40 percent of Americans opposed retaining military bases in Japan in a poll taken soon after the cold war ended. Then imagine a protracted future downturn in the U.S. economy, and that yet another raucous dispute over trade occurs during the same period. It is not hard to see how support for the alliance could slip rapidly in the United States.[54]

Another issue that could change the terms of the U.S.-Japan alliance and force Japan to reassess its national security strategy, which pivots on the guarantee of U.S. protection, is the redistribution of American forces based overseas so as to move resources where they are needed in the post–cold war world. In large part this reassessment follows the shortfall in troops created by the Afghanistan and Iraq campaigns. In response, the Pentagon decided in 2005 to redeploy 12,500 forces from South Korea to Iraq. It also cut troops based in Europe by thousands and redeployed them to the United States so that they are available for missions in areas other than Europe and the North Pacific. In what will be a sweeping change, as many as 70,000 troops are expected to be repositioned by 2015.[55] This is almost certainly the beginning of a longer process, and one must assume that it is only a matter of time before current troop levels in Japan are reassessed; the decision to move the Third Marine Expeditionary Force, along with administrative and support elements, to Guam may therefore be a bellwether. The drawdown of forces from Japan and Korea represents a change in policy announced as recently as during President Bill Clinton's second term, when under the 1995 "East Asia Strategy Report" (or the "Nye Report," after then-Assistant Secretary of Defense for International Security Affairs Joseph Nye) the United States pledged to retain over 100,000 troops in the North Pacific for the long haul.[56]

The reassignment of forces from cold war locations is necessary and inevitable. There are formidable financial impediments to creating a substantially larger military force and they will become more so if crushing budgets become a pattern and if the draft remains the third rail of American politics. A future of faraway military campaigns cannot ultimately be squared with the strategy of staying stuck in the past. Applied to Japan, this prescription would end the alliance as we know it and force Tokyo to devise a new strategy against present and prospective threats.

China as Alliance Savior?

Discussions on the future of the alliance frequently turn to China, which, in effect, replaces (or will replace) the Soviet Union as an antagonist, certainly in the minds of those who see it as the next "peer competitor" of the United States. In this reading, a powerful, belligerent China will provide a new rationale for the alliance and continue binding Japan to the United States.[57] The problem with this account is that there are too many imponderables regarding China's future, and how Japan reacts will depend on what sort of China it faces.

One possibility is the emergence of a Chinese democracy that is created by the long-term, unanticipated consequences of Deng Xiaoping's decision in 1978 to initiate a capitalist revolution of sorts through reforms that introduced markets, private enterprise, and foreign investment to supplant the Maoist model that had persisted for three decades. The possibility that these changes will gradually turn China into a democratic society that is co-opted into the international economic and political order cannot be ruled out, even if the chance of this happening now seems slim. Those American strategists who see small signs of this process want to nudge it along and are, in contrast to the "containers," the "engagers."

Yet the eventual appearance of a mellow, pluralistic China could render the U.S.-Japan alliance superfluous. Of course, a combative nationalism can emerge even in a democratic country, and if that is what happens in China, politicians, unable to rein in their opportunism, may make a practice of mobilizing it for their own narrow ends. Yet the "democratic peace theory" has demonstrated with great success that wars among democracies occur rarely, if ever, and if it continues to be valid, Northeast Asia's two democratic giants will not turn on each other.[58] The view that the baggage of history rules out such a delightful denouement overlooks the replacement in Western Europe over the past half-century of a community of war by a community of peace. Absent the Chinese threat, it's not clear what the value to Japan of the U.S.-Japan alliance qua military pact would be and why Japan would continue paying billions of dollars a year to keep American soldiers on its soil. Likewise, it's hard to imagine how the United States would benefit from doing so. The Atlantic alliance is, as I argued in chapter 3, floundering for lack of clear purpose in a post-Soviet world. The same could happen to America's alliance with Japan, even though the process will take longer.

Yet another prospect, one seldom discussed because it does not fit the dominant dichotomy created by engagers and containers, is China's fragmentation under the weight of chronic instability—a latter-day "Warring States" era, if you will.[59] Here's how China might reach this rocky destination: imagine that Beijing cannot deliver the economic growth of 9 percent that the country has experienced since 1978 and that the social compact the Communist Party has implicitly forged with the population—obedience in exchange for prosperity—unravels and the party, having lost legitimacy, starts ruling through the gun. Imagine further that unrest by Chinese workers and peasants enraged by corruption and economic inequality—a trend already on the rise—reaches a boiling point and the party can no longer retain power, despite its monopoly over the means of coercion. This outcome would also remove the China threat, albeit for entirely different reasons.

A third scenario is that the containers are proven right and a powerful, belligerent China emerges. This outcome is often talked about but will takes decades, at least, to materialize. A gargantuan gap separates China and the United States in every standard measure of power (save population, itself a mixed blessing given the increasing proportion of retirees in China's population) and the People's Liberation Army, with some important exceptions, is equipped with mostly obsolete Soviet armaments, or Chinese modifications thereof. We are a long way from a world where China gains the power required to puts its distinct stamp on the world in much the way Britain did in the nineteenth century and the United States has since at least 1945. Even if it materializes, this outcome may not prove a happy one for the Communist Party. On the one hand, the party would have presided over a profound transformation in China's power—one that could unmake an American-dominated, unipolar world. The economic and technological progress that will propel this ascent will also make the lives of millions of Chinese incomparably better. The party's problem will be that its ideology and institutions will not offer anything relevant to managing and advancing a technologically advanced, complex capitalist economy; worse, its proclivity to stifle pluralism and to control the free flow of information will make it an impediment.

Now, the party could adjust to its creeping irrelevance and gain a new kind of legitimacy by swapping Marxism for nationalism and devising new slogans that envision the supplanting of Pax Americana with a Pax Sinica, thus ending centuries of weakness and humiliation at the hands of the West. There are signs that China has begun to take this road, and those who predict a menacing China point to these signs as perilous precursors. Perhaps they will be proven right. Even so, continuing the alliance with the United States will not be the only conceivable choice for Japan. If the Japanese calculate that the future favors China and that the United States cannot, in consequence, serve any longer as a reliable protector, they may reconcile themselves to the new arithmetic of power and acquiesce to Chinese hegemony. In that case, the alliance would become a hindrance, even a danger, by serving as a symbolic and practical provocation to China. Demands by the United States that Japan expand the scope and nature of its military obligations in East Asia to meet the Chinese threat could, under these circumstances, have the unintended consequence of hastening the demise of the alliance.

The upshot is that the alliance faces too many uncertainties to presume its linear longevity because of threats emanating from China.

Gaullist Japan

The U.S.-Japan alliance could also dissolve if Japanese nationalism becomes so powerful that Japan gravitates toward a defense strategy based on autonomy, one that involves building up its military power based on an independent conception of national interests, not in response to Washington's prods to play a bigger part in an American script. Here, Japan would choose autonomy because it concludes that China's rise has rendered the strategy of seeking safety through the alliance untenable. This strategic choice would shake the foundations of the alliance, which rests ultimately on Tokyo's decision to entrust its security to the United States.

The likelihood of a Gaullist Japan is now seemingly remote. Japan's security calculations are changing, albeit glacially. A defense debate that is unprecedented in postwar Japan has begun, and it will gain momentum as a younger, more nationalistic generation of parliamentarians and thinkers succeeds the older, cautious political elite.[60] Those among them who advocate a more assertive and independent policy point to the JSDF's feebleness, China's expanding military capabilities, North Korea's nuclear weapons, and Indonesia's possible instability (the bulk of Japan's imports and exports flow through the Malacca Straits). They also worry that America's changing interests could make it a fickle ally. Others accept this assessment but go further; they resent the submissiveness of Japan, which they trace to the U.S.-dominated alliance and to a Japanese leadership that seems focused on expressing regrets for Japan's past and treading lightly in deference to regional sensibilities. Nationalists are to be found within the government and in business and academic circles, and their smallness in numbers is misleading when it comes to gauging their influence on policy, which has grown, particularly under former Prime Minister Junichiro Koizumi.

In nationalists' minds Japan must possess military capabilities that reflect and support its status as a front-rank power. They favor removing Article IX and shedding other constitutional restraints and policies that prevent Japan from becoming a "normal country." To them, building weapons that extend the reach of the military, deploying a missile defense system, adopting preemption as a policy to eliminate nuclear threats, and even creating a nuclear deterrent are facets of normalcy.[61]

More than anything, this nascent nationalism stems from rising tensions with China over matters historical and territorial. Beijing continues to insist that Japan revise its history textbooks and accept responsibility for atrocities its troops committed during the occupation of China in the 1930s and 1940s, and that Japanese leaders cease visiting the Yasukuni shrine, a memorial to Japanese war dead that also contains the graves of those convicted by the International Military Tribunal of "class A" war crimes. Japan decided to cool the controversy after Prime Minister Yasuhiro Nakasone's visit to Yasukuni in 1985—the first by a prime minister since the end of World War II—set off a political storm, and his successors stayed away from the shrine. But in a move that reflects nationalist sentiment, Koizumi, unmoved by howls of protest from China (and South Korea), made annual pilgrimages to Yasukuni following his election in 2000. Japan's nationalists have gone further, calling for visits by the emperor.[62]

Japan has been no less defiant on the dispute over the Japanese-held Diaoyu/Senkaku Islands, on rival definitions of the Chinese and Japanese "extended economic zones" (EEZ), and on the conflicting claims to undersea energy fields that have resulted.[63] Japan has shown no inclination to yield, or even to compromise on the islands and it has, following China's lead, authorized private exploration of energy deposits within waters it considers part of its EEZ, refusing to be rattled by Chinese gunboat diplomacy, but also spurning Beijing's proposal for joint development of energy, pending a negotiated settlement.[64]

China's increasing power may, therefore, gradually germinate a feisty Japanese nationalism fed by fears that Beijing's aim is Japan's subservience and that appeasement will merely encourage more demands. Foreign Minister Taro Aso's repeated remarks about the China threat, which have evoked angry responses from Beijing, are emblematic of this logic, but his views are not anomalous within Japan's government.[65]

Anti-Chinese nationalism need not, of course, jeopardize Japan's alliance with the United States; such nationalism could strengthen this alliance and provide cover for increases in Japan's military power. This very argument is advanced by Japanese officials and national security specialists who support an increase in Japanese defense capabilities but want to ensure that it does not set off panic in Asia.[66] But calls for a stronger Japanese military also come from nationalists with a different outlook on the world in general, and the alliance in particular. These nationalists (who are hardly militarists) desire a more powerful and independent Japan, but not necessarily as a means of reinforcing the alliance. Their concern is that the alliance will not remain an effective and reliable source of security for Japan. Moreover, they believe that Japan's military weakness and dependence prevents it from resisting American efforts to shape its foreign and defense policies and perpetuates the pliancy into which it has been socialized. The problem as these nationalists see it is that Japan's dependence on American military power ensures that the nature and extent of threats are defined less by Japanese interests than by American ones and that Japanese security has become hostage to American priorities, which could be reordered by shifts in the regional balance of power.[67] This critique is as much about how the alliance works as it is about whether it will continue to work.

Nationalists of this variety have been avid supporters of the Japanese parliament's 1999 decision to restore official status to the Hinomaru flag (bearing the rising sun emblem) and the Kimigayo anthem, seen by Japan's left and pacifist parties and groups (and by much of East Asia) as emblems of Japanese interwar imperialism.[68] The nationalists, by contrast, "bristle at the continued presence of the American military on Japanese soil . . . and favor 'a true army,' instead of the current self-defense force. . . . [Such attitudes] are notable even in some of the elite educated . . . in the United States."[69] Ultimately, though, the brouhaha over flags and anthems is an epiphenomenon. What shapes the agenda of the radical nationalists is a deep dissatisfaction with the national security strategy Japan has followed for the past half century, which they find increasingly dysfunctional and demeaning.

Neither variant of nationalism yet represents mainstream Japanese thinking. Still, the notion that Japanese public opinion is an immovable barrier blocking a reorientation of foreign and military policy is questionable at the very least. On important issues—the revising of Article IX, building up military capabilities, demonstrating a more assertive policy toward China and North Korea, and discussing the acquisition of nuclear weapons—the range of policy choices now deemed acceptable for debate and discussion within Japan has expanded beyond what even leading Western specialists on Japan would have imagined as recently as twenty years ago.

The Japanese public's support for the U.S. presence also may prove softer than is often supposed. Typically, discussions of Japanese opposition to American bases focus on Okinawa, a neglected periphery that accounts for less than 1 percent of Japan's territory but hosts 75 percent of the U.S. military installations in Japan and more than 60 percent of all U.S. troops. Aside from the noise generated by U.S. military exercises, and the land consigned to American bases, Okinawans' grievances center on numerous incidents of rape, violence, and crime committed by American soldiers. Interestingly, however, while support for U.S. bases is assumed to be widespread in Japan, Japanese elsewhere in the country, adopting the classic "not-in-my-backyard" stance, oppose relocating the forces and bases moved from Okinawa to their neighborhoods. The attitudes toward the U.S.-Japan relationship in general have been remarkably positive, but not overwhelming so, as the annual public opinion polls commissioned by Japan's Cabinet Office show.[70]

Fresh Thinking

The U.S.-Japan alliance may slowly be reaching the end of the road after a long and successful run, even though its pace of obsolescence will certainly be considerably slower than NATO's. Yet the points I made with respect to NATO apply to the U.S.-Japanese military pact as well. The

end of the alliance will not preclude alignments between the two countries on various issues; nor will it segue into enmity. Japan and the
United States will remain linked by dense and multifaceted transactions
(diplomacy, trade, and investment), values (democracy), and strategic
interest (preventing the proliferation of weapons of mass destruction,
battling terrorism, and ensuring reliable oil supplies). Yet as is true of
NATO, cooperation on such issues does not require a military alliance,
merely a convergence of views. While the dissolution of the U.S.-Japan
alliance is viewed virtually without exception in American official and
foreign policy circles as something that will be wholly negative, it will in
fact provide both partners an opportunity to rethink entrenched assumptions and ideas anchored in a bygone era, and to redefine what
they seek in the new century; they will then go about attaining their
goals. That will create a partnership that is better positioned to persist.

In the absence of the alliance, Japan will have to regain the capacity
for independent strategic thinking, which appears to have become a
lost art. Any new Japanese grand strategy must utilize various tools of
statecraft—diplomatic, economic, cultural, and military—to cultivate a
coalition of states that share Japan's assessment of what the threats are
and who poses them. Without that, Japan will face the impossible task
of going it alone. To this end, Japan could join other Asian Pacific
states—including the United States—to create a regional security system that is open to all countries in the region. The new system should
incorporate several elements, all of them designed to increase stability
and to diminish the risk of crises and war. The first would entail negotiations that culminate in formal commitments by members to reduce
their arms in a reciprocal, verifiable manner and to accept ceilings on
destabilizing offensive weapons, such as long-range missiles. A network
of mutually reinforcing "confidence-building" measures—for example,
supplying advance notification of troop movements, observing one another's military exercises, and establishing demilitarized zones—would
be a second. A third feature would be the creation of a regional forum to
promote dialogue on security and regular contacts among militaries
and national security officials so as to build trust, provide early warning

on crises that could create conflict so that diplomatic intervention is possible, and advance the processes of arms control and confidence building. Such proposals are not infrequently dismissed as "feel good" or "talk shop" ventures, but they have a long history and have been pursued with success in cold war Europe. The idea that all we have to fall back on for building peace is the balance of power system is tough-sounding orthodoxy, but it conveniently ignores that deterrence breaks down and, in the wake of the Industrial Revolution that has produced weapons with unprecedented deadliness, often with dreadful consequences.

That said, multilateral security organizations are not a panacea, nor even a substitute for power; indeed it is the power of states that enable these forums by revealing the danger that freewheeling rivalry could segue into war. There is no getting around the fact, therefore, that Japan must have the military means to safeguard its vital interests; no peace-building organization can fill the gap. One such interest, given Japan's extreme dependence on seaborne imports and exports, is ensuring that maritime choke points and sea-lanes (the Malacca Straits, the East and South China Sea, the Sea of Japan) remain unobstructed; another is preventing its territory from being attacked by nuclear-armed states. One could, needless to say, add several other goals to this short high-priority list.

Japan cannot ensure its security needs by acting alone; no state can. Japan does not, for example, have the capacity to independently counter sea-denial strategies that China could develop—and it won't. The good news, though, is that Japan is not the only state with an interest in countering such a threat; nor will it be the only one with the requisite means. The United States will continue maintaining a substantial maritime presence in the Pacific (and indeed elsewhere), even without permanent bases in Japan, by relying on its own bases in Hawaii, Wake Island, Guam, and the Aleutians. India, an emerging military power, has already begun to expand its navy precisely because of its interest in ensuring the unhindered flow of shipping, for economic and strategic reasons that in no small measure are shaped by an awareness of China's growing might.

And consultations between Indian and Japanese officials dealing with matters of national security have begun.

The strategy of combining forces with others to thwart common threats may resemble an alliance, but it is in fact different, for there would be no preexisting commitment, as there is in the current U.S.-Japan alliance, to treat an attack on one member of the coalition as an attack on all. Nor would the like-minded partners play host to the military forces of others in the coalition on a treaty-based, indefinite basis, although it is certainly possible for states with intersecting interests to negotiate arrangements that provide them as-needed access to bases and ports and that even allow stockpiling of arms and supplies to be used by troops once they arrive. Pooling of military resources based on convergent interests amounts to an alignment, not a formal military pact, but it need not be equivalent to be effective.

As for the nuclear threat, Japan could adopt a two-pronged strategy. The first response would be to develop a missile defense network, something it is already doing jointly with the United States.[71] In extremis it could—and this would be the second part—deploy a minimum nuclear deterrence so long as adversaries in the region retain nuclear forces. Merely suggesting this latter choice invites accusations of recklessness. But consider Japan's plight if extended deterrence provided by the United States became unreliable while the threat of Chinese (and North Korean) nuclear weapons remained. Japan's recourse to a limited deterrent would then amount to prudence.

No matter the particulars of Japan's post-alliance strategy, the points to keep in mind are that Japan and the United States will have ample room and occasion to cooperate even though they are not bound by a formal military pact. An unallied Japan will not stand alone, bereft of partners. The threats it faces—and may face—will be other states' problems as well. Dealing with dangers by effecting a changeover from alliance to alignment will merely usher in a new phase in Japan's national security policy. Despite the consensus in American and Japanese foreign policy circles that the end of the alliance will bring all manner of crises and conflicts to East Asia, the reality will be quite different.

A Japan that can better defend itself while remaining friendly toward the United States—and the two conditions are certainly not mutually exclusive—will free up American resources and enable a U.S. national security policy attuned to the realities of a new world. Seen thus, an equitable partnership shorn of asymmetric benefits and burdens is the best way to ensure that Japan and the United States work in harmony well into the future. And they should.

Korea: Coming of Age

5

The alliance between the United States and South Korea (or the Republic of Korea, its official designation) served each government's interests well during the cold war and mirrored America's alliances with Europe and Japan in this respect. The 1954 Mutual Defense Treaty prevented attacks against South Korea and provided it with security.[1] By creating a favorable environment for South Korea's spectacular economic transformation over the past fifty years, America also contributed to its prosperity. And despite Washington's embrace of repressive South Korean regimes, stability and prosperity eased the eventual passage from authoritarianism to democracy.

At the end of the 1950s, South Koreans had a per capita income comparable to Ghanaians. Not only has South Korea long since left Ghana far behind, it has become a global economic power. Its Gross Domestic Product (GDP) of $605 billion makes it the world's eleventh-largest economy; only five members of the European Union (EU) rank above it on this measure. Not long ago, South Korea's economic profile resembled that of a third-world country; now it competes with the world's foremost economic powers in the manufacture and export of a host of industrial goods, many of them high-tech.[2] This is, above all, a South Korean achievement: successive governments enacted land reform, implemented policies that created an educated society, and nurtured successful export-oriented industries. These initiatives propelled South Korea's extraordinary ascent—one so rapid that its neighbor and antagonist, North Korea (the People's Democratic Republic of Korea), has been left standing as a monument to failure.[3] There is no doubting the winner in the Seoul-Pyongyang competition.

The economic success has had important political consequences. The rise of a large middle class enabled democracy to emerge by the early 1990s, ending decades of often-brutish authoritarian rule. Open elections, a free press, robust civic organizations, raucous student groups—these are now commonplace in South Korean society. North Korea, by comparison, remains a Stalinist stronghold where both goods and freedom are scarce. When South Korea hits the headlines, the story is more often than not about something good—the outcome of an election or rising exports. When North Korea makes the front page, the news, by contrast, is almost always bad—famine, failing industries, bellicosity, or covert nuclear weapons programs.

America the Enabler

While South Korea's success was and remains homegrown, an account that omitted the contributions of the United States would be incomplete, even distorted. Some are evident; others less so. The most important one is the defense of South Korea, starting with the 1950–1953 Korean War. Its roots can be traced to the division of the Korean peninsula, and therefore the Korean nation, along the thirty-eighth parallel after the United States and the Soviet Union could not agree on a formula for unification. (Japan, which had colonized Korea since 1905, surrendered to the United States and the Soviet Union following its defeat in World War II.) That much is true, but some elements in the standard rendition of the war's background need correction. The United States actively contemplated dividing the peninsula well before the North Korean attack, and while the war itself was begun by Pyongyang, it was hardly an unprovoked bolt from the blue; to be sure, North Korea was not an innocent bystander, but South Korea was not passive and had initiated a series of attacks, inflicting significant casualties on North Korea.[4] It was not Pyongyang alone that saw war as a rightful means to unification, and the United States was quite concerned that Seoul would be the one to start a war to this end. Nevertheless, it was North Korea that made the all-out bid to forcibly unify the Korean peninsula, and its gambit would have worked had a force led by the United States and sanctioned by the United Nations (UN) not rushed to the scene. The Korean War brought American combat troops back—they had been withdrawn in 1949—and once the guns fell silent, they remained, under the terms of a bilateral alliance that would shape South Korea's internal order and external environment, while also serving as a critical component of containment.

The advantage of being able to supplement its own defenses with the might of the world's wealthiest and most powerful country reduced the proportion of GDP South Korea would have had to spend to defend itself against North Korea had it stood alone. That, in turn, increased the capital the state had available to invest in key economic sectors and helped prepare the groundwork for the revolution that would catapult South Korea into the ranks of the world's foremost economic powers in less than a generation. And as this economic transformation proceeded, the American military presence shielded Seoul from the coercive diplomacy that China and the Soviet Union, North Korea's patrons, could have applied to shape its policies at home and abroad with the aim of drawing it into their spheres of influence. It also prevented them from backing Pyongyang's bid to forge a single Korean state by force of arms.

There were also benefits of a less obvious sort. One need only ponder whether democracy would put down roots in South Korea had the country been trapped in a cycle of war, and whether the foreign investment that accelerated South Korea's economic advance would have flowed in so freely had the American military presence not reassured companies that they could conduct business expecting that peace and stability would endure. South Korea's economy also benefited from the substantial payments the United States made for the tens of thousands of troops Seoul sent to support the American military campaign in Vietnam and the array of goods and services it provided to help sustain the war.

Rare is the alliance that favors only one party, and the one uniting South Korea and the United States certainly was no exception, because it benefited America in several ways. Particular sectors of the U.S. economy profited from selling the weapons, goods, and services needed to maintain the open-ended military presence on the Korean peninsula, even though the overall effect on the American economy was modest, given its gargantuan size. The gains on the strategic front, however, were more palpable and prominent, and mattered for U.S. policy more generally. Washington's indefinite access to South Korea as a platform for projecting military power onto Chinese and Soviet territory was critical to containment. Together with Japan, South Korea denied Soviet strategists the luxury of concentrating solely on the western front and forced them to confront a citadel of American power in the Far East while also allocating resources to their distant European flank to counter NATO. The contractual right to use Japanese and South Korean ports, airfields, and logistical installations proved essential in enabling the U.S. Navy to dominate Pacific sea-lanes and to maintain a perennial presence. The defense of South Korea also preserved a balance of power in Northeast Asia that favored the United States and that, in turn, had wider strategic significance. Furthermore, the Soviet Union and China were deprived of the geopolitical advantages that would have accrued to them had they been free to help Pyongyang unify the peninsula and to establish a unified and dependent Korean client state. That would have transformed the milieu in which American military forces operated in the Western Pacific, particularly because Vietnam was already aligned with them.

American policy was, of course, not guided by sheer benevolence; there was plenty of Realpolitik in play. Throughout the cold war the United States lent fulsome support to a succession of dictatorial and repressive South Korean regimes, civilian and military, turning a blind eye to their serial brutality: Washington's first order of business was not the liberties of Koreans but maintaining its strategic position in South Korea for wider goals related to the cold war; Korea was a means, not an end. The eventual blossoming of democracy in South Korea does not nullify this fact or justify the sufferings endured by South Koreans at the hands of brutal governments, and it would be crass teleological reasoning and rationalization to depict decades of repression as a painful but unavoidable pathway to liberty. To this day, millions of South Koreans are persuaded that misfortunes at the hands of authoritarian governments during the cold war are inseparable from the alliance with the United States, and that Washington was therefore complicit in the repression. As we shall see, the animus that this breeds toward the United States bodes ill for the alliance's future at a time when it faces new circumstances.

The Tide Turns against Pyongyang

The conditions that supported an alliance between successive American and Korean governments and that both sides found mutually advantageous have disappeared, as they have in the case of NATO and the U.S.-Japan defense treaty. Consider the lingering status quo: in 2004, fifty years after the Korean War, 37,000 American troops remained ensconced in ninety-six South Korean bases, with a good proportion pressed up against the 155-mile demilitarized zone (DMZ) to remind North Korean leaders that an attack on South Korea would kill Americans and draw the United States into the war. And in the event that Pyongyang casts caution to the wind, defying the doctrine of deterrence, the next mission of American forces remains the defeat of North Korean forces. This strategy—relying on dissuasion to the extent possible, but waging war if unavoidable—has stood the test of time, and is no trivial accomplishment considering the Korean peninsula's reputation as the planet's most militarized and dangerous place. An inter-Korean war would take a horrendous human toll even if only conventional armaments were used. Despite the withdrawal of American tactical nuclear weapons from South Korea, however, the escalation to nuclear conflict cannot be ruled out and neither can the possibility that China and Russia might be dragged into the fracas. Under these latter conditions, the consequences would be even more terrible.

So why fix what's not broken, particularly when the problem the alliance was meant to address—an opaque, militarized, totalitarian, dysfunctional entity, North Korea—persists, despite intermittent predictions of its imminent demise. Pyongyang's armed forces and arsenal remain huge, and while the regime's opaqueness renders reliable calculations impossible, it devotes close to 20 percent of its GDP to military spending to keep it that way—this despite an economic crisis that has caused its economy to contract since 1990 and the ravages of famine that forced it to appeal, openly and uncharacteristically, for help from abroad.

But for all of Pyongyang's bombast and vitriol, the reality is that things are not going its way, and the regime can hardly be unaware of this and the reasons why this is so. South Korea now disposes of economic resources far larger than North Korea possesses and can outspend its adversary with minimal additional economic strain; this cannot be said of North Korea. Pundits and policymakers in Washington may debate the outcome of a war between North Korea and South Korea, but the imbalance between the two countries in the capacity to mobilize war-related resources is incontrovertible. For conflicts that end relatively quickly (within several months, say), what matters is the ability to inflict in short order losses so severe that the adversary sues for peace to avoid catastrophic defeat. The ability to present an opponent with this stark choice is a function of payoffs from long-term investments in research and development (R&D) that harness advanced technology to transform the speed and lethality of weaponry. Spin-offs from a vibrant civilian economy featuring state-of-the-art technology are also of cardinal importance here, quite apart from the efforts of a government. South Korea is in a different league altogether than North Korea in both respects, and one indicator of this is its investments in R&D. In 2003, its governmental appropriations for R&D amounted to 0.78 percent of its GDP, of which 14.2 percent was allocated to defense. Only five other members of the Organization for Economic Cooperation and Development (OECD), the club of the leading economic powers, surpassed the former figure and only four OECD members the latter.[5] North Korea cannot hope to match this level of investment; nor can its shopworn economy produce investment capital or technological innovations remotely comparable to South Korea's. Quite apart from governmental initiatives to boost military power, South Korea's economy boasts an array of world-class industries that generate all manner of technologies pertinent to military modernization. In a war of attrition, the capacity to marshal the financial resources needed to fight on at a bearable economic cost while also managing the maladies of inflation and indebtedness that often accompany protracted campaigns is the sine qua non for victory. While wealth alone may not always determine who wins wars, it remains the single best predictor despite aberrant cases.[6] Here again the news for Pyongyang is bad. Every indictor relevant to assaying the comparative economic prospects for sustaining a lengthy war shows that it is in a vastly inferior position. Worse, its relative position is deteriorating as the South Korean economy races ahead.

The second sobering reality—and one related to the first—for Pyongyang is the widening technological chasm between North Korea and South Korea. Although the two Koreas started off on a roughly equal footing in the early 1950s, North Korea has long since proven incapable of advancing beyond what might be called nineteenth-century industries. South Korea, by contrast, has mastered the domain of cutting-edge, knowledge-intensive twenty-first-century technologies, while also harnessing them to revolutionize traditional industries, whether steel making, shipbuilding, or automotive production. Both categories of production matter for military might, especially now that the much-vaunted "Revolution in Military Affairs" (RMA) has redefined the terms of war by introducing precision-guided munitions, advanced surveillance and battle-management systems, weapons that strike from beyond the horizon, pilotless drones that gather information and destroy targets, and advances in electronic warfare that have transformed targeting and jamming techniques. North Korea has failed to enter this arena, much less master it: its arsenal is stocked largely by outmoded aircraft and tanks of Soviet and Chinese vintage. This inferiority may be among the reasons why it has apparently chosen to build nuclear weapons on the theory that they constitute the great equalizer.

North Korea's third problem is that its strategic environment has been changed irrevocably, and to its detriment, with the most important development being the new relationship between China and Russia, North Korea's principal patrons, and between them and South Korea. The triumph of practicality over ideology in Beijing and Moscow accounts for this change. While China's leaders continue to pay ritual homage to Marxist precepts and to condemn capitalism's evils, they have in effect abandoned Marxist-Leninist-Maoist ideology as a guide to quotidian public policy. Unlike in the era of Mao, Beijing's preoccupation now is not the export of revolution, but the export of goods. It sees foreign investment, once shunned as exploitative and corrosive, as a key ingredient for economic success, and cultural and educational exchanges with the capitalist world, which were spurned for three decades after the revolution, as sources of economic advancement. Whatever Beijing may say about ideological solidarity with Pyongyang, its policies are driven by an entirely different calculus than they were when the Mao suits, the Great Leap Forward, and the Cultural Revolution defined Chinese reality. For the future that the Chinese leadership hopes to create, wealthy, scientifically advanced South Korea is an asset while North Korea, which depends on Chinese largesse for the most basic of needs, has little to offer and is in fact a drain on resources. But Pyongyang has been dealt a double whammy, for if China has changed its priorities, its other patron, the Soviet Union, simply vanished, and its successor state, the Russian Federation, has jettisoned communism in favor of consumerism. As with Beijing, it is trade, investment, and technology transfer that matter now for Moscow, and it's apparent to the Kremlin which Korea counts for more when it comes to these necessities.

While China and Russia have not abandoned North Korea outright, they have stopped shunning South Korea out of ideological fealty to Pyongyang. Given their priorities, South Korea is too consequential a state to ignore, let alone alienate; there are numerous reasons to build substantial ties with it, and that cannot happen if the old political atmosphere persists. So it is not surprising that Russia and China decided on a volte-face and changed their long-established course to establish diplomatic relations with South Korea, in September 1990 and August 1992, respectively. They also ceased backing Pyongyang's position that two Korean states could not be allowed to enter into the United Nations simultaneously—on the theory that that would have conferred legitimacy on the division of Korea—and welcomed Seoul's admission to the world body. Russia delivered an even blunter message to Pyongyang in 1996 when it unilaterally scrapped the military assistance clause in the 1961 Soviet-North Korean Treaty of Friendship and Cooperation and pressed for negotiations to replace the treaty itself with an anodyne alternative, which was signed in February 2000.[7] No less significant was Russia's decision to cease the Soviet practice of serving as North Korea's reliable supplier of weapons and its decision to sell arms to South Korea—in part to liquidate Soviet-era debt; in part for profit.[8] Russian arms sales are now determined by the cash nexus, and that's bad for cash-strapped North Korea.

But recalibration must not be confused with rejection, for China and Russia are not about to sever economic and political ties with North Korea. Each wants to use its influence with Pyongyang—especially now that it is playing a nuclear cat-and-mouse game—as leverage against the United States and South Korea; to ensure that any settlement on major political issues on the peninsula involves their full participation; and to avoid giving Washington the impression that it could attack a friendless North Korea preemptively, so as to demolish its nuclear weapons program, with few risks.[9] Still, it is clear that Beijing and Moscow will no longer bear major economic burdens or take military risks in behalf of

North Korea and that Pyongyang's strategy of manipulating the competition between them to extract benefits from both won't work as it did when they were at loggerheads. That game is over. Russia and China are no longer at daggers drawn as they were from the late 1950s to the late 1980s. The volume of their bilateral trade is up (albeit from the very low baseline of 1991). The once hotly contested border, along which their military forces clashed in 1969, has been delimited. Russia is now China's largest arms supplier by far, while China is becoming a big market for Russian energy. Indeed, both countries' interests intersect to the point that they have proclaimed a "strategic partnership."[10]

Together, these disparate developments have recast what Soviet strategists used to call the "correlation of forces" between North Korea and South Korea.[11] Seoul, incomparably wealthier, technologically more advanced, and strategically more consequential, is in a different position than it was in the 1950s and 1960s, when the American alliance was indispensable to its defense because it faced three hostile, well-armed states. This means that the justification for continuing the U.S.-South Korean alliance is grounded less in fact than in inertia, and the comfort South Korean and American foreign policy and national security officials and mavens derive from reenacting received routines. The assumption underpinning the alliance was that South Korea could not survive without an American commitment to defend it against the North Korean juggernaut. While that may once have been true, the new strategic landscape places in relief the contrast between a static alliance and new realities. This outmoded status quo must and will change. The proposition that the forward basing of thousands of American soldiers and a multitude of materiel in Korea remain essential is particularly flawed now that the threats facing the United States are so different from what they once were and now that Seoul is fully capable of mobilizing the resources needed and devising strategies appropriate for its defense. Quite apart from the costs related to continuing the deployment of thousands of U.S. troops on the Korean peninsula, the logic for spending $11 billion to bolster American capabilities to defend South Korea in the wake of President George W. Bush's plan to downsize U.S.

forces there is shaky given the country's emergence as an economic heavyweight.[12]

Commitment versus Continuance

Even though South Korea's economic achievements made its ability to defend itself apparent even before the cold war formally ended, efforts by American presidents at various points to reduce, let alone relinquish, Washington's responsibility for guaranteeing South Korea's security largely came to naught. The arguments made in support of the alliance by officials and national security experts in both countries prevailed, no matter their predictable refrain and list of particulars. The foes of exit averred that disengagement would damage American credibility—an old standby trotted out whenever proposals are made to reassess foreign commitments that have long been in place but are no longer meaningful or necessary. The departure of U.S. forces would, they added, leave South Korea exposed to attack by North Korea and allow Pyongyang to unify the peninsula on its terms, strangle the freedoms of millions of South Koreans, and transform the balance of power. These outcomes would, the critics continued, have incalculable adverse consequences for the United States and its allies in East Asia; in particular, the Korean peninsula would become a dagger aimed at Japan's heart, causing it to lose faith in the efficacy of American power and pushing it toward full-scale rearmament and setting off alarm bells and provoking arms races that would unsettle regional equilibrium. In short, very many bad things would happen. These assertions, made with force and persistence by senior policymakers and experts, have become axiomatic truths, so much so that criticisms of the status quo by definition appears unrealistic, naive, even irresponsible. The similarity between the case for maintaining the alliance with South Korea and for the continuing relevance of NATO and of the U.S.-Japan alliance is striking, as is the American foreign policy establishment's abiding attachment to existing concepts and structures.

The indispensability of the alliance is so rarely disputed within the

American foreign policy community that contrarians have been relegated to a "voice in the wilderness" status.[13] Is it surprising then that the United States has invested so much in the defense of Korea for so long despite the changes in Seoul's strategic environment and capabilities? True, in 2005, the Pentagon did cut troop levels in South Korea to reduce the stress that the war in Iraq had placed on the U.S. military. Moreover, further reallocations are scheduled. This is a welcome and much overdue change, but it will still leave many Army, Navy, Air Force, and Marine Corps units in place, including the Eighth Army, the Second Infantry Division, and the Seventh Air Force (plus additional forces based nearby in Japan)—in all, still a substantial commitment.[14]

To underscore the seriousness of this investment and to demonstrate that South Korean and American forces are ready and willing to operate together, the two countries have held the annual, joint "Team Spirit" exercises since August 1976 (although they were canceled between 1994 and 1997 as a good-faith gesture to advance negotiations aimed at ending Pyongyang's nuclear program). Some 200,000 forces participate in the exercise, with additional American forces being ferried in from elsewhere for the occasion. To make it even clearer to North Korea just how much danger it would court by starting a war—as if that were needed—the United States stationed tactical nuclear weapons in South Korea for most of the cold war, while also retaining the capability to launch nuclear strikes against North Korean targets from elsewhere in the Pacific. The deployment of nuclear weapons on the peninsula began in 1957 under President Dwight Eisenhower and continued until September 1991, when President George H. W. Bush—taking account of the end of the cold war as well as advice from the commander of U.S. forces in Korea and the American ambassador, who argued that there was a mismatch between the utility of these weapons and the risks they posed—ordered their withdrawal.[15] But Bush assured the South Korean leadership that the deterrence provided by the main American nuclear arsenal remained reliable (which statement should have raised the question of why it had been necessary to maintain U.S. nuclear arms for decades).

Not only did South Korea, like Europe and Japan, delegate its defense to the United States, it also ceded extraordinary control over its national security to American military and political leaders. South Korea's armed forces, which were placed under the U.S.-led United Nations Command at the beginning of the Korean War, remained under the control of the commander of U.S. forces in Korea until 1994, and his permission was required, in theory, before South Korean officers could order large troop movements within their own homeland. Even today, the South Korean military would revert to American command in wartime, and despite discussions between the two allies about ending this anachronistic arrangement, a decision has been deferred indefinitely.[16] In a similar fashion, basic information about the location of American nuclear weapons, and policies governing their use, was tightly held (no matter that millions of Koreans would have been killed had these arms been used), and not just from average Korean citizens: the secrecy was so stringent that until the circle was widened in early 1991 to include top South Korean national security officials (that is, less than a year before the weapons were removed), the South Korean president was briefed alone, without the presence of anyone else from the South Korean government.[17]

Taken as whole, then, the United States has made a substantial investment in South Korea's defense. The idea that South Korea can take care of itself has been, in effect, dismissed out of hand within the highest reaches of the American government—with some notable exceptions.[18] In 1971, President Richard Nixon withdrew the Seventh Infantry Division's troops from South Korea, but Secretary of State Henry Kissinger scrapped the Pentagon's plans for further substantial cuts centered on the Second Infantry Division. The Ford administration commissioned studies to reevaluate the size of the American deployment in South Korea, but no change in actual policy followed. The most far-reaching reconsideration by far occurred during the Carter administration. Carter had advanced the idea of withdrawing ground forces from South Korea in stages, even during his campaign. He believed that the South Koreans had the capability to protect themselves and was also aware that the Vietnam debacle had eroded public support for military commitments overseas. Despite his dogged determination, his plans were scuttled by his national security officials, for whom the reasoning behind the military presence in South Korea was, in effect, sacred scripture. The result was that only 3,600 troops were removed and the president's effort to break new ground was stymied.

Yet the reductions by Nixon and the radical cuts proposed by Carter occurred when cold war imperatives still reigned. Now the circumstances are dramatically different: the cold war has ended, South Korea is an economic colossus, and North Korea's strategic and economic position has deteriorated. It is this new context that has enabled George W. Bush to reduce U.S. forces in South Korea by 7,000. More generally, 9/11 and the campaigns in Afghanistan and Iraq have recast the strategic realities and America's perspectives and needs regarding security, and the new environment will necessitate even larger reductions in the forces based in Korea.

What the Numbers Show

Even if one concedes straightaway that a substantial American military presence under the extraordinary terms just described was necessary during the cold war, the mainstream view that South Korea cannot protect itself even today strains credulity. Despite the ever-widening gap in power between North Korea and South Korea, however, this perspective prevails in our corridors of power.[19] But a comparison of the two states using standard measures of military capability casts grave doubt on the commonplace assertion that North Korea's stark numerical lead in military manpower and weaponry makes it impossible for South Korea to defend itself alone, let alone defeat North Korea, in the event of war.

Let's begin by examining the gap in the economic foundations of military power, using some basic measures. South Korea's GNP in 2004 was $673 billion; by comparison, North Korea's was $22 billion, a ratio of 30:1 in favor of South Korea. On a per capita basis, the disparity is not as large, but is still stark: South Korea's, in 2004, was almost $14,000;

North Korea's, $969, a ratio in excess of 14:1. The gulf reappears in defense spending, despite the North Korean regime's (well-deserved) reputation for an "all guns and no butter" mentality when it comes to resource allocation. Pyongyang's military budget approached $6 billion in 2004; Seoul spent $ 16.3 billion, giving it a 2.7:1 edge.[20] Because North Korea's polity is opaque, one must consider the possibility that its true expenditure is larger, but a major miscalculation seems implausible, especially given the considerably smaller size of its overall economy. A vastly larger defense budget would be unsustainable for a country that already devotes one-fifth of its GDP to military spending, giving it the dubious distinction of holding first place in a ranking of 169 countries in this category. South Korea, by contrast, devotes 2.9 percent of its GDP (which is, incidentally, a significantly smaller proportion when compared with the United States) to military spending. Not only can South Korea bear this burden easily, given the size of its economy, even a small increase will easily yield substantially larger sums for military spending, and with minimal sacrifice. Neither of these conclusions applies to North Korea.[21]

The picture is somewhat different and less straightforward when one moves from money to manpower and materiel. North Korea's soldiers, tanks, and submarines heavily outnumber South Korea's, often by a sizeable margin. The only exceptions are combat aircraft, where the balance is about even, with a slight edge favoring North Korea, and frigates and destroyers, where South Korea leads almost 5:1.[22] Yet the raw figures mask important qualitative contrasts that overwhelmingly favor South Korea. First, South Korea is in an altogether different technological league given the moth-eaten North Korean economy; second, its greater wealth puts it in an incomparably better position to purchase advanced weaponry from abroad and to modernize its forces through efforts at home. The qualitative contrast becomes clearer if, for illustrative purposes, we consider three pillars of military prowess: tanks, combat aircraft, and naval vessels. On the face of it, North Korea, with 3,500 main battle tanks as opposed to 2,330 for South Korea, seems to have a clear advantage. But the overwhelming majority of North Korea's inventory consists of outmoded Soviet models: the T-34 was built in 1936–37 and served as the mainstay of the Soviet tank force during World War II; the T-54 and T-55, replacements for the T-34, appeared in 1949, and were phased out in the mid-1970s to make way for the incomparably more advanced T-72 and T-80, neither of which is present in the North Korean tank force, even though Russia has sold South Korea the latter model. South Korea's tanks are far superior in decisive battlefield properties: fire control and target acquisition, mobility, laser-based range finding, quality of armor, night vision capabilities, and thermal imaging technologies. They are also newer—none was in production before 1980—and far more technologically advanced. There is little doubt where the qualitative advantage lies if one examines the technical traits of the indigenously designed and built Type 88 K1, the American M1A1 Abrams, and the Soviet T-80.[23]

The story is similar when it comes to combat aircraft. The bulk of North Korean fighter and ground attack aircraft are Chinese knockoffs of old Soviet models made under license: the Jian-5, based on the Soviet MiG-15, which emerged shortly after the Korean War; the Jian-6, a copy of the MiG-19, which was first tested in 1958; and the Jian-7, for which China received a license in 1961. Compared to these old models, South Korea's fighters (the American-built F-16C and F-16D Fighting Falcons) and ground attack aircraft (Phantom F-4Ds and F-4Es and the Tiger F-5Es, F-5Fs, and F-5Ks) are far more advanced in speed, agility, avionics, and targeting capabilities—and are newer, especially the F-16s and the F-5Ks. North Korea does not even have the quantitative lead in the realm of airpower that it does in armored warfare. Its fleet of 590 combat aircraft exceeds South Korea's by only fifty; on top of that, because of North Korea's severe economic constraints and chronic fuel shortages, its pilots fly far fewer training missions than their counterparts in South Korea.[24]

The naval balance favors South Korea even more.[25] Although North Korea has a 4:1 numerical advantage in patrol submarines, they consist of Chinese-built boats of the Soviet Romeo class, dating back to the 1950s. By contrast, South Korea's *Chang Bogo*-class, home-built with assistance from Germany, was commissioned in 1993, and nine had been delivered to the fleet by the end of 2005. Likewise, South Korea's inshore submarine force, consisting of the German Type 214, is much more advanced than its North Korea's counterparts. The most glaring contrast appears in large surface vessels, frigates, and destroyers. North Korea's fleet is essentially an aging coastal defense force. By comparison, in 2001, South Korea committed itself to building a modern oceangoing fleet. The *King Kwanggaeto*-class destroyers and *Ulsan*-class frigates, which incorporate various advanced Western technologies—in particular the American-built AEGIS defense system that can locate and track numerous threats simultaneously, whether submarines, ships, or aircraft—but are built in South Korea, continue to join the fleet, reflecting both South Korea's commitment to construct a "blue water" navy as well as the technological prowess of its economy.[26] Apart from the qualitative gap separating South Korea's warships from North Korea's aging and outmoded *Najin*- and *Soho*-class frigates, Seoul has almost five times as many major warships, and the numerical balance will only tilt further in its favor in the years ahead given the disparity in economic power between the two countries.

There are other realities that work to South Korea's advantage. With much greater wealth and a far more sophisticated technological base, it can develop, or acquire from the West, military technologies in ways that are simply not open to North Korea. In particular, the United States will continue to be a major supplier of arms and defense technology to South Korea whether or not there is a formal alliance—and for two basic reasons: one economic; the other, strategic. First, South Korea has the cash on hand to pay for what it needs: its foreign exchange reserves at the end of 2005 amounted to $207 billion, or nearly ten times the value of North Korea's entire GDP. Of the "emerging" economies, only China ($769 billion) and Taiwan ($251.8 billion) had larger sums, and South Korea has considerably more per capita than China does.[27] The United States is the world's largest exporter of weapons by far, and its defense contractors are keenly aware that South Korea offers a lucrative market for their wares. Second, America's stake in ensuring that South Korea is militarily strong will continue even without an alliance: sheer balance of power considerations ensure that the United States will assist South Korea in the unlikely event that it proves unable to defend itself. The same cannot be said about Pyongyang's traditional allies, China and Russia. Why, given the change in the relative strategic significance of North Korea and South Korea, would they jump into a war initiated by Pyongyang and jeopardize their flowering relationship with Seoul? Perhaps more important, why would they encourage such a war to begin with, or imply that they would assist North Korea once its guns start firing? Given their current priorities, China and Russia have little to gain and much to lose from a war on the Korean peninsula. Quite apart from the chaos it would wreak in their neighborhood, both countries have borders with North Korea and would almost certainly face massive inflows of refugees. A clash between the two Korean states would also rattle investors, disrupt trade, and harm the Chinese and Russian economies. The upshot is that North Korea not only faces a military balance that favors South Korea, it also cannot count on its traditional allies to help offset the disadvantage.

The Shift in Public Sentiment

In assessing the prospects for the alliance, two other propositions that permeated cold war thinking need to be reconsidered because they continue to pervade the American foreign policy establishment. The first holds that the South Koreans' support for the American military presence in their homeland remains strong and reliable; the second that American and South Korean interests will converge on the issues that truly matter, just as they have for decades. Together these beliefs produced and perpetuate a consensus that the alliance is in fine fettle and that views to the contrary are superficial, alarmist, or both.

Yet the reality is different. Contrary to the first supposition, anti-American sentiment has gained ground in South Korea in the aftermath of the cold war, and is now embedded in the body politic.[28] As a summary report of a conference on the Korean peninusla put it, even though dissatisfaction with the United States is greater in other parts of the world, South Korean anti-American sentiment is "intense" and "real" and "evidence from public opinion polling by organizations ranging from left to right indicate the growth of [such feelings] . . . which several decades ago had been confined to the fringe element of the youth, is now far more widespread and permeates society."[29]

This does not mean that the alliance teeters on collapse, and some caveats are in order to place these attitudes in perspective. There have always been highs and lows in the history of the pact, and it would be incorrect to speak of a steady, steep, and irretrievable descent; nothing in life is inevitable, and this certainly applies to the Seoul-Washington alliance. Moreover, the very term *anti-Americanism* is too capacious: it can become a big pot into which too many different things are thrown. It's important, therefore, to differentiate among beliefs that originate in an ideological position and that have an across-the-board quality and transcend particular issues; ones produced by specific features of the relationship (such as the effect of American bases on the quality of life in nearby communities); and others that are sparked by discrete events, such as incendiary incidents involving encounters between American soldiers and South Korean citizens.[30] Then there's the problem with television as a medium. Footage of anti-American demonstrations featuring angry slogans, flag burnings, and clashes with police make for "sit up and take notice" headlines, but they can convey the impression that such protests are routine, or that they reflect spiraling hostility toward the United States on the part of South Koreans generally. In news coverage, a picture, which necessarily omits complexities and nuances, is not worth a thousand words.[31]

Ill will toward the United States among South Koreans has certainly increased since the end of the cold war, as has the belief that the American military presence in South Korea actually reduces their safety, but these sentiments have their deepest roots among those born after the Korean War; their understanding of that conflict and the part played by the United States (and many other states) in defending South Korea has been shaped by stories, texts, and photographs, not visceral experience. South Koreans also still remain apprehensive about North Korea, in general, and a nuclear North Korea, in particular. When the Pentagon, faced with a shortage of troops in Iraq, redeployed some forces from the Korean peninsula, South Koreans did not react with full-throated glee. There is, moreover, no shortage of South Korean commentators warning against an American disengagement and hailing the continued value of the alliance, especially when faced with American voices advocating disengagement.[32] Koreans are not marching in lockstep when it comes to their views on the alliance.

This having been said, the end of the cold war and the transformation that has occurred in South Korea's relationships with Russia and China have enabled antagonism toward the United States among South Koreans to emerge more easily and to gain greater depth: the cost of criticism is simply less prohibitive now that the neighborhood is less dangerous. As a result, support for the alliance is weakening and antipathy toward the United States is becoming stronger, and a more prominent part of South Korean politics. The ranks of anti-American demonstrators are no longer populated mainly by student radicals and others from the far left; they include a larger and more representative slice of the population.[33] Furthermore, the fear that the presence of American troops actually increases the likelihood of war appears to be on the rise. (If this seems irrational, it is well to keep in mind that Seoul, which is home to almost a quarter of all South Koreans, is less than fifty miles from the DMZ and would be hard hit were war to break out.)

Public opinion polls taken in South Korea between 2000 and 2005 show that unfriendly attitudes toward America are strong and exist for several reasons, and that some are quite surprising. Furthermore, now that South Korea is a democracy, citizens' attitudes matter: the alliance's future ultimately depends on whether support for the continued presence of American troops remains solid and persistent. Polls that plumb this topic need to be treated with care, of course: as with polls generally, much depends on how the questions are formulated, and the political context in which they are posed. Attitudes do not remain frozen over time; they reflect the state of the bilateral relationship; and polls permitting a range of responses—as opposed to a "stay" or "withdraw" dichotomy—show that only a small minority of South Koreans favors immediate, unconditional withdrawal.[34] Even allowing for these nuances and caveats, one would be hard put to make the case based on data from opinion surveys that the American military presence enjoys solid support among South Koreans and that there has been no change in their attitude.

Five surveys conducted by South Korea's *JoongAng* newspaper between the fall of 1990 and the summer of 2003 showed that a majority supported keeping U.S. troops in place only in two years, 1997 and 2003, when 60 percent were in favor, and that the percentage ranged between 35 and 45 in the remaining three years.[35] Other polls reveal a different and no less important side of the same issue: the percentage who favored the withdrawal of American forces was 67.3 percent in 2000, 68.4 in 2003, and 54 percent in 2005.[36] Even allowing for the background conditions that create variations in the strength of sentiments and for polls showing continued backing for the alliance, the picture that emerges is clear. Support for the presence of America troops is far less solid than is generally assumed, while outright opposition is remarkably high—and these attitudes are not ephemeral.

Another question central to the outlook for the alliance is the degree of goodwill toward the United States. Here again the news is not positive. A 2002 poll showed that 53 percent held a very or essentially positive attitude toward the United States, while 44 percent were "somewhat unfavorable" or "very unfavorable"—about an even split in sentiment toward a key and longtime ally. These results were mirrored in a survey taken the following year: 47 percent had a favorable view of the United States, to one degree or another; 50 percent did not.[37] In polls taken in 2005, only 20 percent of those surveyed said that they trusted the United States (44 percent reported a lack of trust; the rest gave no response), while 77 percent believed that the state of the alliance was worse than it was two years ago.[38] And when asked in 2003 whether the American troops helped keep the peace, those who volunteered a view were divided roughly evenly: 34 percent opined that they did; 30 percent said that they did not.[39]

Two polls conducted in 2005 showed even more surprising results. The first, which focused on individuals born between 1980 and 1989, asked whether South Korea should side with Pyongyang or Washington in the event that war erupted. Fully 65.9 percent of the respondents chose the former country, not their ally.[40] In the second survey, which was not pegged to the age of respondents, 37 percent said that any war on the peninsula would be started by the United States and 49 percent believed that it would be initiated by North Korea. One way to assess this result is to conclude that the alliance remains strong because more people still see North Korea as the more dangerous party; another is to wonder why, despite the history of war, crises, and hostility between North Korea and South Korea, and the alliance uniting Seoul and Washington, over one-third of South Koreans polled considered the United States the true threat to peace, with the percentage increasing when those responding were below age thirty.[41] The latter conclusion, I would argue, is the one that bears thinking about.

Also striking is the difference in perspective between Americans and South Koreans on how best to deal with Pyongyang, the common threat that is supposed to keep the alliance in business. An overwhelming majority of South Koreans oppose a hard line toward North Korea, particularly if it involves the use of force. This is true even when it comes to preventing a nuclear-armed North Korea: most South Koreans are convinced that the threat or use of force will only provoke North Korea and increase the risk of war—an outcome that they desperately want to avoid, but fear may occur because of events beyond their control.[42] Quite apart from a divergence on tactics, South Koreans have a decidedly more positive image of North Korea—precisely when their attitude toward the United States seems to be changing for the worse.[43] A poll that has tracked South Korean perceptions of Pyongyang since 2003 shows that the percentage who believed that it was possible to cooperate with North Korea rose steadily from 36 in 2003; to 39 in 2004; to 43 in 2005. Suspicion toward North Korea also declined over this period, with only 36 percent expressing wariness or hostility in 2005. Astonishingly, when asked to identify countries that they viewed positively,

North Korea placed second behind the United States in each of the three years.[44] This is not an aberration; other opinion surveys confirm that North Korea is now seen by South Koreans through kinder, more hopeful eyes.[45]

Parting Ways on Policy

It should come as no surprise that with the consolidation of democracy in South Korea, the government's policies reflect these changes in public perceptions, and its policies toward North Korea exemplify this. Seoul has continued providing food and other forms of economic assistance to North Korea even when the West and the World Food Program have held back, thus effectively reducing the pressure Pyongyang faces on this particular front. South Korea has also vigorously promoted cultural contacts and trade and investment with North Korea on the premise that carrots will prove more effective than sticks in dissuading Pyongyang from developing nuclear weapons, and thus evoking its cooperation on other issues—a position in decided contrast to the Bush administration's. An American expert summed up the variance in attitudes toward handling North Korea as follows: "Whatever the public relations facades that both South Korea and the U.S. governments may wish to set up about the convergence of views . . . the differences are apparent and troubling, and obviously important to a large segment of the Korean public." As one Korean academic said, "If Americans are considered friends North Koreans are considered brothers. The U.S. should remember this."[46] The differences on how to deal with North Korea have become more pronounced with the end of the cold war, and they have not turned on which party controls the White House. This is apparent from Seoul's frustration at being left out of the loop as the Clinton administration tried to persuade Pyongyang to freeze its nuclear program in exchange for light water nuclear reactors (to address North Korea's claim that it needed nuclear power to supply energy for the economy) and political normalization. At bottom, what is at work is South Koreans' belief that they have come into their own and must now manage their own fate and refuse to be a means to serve the larger ends of great powers, no matter if they are longtime allies. Opinion surveys show that South Koreans are eager for a policy toward North Korea that is independent from and not contingent on American preferences, or the constraints created by the alliance.[47]

True, dislike of the United States rises and falls and is found disproportionately in younger, well-educated Koreans, but this does not mean that anti-Americanism does not matter to the alliance's future viability. While there certainly have been peaks and valleys in South Korean public attitudes, unfavorable attitudes in areas central to the alliance have remained remarkably persistent in recent years. Oddly enough, familiarity could be the foible for an alliance that has lasted for decades but has been slow to adapt to the increasing power and influence of South Korea. South Koreans want greater autonomy, but Washington is loath to alter what it sees as an arrangement that, from its standpoint, has worked well and that it does not consider hierarchical in the way that South Koreans increasingly do. Nor should Washington seek solace from the fact that it is young, educated South Koreans who are most likely to harbor ill will toward the United States, for they are precisely the ones who will soon occupy positions pivotal to the alliance and whose views will matter most in shaping South Korea's political climate and policy toward the United States. If their current attitudes are any guide, they will be far more apt than their elders to hold the view that South Korea no longer needs American tutelage and protection and should therefore not act as a subordinate.[48] The passage of time guarantees that older Koreans who experienced the Korean War and who most value the American connection will play a diminishing role in South Korean politics. Senior military, diplomatic, and national security officials, and academic experts, who polls show strongly support the alliance, not least because their careers have been shaped by it, will move into retirement, passing the torch to a younger generation with markedly different attitudes.[49]

To the generation approaching retirement, the Korean War demonstrated the danger presented by North Korea and the importance of American protection. By contrast, the younger generation grew up in a country that is economically prosperous and politically self-confident and less fearful of North Korea as a result. A large proportion of these young men and women were born after the Korean War—half of all South Koreans are under age thirty-five—and reached political consciousness in a democratic South Korea.[50] They share a deep distaste for the authoritarian governments, civilian and military, that ruled South Korea from its foundation until 1987 (when South Korea held its first democratic election) and that disregarded democracy and human rights. And many tend to blame the United States for the survival and conduct of these regimes precisely because they are persuaded that the United States dominates the alliance. And who can blame them for holding this view?

One consequence of generational change is that long-standing irritants, controversies, and suspicions have a newfound capacity for creating discord within the alliance.[51] Among them are the following: whether the United States traded recognition of Japan's colonization of Korea in 1905 for Japanese acceptance of American control of the Philippines; the precise role (through prior knowledge, complicity, or negligence) that American civilian officials and military commanders played in the massacres perpetrated by U.S.-backed authoritarian South Korean governments in Cheju and Yosu (1948) and Kwangju (1980); the repression that marked the rule of the civilian and military dictatorships supported by the United States; intermittent altercations between South Korean civilians and American soldiers; the opposition to the Yongsan military base in central Seoul (which eventually led to a 2004 U.S.-South Korea accord to relocate the garrison); the perceived inequities in the "Status of Forces" (SOFA) agreements governing the U.S. military presence; extraterritorial agreements that place American soldiers beyond the reach of South Korean laws; and whether the United States used the 1997–1998 East Asian financial crisis and its support for the $55 billion bailout provided by the International Monetary Fund (IMF), the World

Bank, and other international financial institutions as a lever to pry open South Korea's markets and to loosen official restrictions covering foreign equity in its companies.[52]

Oddly enough, another source of disagreement is North Korea, long the enemy and unifier. While North Korea's nuclear weapons program has created anxiety in South Korea, the differences between Seoul and Washington on how best to deal with the threat have become downright divisive.[53] Within American foreign policy circles, skepticism about using economic and political incentives to moderate North Korean behavior has always been plentiful. It reached new heights under the administration of George W. Bush, which abandoned the Clinton administration's approach—embodied in the 1994 "Agreed Framework"—of providing political and economic incentives to induce North Korea to renounce nuclear weapons and to accept stringent International Atomic Energy Agency (IAEA) inspections. But the South Koreans were not enthusiastic about Bush's get-tough policy. They made it clear that conciliation and cooperation were better means, both to keep the peace on the peninsula and to gains concessions from Pyongyang. In essence, this approach reaffirmed the "Sunshine Policy" initiated by former president Kim Dae jung, himself a prominent leader of the movement for democracy during the decades of dictatorship.[54] Kim's approach, which was marked by a June 2000 meeting with North Korea leader Kim Il-sung—the "Kim-Kim summit" as it came to be known—stirred excitement and hope in South Korea about reconciliation and even reunification; but it was considered naive, even dangerous in much of Washington, certainly by the Bush foreign policy team. The premise of the "Sunshine Policy" was that isolating Pyongyang would only make it even more intransigent and accelerate its pursuit of nuclear weapons, and that trade, cultural exchanges, and political dialogue between the two Korean states would reduce the danger of war on the peninsula and keep it free of nuclear weapons. This view is shared by Kim Dae jung's successor, Roh Moo-hyun—and, as opinion polls show, by much of the South Korean public.

During the 2002 presidential campaign, which ended with his victory over a conservative candidate and advocate of a hard line toward Pyongyang, Roh Moo-hyun stressed his opposition to policies designed to pressure Pyongyang and his determination to deal independently with North Korea despite American reservations.[55] The differences on how to handle Pyongyang became public in early 2006 when reports that North Korea was engaged in an extensive campaign of counterfeiting American currency and U.S. intelligence assessments that North Korea's nuclear program remained active created a hubbub. South Korean officials distanced themselves from American efforts to bring Pyongyang to account, with President Roh going so far as to assert on television that squeezing North Korea would produce "friction and disagreement between the United States and South Korea."[56] This statement in itself reflects the consequences of generational change and the emergence of viewpoints quite different from those that have prevailed within the traditional foreign policy and national security elite: Roh, a human rights lawyer and democratic activist, was fifty-six when he assumed the presidency, and was a child during the Korean War. He represents a wider change in attitude within South Korean society on issues of security, in particular the preference for engagement in dealing with North Korea. This is why South Koreans saw the Clinton administration's consideration, prior to the 1994 accord, of preemptive attacks on North Korea's nuclear installations as reckless and dangerous. It explains, as well, their view of George W. Bush as a gunslinger, whose allusions to using force to forestall the North Korean nuclear weapons program and labeling of North Korea as part of the "axis of evil" presented greater hazards to their lives than the dictatorial North Korean regime itself. (Even the 2003 decision by the Bush administration to relocate American units stationed near the DMZ to the south is seen in an unfavorable light; the fear among South Koreans is that the United States was removing its forces to safer areas so that it could launch long-range strikes against North Korea if need be.)

Why Past Won't Be Prologue

Better mutual understanding and greater efforts to minimize differences on "the facts" may help bridge the divide, but only up to a point. It may well be, for example, that South Koreans are wrong to fear that American toughness toward Pyongyang, particularly if its involves economic pressure, will bring about North Korea's collapse and saddle them with burdens that threaten their economic prospects, strain their social fabric, and promote political upheaval as a result. The fear bred by this possibility will not, however, be allayed by the calculations of American scholars who, sitting thousands of miles away, offer confident assurances that South Korea has the wherewithal to pick up the tab that would be left if North Korea unravels.[57] The contest between facts and fears is never won so easily by the former.

While American policymakers are unconvinced by the idea that North Korea no longer represents a serious military threat, this assessment has far greater purchase among South Koreans, or so some of their important decisions would indicate, a case in point being the brisk home building occurring right near the DMZ, long viewed as a prime venue for war.[58] While American officials tend to be skeptical that steps promoting interdependence and various forms of contacts will increase goodwill between Seoul and Pyongyang and allow disputes to be settled through negotiation and compromise, South Koreans increasingly take a different view. They are enthusiastic about family reunification programs and cultural exchanges, investments by South Korea in the special economic zone created by North Korea at Kaesong, and the reconnection of discontinued rail and road links and the building of new ones. They believe that these steps will not only reduce the risk of war but also create a climate conducive to pursuing peaceful reunification.

By contrast, American officials regard the upbeat assumptions underlying these actions and ideas as naive at best. For example, in his 2001 testimony before the Senate Armed Services Committee, the commander of U.S. forces in South Korea expressed his concern about the "reconciliation euphoria" that had gripped South Korea, and underscored the continuing North Korean threat by pointing to Pyongyang's massive military, its development of the Nodong missile and its longer-range successors the Taepodong 1 and 2, its ongoing nuclear weapons program, and its failure to implement agreements aimed at reducing the risk of war. That South Korea nevertheless pursues policies of engagement while also reducing the proportion of GDP allocated to defense was an evident source of frustration to him.[59] The general's testimony brings to light a larger problem: the divergence of view between Washington and Seoul on North Korea, which, with the Soviet Union gone and China and South Korea on good terms, remains the principal reason for the American military presence in Korea.

True, Americans are not as divided over the alliance as South Koreans, but in time they too will start questioning its relevance.[60] There is no getting around the reality that the practice of underwriting South Korea's defense has become increasingly odd now that it is a modern, prosperous, highly educated society, whose products are ubiquitous in the American marketplace, while North Korea remains a stagnant backwater. The refrain that South Korea cannot defend itself against such an adversary will wear thin, particularly if anti-Americanism becomes a fixture in South Korean politics. Americans' patience will be taxed even further if disharmony within the alliance rises as the U.S. economy's competitiveness in an increasingly crowded global marketplace declines, and politicians play to the galleries by resurrecting stereotypes of "unfair" competition from "ungrateful" alliances. Such demagoguery will be particularly persuasive if spending on social programs needed to support an aging population places increasing pressure on the federal budget and jobs become harder to find or keep as allies prove to be increasingly strong economic competitors.

Public pressure will then mount to cut expenditures abroad so that problems at home can be addressed, and statistics on South Korea's contribution to the costs of stationing American troops on its soil will have little effect. In any event, Seoul's payments to reduce the burden that the United States has assumed for the defense of South Korea began only in 1991, some four decades after the alliance was formalized, and amounted to $150 million. By 2002 it had almost doubled—albeit in nominal terms—but still amounted to only $350 million, or one-sixth of the overall costs incurred by the United States. Three years later, it stood at $623 million, a significant increase, even taking account of inflation, but still well below the increased sum spent by the United States for its troops in South Korea. American efforts to secure larger payments from Seoul—which Washington would like to increase so that it covers 75 percent of the costs, as Japan's contribution is said to do—were resisted by South Korean negotiators on the grounds that the United States was demanding more while cutting back its presence.[61]

For now, regardless of the costs, Americans favor the deployment of troops and the retention of bases overseas, but they are unwilling to see the United States play the global sheriff and, by a sizeable majority, favor the use of force in cooperation with other countries and with UN approval. This has ramifications for our allies. In the case of South Korea, for example, 56 percent of those surveyed in a major study of Americans' foreign policy views released in 2002 opposed the use of force to defend South Korea, the defense treaty notwithstanding, if it meant that the United States would have to act alone, and only 36 percent were in favor; but the results were almost exactly reversed when the question specified that the defensive effort would be undertaken multilaterally and with the imprimatur of the United Nations.[62]

As with our alliances with Europe and Japan, our existing military commitments in Korea will in time come to be seen as relics ill-suited to the post- 9/11 world. The argument that thousands of soldiers must still remain in South Korea will then gradually begin to lose its persuasiveness, while the views of those who challenge it will fall on more receptive ears. Already, the strategic logic for maintaining U.S. forces on the peninsula is shaky. Consider, for example, that these troops are trained and equipped only to fight North Korea and cannot usefully or easily be transported and utilized elsewhere;[63] that even potential Pacific trouble spots such as Taiwan or Southeast Asia are too distant; and that South Koreans do not want, and will not allow, their military installations to be used for defending Japan or fighting China. Moreover, our policymakers will find it hard to rationalize a policy that ties up many thousands of troops in South Korea (and in Europe and Japan) when the campaigns in Afghanistan and Iraq have shown that the loci of threats and the theaters of war have changed, and that the U.S. military cannot be ordered to undertake new missions while being required simultaneously to continue carrying out old ones.

The idea that the United States could disengage from South Korea is hardly far-fetched. We have seen that forces based there were cut even during the cold war by presidents Richard Nixon and Jimmy Carter. Additional cuts are certain to follow. The Bush administration announced in 2003 that 3,600 troops from the Second Infantry Division, which has been stationed along the DMZ, would be transferred to Iraq, that the rest of the division would be relocated to bases south of the Han River (which runs through Seoul, the capital), and that one-third of the 37,000 soldiers now based in South Korea would be removed and deployed elsewhere.[64] The new strategic environment that the United States confronts and the changes in South Korean attitudes toward America, the alliance, and North Korea all but guarantee that these latest reductions will not be the last.

Ultimately, the true test for the alliance is whether it will serve American national security interests in the twenty-first century. South Korea's decision to send more than 3,000 troops to aid Iraq's reconstruction may suggest that the answer is that it will; American and South Korean officials certainly hastened to present it in that light. But that did not alter the reality that the Bush administration's decision to attack Iraq was deeply unpopular among South Koreans. When polled for a thirty-five-country survey commissioned by the BBC and conducted between October 2005 and January 2006, 70 percent said it had been a mistake and 84 percent believed that it would increase terrorism. A South Korean poll conducted almost a year after the war began did show significant support for Seoul's decision to send troops to help stabilize Iraq, with 60 percent favoring it. But 37 percent were opposed, suggesting a strong basis for a shift in sentiment if the situation in Iraq deteriorated. As evidence mounted that the United States was getting bogged down in an Iraq increasingly defined by anarchy and violence, and as terrorist groups threatened to attack South Korea for its military presence there, South Koreans' mood did indeed change. The BBC poll showed that 51 percent of them had concluded that the United States and its allies should withdraw from Iraq. It was not surprising in light of these attitudes that in late 2005—and hard on the heels of a visit by President Bush—Seoul announced that its contingent in Iraq would be cut by one-third. The lesson here—and one that applies, as I have noted, to NATO and Japan as well—is that the notion that the U.S.-South Korean alliance will reinvent itself to support American missions beyond the North Pacific is chimerical. Not only did most South Koreans oppose the war in Iraq and the dispatch of their troops there, they also do not want to be part of similar American missions in the future. As an editorial in a South Korean newspaper put it, "the character of a USFK [United States Force in Korea] which is devoted to the defense of the Korean peninsula is different from that of a USFK which defends against threats from the world's rogue states and terrorist organizations. In spite of America's global strategy, the primary role of the USFK must clearly be the defense of the Korean peninsula."[65] This is a wholly reasonable position for Seoul to take. But Americans—most of whom already seem unwilling to go to war unilaterally in defense of South Korea—could be forgiven for wondering why the United States should defend a country that is capable of defending itself but whose government continues to insist that a fifty-year alliance remain unchanged.

Proposals for reforming the alliance to make it relevant to new realities fall into two categories. The first recommends expanding the alliance's military scope so that it provides security to the wider Asia Pacific region. But this begs the question of whether and why Koreans would agree to become entangled in distant and possibly dangerous missions and why East Asia's security could not be accomplished more effectively and with less risk by a multilateral security arrangement, the approach that South Koreans seem to favor anyway.[66] A second set of proposals would have the alliance retain its traditional missions of deterrence and war fighting on the peninsula but while assuming nonmilitary responsibilities in East Asia, among them promoting markets, democracy, and human rights. Here, the questions I raised about NATO's future are apposite: Why do these goals, laudable though they are, require a military alliance? And why is the U.S.-South Korean alliance, as opposed to a larger coalition of wealthy states, not better suited to realizing them?

Whither Pyongyang and Beijing?

The most serious challenge facing the U.S.-South Korean alliance is North Korea—not its menace, but its mortality. The seriousness of North Korea's economic problems is increasing. Its GDP shrank by 50 percent in the course of the 1990s, approximately a million people died in the famine that gripped the country in the latter part of the 1990s, and in every respect the economic system is ill-equipped to deal with the competitive world market created by globalization.[67] While North Korea's obituary has indeed been written many times, the unraveling of the country and the subsequent emergence of a unified Korean peninsula is no longer a fantasy. North Korea's end may prove quick or slow, violent or peaceful, and the consequences for South Korea could be manageable, economically and politically, or chaotic and expensive.

The possibility that a unified Korean state could emerge on account of changes within North Korea should not be ruled out. There are many influences that could change the direction of a regime that, until the 1990s, seemed determined to avoid economic reform and to minimize contact with the outside world. They include the increase of travel to and from South Korea (2,500 North Koreans visited South Korea in 2000, and 5,385 in 2004; while 26,534 South Koreans visited North Korea, compared to 7,280 in 2000); the circulation in North Korea of tapes and DVDs of South Korean television programs; slow increases in trade between the two Koreas; and increasing South Korean investments in North Korea.[68] Cumulatively, these transactions could accelerate the incremental and minimal economic and political changes already visible in North Korea. Before this denouement is dismissed, it should be recalled that the post-Stalinist Soviet Union's progressively greater openness to external influences was an important catalyst for the political ferment that eventually led to its demise and that the end came, for the most part, peacefully, taking virtually everyone by surprise. Even those who predicted an eventual collapse said that it would be the result of different causes, such as a war with China.[69] In light of this, can we rule out the possibility of a dramatic and unforeseen change in North Korea that redefines the peninsula environment?

Nobody knows, of course, whether or when a single Korean state will emerge. But this much is certain: if it does, the case for permanent U.S. bases and troop deployments will crumble soon thereafter. American military forces may remain on the peninsula for a transitional phase, but Korean nationalism and China's eagerness to remove the American beachhead on its southern rim will make it a brief one. And once the peninsula's politics are transformed in this manner, even the most fervent American advocates of keeping U.S. forces in South Korea will be hard put to insist that a past practice must persist.

As I have observed in discussing the U.S. alliance with Japan, China is widely expected to become a powerful country that challenges American primacy and becomes the next big threat.[70] Those who are sure about this scenario insist that the retention of American forces in Northeast Asia is essential for this reason. The problem, however, is that South Koreans do not want to turn the alliance into a mechanism to balance an ascendant China, just as they have no appetite for reshaping the alliance to support far-flung American military interventions. This is because they do not see China as the equivalent of the Soviet Union. To the contrary, for several reasons, they view it as a state with which they can live amicably and on a mutually beneficial basis. China has replaced the United States as South Korea's biggest trade partner, it represents a civilization with which Koreans share centuries-old cultural and historical ties, and it has become more popular in South Korean society than the United States. Moreover, as Koreans cast wary eyes on Japan and worry that it could turn nationalistic and pump up its military might, they see China as a strategic soul mate, perhaps even an ally.

China is, in short, fast becoming the country South Koreans consider most important in the new century.[71]

The bottom line of this chapter, then, is that the U.S.-South Korean alliance is fast losing its strategic purpose and is starting to flounder. It will not be reinvigorated by new adversaries; the new missions offered to ensure its relevance lack support among South Koreans and will, in fact, create tensions between the two allies; and the perspectives and priorities of Americans and South Koreans are pulling in different directions. What lies ahead is not enmity, however, but—as with NATO and the U.S.-Japan military pact—the end of a once-effective and now-obsolete alliance.

Conclusion

6

At the end, we return to the beginning—to impermanence, which evokes excitement because it brings newness, but also anxiety because it displaces familiar routines. Impermanence is a double-edged sword. We like it—and don't. Paradigm shifts, dramatic manifestations of impermanence, appear in various walks of life, including, as we observed in the introductory chapter, the history and grand strategies of nations. The changes in established grand strategies created by paradigm shifts can be sharp, though not necessarily sudden, and the accompanying reorientations are often unforeseen, so implausible did they seem before signs of their arrival became undeniable. Not infrequently, these shifts are resisted, for they steer states into unfamiliar waters, making existing maps obsolete.

Recall, from chapter 2, the advocates of continued neutrality in the 1930s, who campaigned mightily to prevent the United States from entering the war in Europe as an ally of Britain. They invoked the longtime American renunciation of alliances and argued that abandoning that policy would plunge the nation into a war that it should have no part of and that would endanger its security. American policy took a new tack nevertheless and set a course that eventually led to the era of containment, during which permanent alliances became the hallmark of U.S. policy. This new strategy departed wholesale from the precepts of Washington's Farewell Address, which stressed the evils of alliances and had served as the nation's compass for over a century and a half.

A Summing Up

Of the many cold war alliances formed by the United States, the pivotal ones were in Western Europe, Japan, and South Korea—centers of power that American policymakers deemed too important to allow to drift into the Soviet sphere of influence, let alone to be occupied by the Red Army. So it was that the vast majority of American troops stationed abroad came to be ensconced in these three places. Despite the collapse of the Soviet Union and the consequent end of the cold war, there has been no fundamental change: as recently as 2003, of the 199,334 U.S. troops posted abroad, 187,000, or 94 percent, still remained in these three places.[1]

This makes little—if any—sense. It's time for America to stop being a nanny state and for our wards, now among the richest, most advanced places on earth, to fend for themselves. If we continue a cold war strategy in a post–cold war world we will inevitably run up against the iron law of impermanence. Sooner or later, the mismatch between reality and policy will become apparent. Either we make new maps or we come to resemble the moth in John Tarrant's story. Happily, it looks like we won't, as witness the redeployment of American forces from Europe, Japan, and South Korea in the wake of the war in Iraq, which I believe is the beginning of a trend.

The claim that America's allies cannot do more, or that they are already doing their utmost to take charge of their security, is simply false.

There is certainly no lack of capacity. Their gross domestic products (GDPs) are among the world's largest; but in most cases the proportion they allocate to defense spending is well below what the United States does, in many cases substantially so. Their budgetary priorities remain where they have been. In fact, in several instances, defense spending as a percentage of GDP has declined.

Let's look at some pertinent data.[2] Between 1995 and 2003, with the exception of Norway, Luxembourg, Spain, and Turkey, of the fourteen non-U.S. North Atlantic Treaty Organization (NATO) states for which information is available, defense spending (calculated in dollars at 2003 exchange rates) fell in every case. So did defense spending as a percentage of GDP for twelve out of seventeen states for which there are figures. While U.S. defense spending declined by 2.6 percent from 1995–2001 because of the increased spending after 9/11 it actually increased by 16 percent between 1995 and 2003. American expenditures as a percentage of GDP did decline by 9.9 percent over the same time span, but only two non-U.S. NATO states, Turkey and Luxembourg, showed an increase, and with the exception of two allies (Greece and Norway), the others registered an even greater reduction. Japan and South Korea present a somewhat different picture. Japanese defense spending increased by 11.5 percent between 1995 and 2003, but the increase represented a mere 0.8 percent measured as a proportion of GDP. South Korea's spending grew by 38.6 percent over the same period, but declined by 2.9 percent as a proportion of GDP.

There is also a large gap between the United States and its NATO allies when it comes to key categories of military power, and again, it cannot entirely be explained by pointing to differences in capacity. To begin with, the populations of the United States and its NATO partners are of roughly equal size. While American per capita income was about $10,000 greater than the total for non-U.S. NATO states in each year between 1995 and 2002, the latter's increased by a larger percentage. The increase in the combined GDP of non-U.S. NATO countries and the GDP of the United States between 1995 and 2003 was equal (28.8 percent apiece), but the increase in non-U.S. NATO countries' combined GDP per capita was greater by two percentage points, 18.7 percent versus 16.7 percent. Yet, even if one takes into account that the United States is a superpower with a global military presence, there is a significant imbalance when the United States and its NATO partners are compared in terms of their share of the total provided by all allies (non-U.S. NATO, Japan, South Korea, and various Arab countries) in major components of military power. The share of non-U.S. NATO is respectable for ground forces (40.8 percent), but it is barely one-third in naval and airpower and well below 20 percent in military transportation and logistics. As for expenditures on weapons and military research and development (R&D), the United States accounts for 73 percent of NATO's total. (Japan's and South Korea's shares are omitted given that the number of non-U.S. NATO states is so much larger.)

This lopsidedness will not change if business proceeds as usual, something American leaders have conceded. Noting the allies' cuts in defense spending and the demographic realities—aging populations, increased claims on budgets for programs needed to support the aged, and shrinking tax bases—former Defense Secretary Donald Rumsfeld expressed pessimism about the prospects for increases.[3] Something is amiss here. Either America's allies don't feel as vulnerable to the threats they will allegedly confront if we depart, or they don't need to do more because American protection continues to be available. Neither conclusion is, to put it mildly, a ringing endorsement of our alliances.

The invariable response to this observation is that the charge of inequity is unfair because our allies share the costs of deploying American forces on their territories. Indeed they do, but their contributions should be placed in context. In 2002, members of NATO covered—there were, of course, individual variations—an average of 28 percent of the costs involved, while South Korea and Japan did much better, paying roughly 50 percent and 75 percent, respectively. As we have seen in chapter 4 in the case of Japan, however, tallies of allied contributions exclude other significant expenditures paid for by the United States. Nor is there reason to expect substantially greater contributions in the future, from Japan or from the others.

The claim that our allies still face threats and that the United States must therefore retain troops on their soil is common but increasingly threadbare. What are the threats Europe faces that require the positioning of some 100,000 American troops there? The Soviet Union has vanished. The military forces of its successor state, Russia, lack materiel and morale—the lifeblood of armies. Moscow does not threaten Europe; it wants a constructive relationship for reasons of economics, politics, and security. Its aim, aside from reaping specific benefits (increased energy sales, for example), is to wean Europe from the United States, not to rattle sabers and revive old fears.

Historically, Europe's biggest problem when it comes to carnage has been itself. Yet its wars, which consumed blood and treasure at a monstrous rate for centuries on end, have receded into the mists of time. War-mongering Europe has yielded to peace-loving Europe, in what is a miraculous example of a paradigm shift. In a Europe where old enemies such as France and Germany are fast friends, war has become inconceivable. No matter its recent setbacks, the European Union (EU) has created the world's only Kantian community of peace.

Japan and Korea are in a different circumstance; as I noted in chapters 4 and 5, they live in a neighborhood that remains dangerous. Granted. Yet Japan is doing much less than it could to defend itself. The retort that it will start down the slippery road to militarism if it does more amounts to a crude stereotype that suggests, whether by design or default, that imperialism is an irreducible attribute of Japanese "national character." Japan's choice is not limited to minimalism or militarism. There is a healthy, reasonable middle ground, and Japan, which increasingly wants to become a "normal" country, must find it and develop a strategy that combines power with reassurance, military might with diplomacy.

Among the points made in chapter 5 is that South Korea can already protect itself against North Korea much more effectively than run-of-the-mill analyses suggest. Every economic and technological indicator shows that it is leaving North Korea, which can't produce a decent refrigerator, let alone modern weapons, ever farther behind. Moreover, whatever Washington may think, South Koreans, while they understand that North Korea must still be deterred militarily, also believe that it must be engaged economically and politically. And that's what they are doing—in contrast to American policy, indeed in defiance of it.

The real question is whether there is a sound case to still deploy a total of some 70,000 U.S. troops in Japan and Korea. I do not think there is.

The chapters on NATO and the U.S. pacts with Japan and South Korea also show that the chances of redesigning them for new missions are slim.

The citizenry of NATO countries does not—as was noted in chapter 3 —want the alliance to morph into a U.S.-led posse that operates outside Europe. The Iraq war—largely an American undertaking anyway—split the alliance. Even most of the NATO allies that provided troops for the postwar occupation have pulled them out, or are doing so as I write. The Afghanistan campaign is a special case because it is covered by a UN peacekeeping mandate. Despite that, there were sharp divisions over the issue of moving from the original mission, providing stability in the north and west to enable economic reconstruction, to fighting the Taliban in the southeast. It remains to be seen how long those NATO allies that have agreed to assume counterinsurgency missions will actually remain steadfast—and for how long—if the Taliban becomes an even more formidable foe.

What about NATO's future as a global peacekeeping organization? In a word, for reasons mentioned in chapter 3, it's not promising. The lesson of Rwanda, Liberia, and Darfur is that European NATO—or the United States, for that matter—has no desire to become a global policeman, sorting out civil wars and keeping the peace among warring parties. These are dangerous tasks that can last for years and prove futile in the end, which explains the noticeable lack of enthusiasm Europeans have for such assignments. They worry about being pulled into quagmires, they do not want to spend the money needed to develop military capabilities for mounting and sustaining such far-flung missions, and their attitudes toward the United States do not bode well for a U.S.-led NATO that looks beyond Europe as a way to stay in business.

The situation is similar in Japan and Korea. Japanese strongly support the alliance but they do not want to transcend the terms of the defense treaty and undertake combat missions with the United States in parts of Northeast Asia that lie beyond their homeland. (Why do so when the United States will make sure Japan's extended perimeter is safe?) American strategists who believe that a rising China will serve as a common threat and ensure the longevity of the alliance wrongly assume that Japan will adopt a more capacious conception of defense within the framework of the alliance. I believe that the alliance, far from facilitating such a change, will prevent it by preserving the status quo.

South Koreans, for their part, are much less supportive of the alliance and much more out of sync with the United States on how best to deal with North Korea. Once the Korean peninsula is reunified, they are quite unlikely to support the continued presence of U.S. troops. Nor will they join any future American plan to balance China, which they regard as a friendly state.

These are the reasons why the cold war alliance system will unravel. But this will not occur all at once or at the same pace. NATO faces the biggest challenge when it comes to defining a new rationale for its continuation as a military pact. Japan is at the other extreme because public support of the alliance remains strong. Korea is in an intermediate position, but one that is more similar to Europe's. American military disengagement from this strategic triangle won't happen suddenly; nor should it. But if by 2020 U.S. troops are still in Europe, Japan, and South Korea, and America's alliances there remains intact, the argument I advance in this book will be proven wrong. Needless to say, I don't think it will be.

Guidelines for the Future

Someone who writes about the inadequacies of our present policies has an obligation to provide an alternative, even if all that can be realistically done in a short conclusion is to offer some general ideas, rather than a nuts-and-bolts operational plan. Before offering some thoughts on what the planks of a new American grand strategy should be, a point made earlier bears repeating: the sequel to the end of alliances is not the advent of isolationism. As I have argued in chapter 2, American foreign policy has never really been isolationist; the Republic was deeply engaged in the world from the day it became independent—indeed even before that. Herein lies a lesson: alliances are not the only means for being active and effective in the world, and they certainly are not indispensable. The question is not whether the United States engages the world after the end of alliances, but how. I should also reiterate that the end of alliances will not lead to estrangement between the United States and its partners. To the contrary, it can set the stage for creative cooperation among states that share many common interests and that have shifted from alliance to alignment to combine their resources and wits to address an array of issues encompassing politics, economics, and security.

In what remains—and will remain—a Hobbesian international system, security is the sine qua non for all else, and having military power sufficient to defend the homeland as well as vital interests abroad is essential for the United States. Nothing I have said in this book should be taken as suggesting otherwise. The unassailable proposition that we need military power does not, however, tell us what kind of military power we need.

Let's start with nuclear weapons. Despite the deep cuts made in our strategic arsenal pursuant to START I (Strategic Arms Reduction Treaty), we continue to deploy just over 5,000 strategic nuclear warheads (and to retain an equal number that constitute a reserve or have been disabled). Paradoxically, the history of nuclear weapons demonstrates that their only value lies in preventing their use—deterrence, in other words. Seen thus, the U.S. strategic arsenal is far larger than needed to prevent a nuclear attack against us. So the first order of business should be cutting the number to a few hundred and deploying them in ways that make a successful first strike impossible. If that is done, we will be safe; only a state set on suicide would attack the United States with nuclear arms.

There may be another benefit, namely, reducing the appeal of nuclear weapons and, in consequence, the perils of proliferation. States do not, of course, acquire nuclear weapons (India, Israel, or Pakistan) or try to (Iran and North Korea) merely because the United States and others happen to have them, and cuts in the existing stocks of nuclear weapons are not a panacea for proliferation. Still, reductions implemented by current nuclear powers could help create a symbolic change, for there's no denying that nuclear-armed states, while preaching the evils of proliferation, have wrought a world in which the possession of nuclear weapons confers the prestige and the badge of great-power status. It's hardly a coincidence that each one of the United Nations (UN) Security Council's permanent members has nuclear weapons and that China began to be regarded differently once it acquired nuclear weapons. Because symbols of status are not unimportant as motivators of behavior, we have an opportunity to lend credibility to our nonproliferation policies by reducing our nuclear arsenal sharply and, on the strength of that bold move, negotiating with the other nuclear powers to reach a common ceiling that is low but sufficient for a minimum deterrent. That is as far as we will get, for no state with nuclear weapons will give them up, but that's still pretty far.

America's current conventional forces were created in a cold war environment and are mainly heavy units built with the Soviet-led Warsaw Pact in mind. There is no such adversary anymore and none on the horizon. A reconfiguration to create a "force structure" defined by lightness, agility, and mobility is in order. Efforts to achieve this have begun and they should be ramped up and sustained. This is not the place to spell out operational details; there is no doubt that a reassessment along these lines implies major changes for the Navy and Air Force as well (though not so much for the Marines, who are already in the mobility business) and a future with smaller forces and different kinds of weapons systems. Given that the United States is a maritime nation, we will always need a substantial navy, but that does not mean that it should necessarily remain in its current form or size, and so the U.S. Navy will also have to face a different future. As all bureaucracies do when faced with the prospect of unfamiliar changes, the armed forces will resist change and attempt to thwart it at every turn. That is not disloyalty; it's normalcy.

No matter their size and configuration, U.S. forces may have to be dispatched abroad when important interests are at stake. On occasion, the distance involved will be considerable, and the United States will need to work out standing agreements with its former NATO allies, and other states with which the United States will come to have convergent interests, for access to ports and airfields, and for storage of equipment and supplies. The end of alliances is not synonymous with the end of access; but access cannot be had without prior understandings.

This raises the question of how and when American military power should be used. That it should be employed to repel attacks on the homeland goes without saying. The harder part involves identifying essential interests, those that must be defended by force if necessary, from secondary ones, those over which reasonable compromises through diplomacy are possible. Of obvious importance in this respect is the alignment of means and ends so that grand strategy is not hijacked by extravagant goals defined by grand conceptions of how the world should look. America must not undertake to remake entire societies, to say nothing of entire regions, which is what the intervention in Iraq was supposed to do in the minds of its most fervent supporters. No matter how eloquently proponents of such revolutionary missions invoke democratic ideals, social engineering by force of arms is a fool's errand, not an element of a viable grand strategy. Armed Wilsonianism is the path to overextension and quagmires, perhaps even insolvency; it soon loses support at home and quickly amasses enemies abroad.

As a rule, the United States should also avoid preventive war. The quandary we face in Iraq is a product of the Bush administration's decision to destroy a government—admittedly a brutish one—even though there was no evidence at the time (nor has any been produced since) that it was about to do us harm. Saddam's horrific deeds have now become the justification for the war because the claims that Iraq had weapons of mass destruction and was providing a haven for al-Qaeda have been proven false. The problem with the "taking down the bad guy" argument is that the world will never lack for thugs; indeed, we have a long record of befriending many, including even Saddam. During his 1980–1988 war with Iran, Saddam received credit to buy American agricultural products and was provided with intelligence information, even though we knew that he was committing massive atrocities against Iraqi Kurds.

The war in Afghanistan belongs to a different category and was not a preventive one. The Taliban was a belligerent: it had long played host to a terrorist organization that eventually carried out a horrendous attack against the United States, killing more than 3,000 innocent people in what was the single biggest attack on American soil, and therefore bore responsibility for the 9/11 massacre. The regime then refused to surrender Osama bin Laden when asked to do so and, in effect, thus spurned the opportunity to avoid war. In this instance, then, the United States had been attacked, and another state had given the attacker sanctuary. Most reasonable people in the world understood that. A far more reasonable criticism of the war is that its air campaign, while it destroyed the Taliban regime, also inadvertently killed many innocents— perhaps more than perished in 9/11—who themselves were victims of that despotism. From an ethical standpoint, that consequence cannot be finessed by antiseptic statements about the unavoidability of "collateral damage" or the liberation of Afghans from Taliban tyranny.

Eschewing preventive attacks is part of a strategy for using power wisely and is not the same as ignoring the realties of power. In a world of armed competitive states, rivalry and war are ineradicable, and the United States must be attentive to the equilibrium in key regions and join like-minded states against those who threaten stability and peace by preying on the neighbors. As the world's premier power, its role in gathering countervailing coalitions will be more important than that of other states. This is illustrated by the Gulf War, which was a skillful achievement in this respect because it answered the aggressor's challenge by orchestrating a diverse UN-sanctioned coalition, combining power with legitimacy, and setting clear limits for the mission.

In the twenty-first century, the state that is considered most likely to contest the existing distribution of power, itself the product of Pax Americana, is China. What's not clear, however, is just how it will do so, to what degree, and when. The advocates of containment believe China aims to displace the United States as the dominant state in the international system. To them China is, ipso facto, an adversary. By contrast, promoters of engagement favor increasing contact and cooperation with China in all spheres, in the hope that it will eventually become a pluralistic polity—if not necessarily a democracy—that is so enmeshed in the global economic and political system that it acquires a stake in its stability and therefore acts constructively within it. In this view, the appropriate task is bringing China into the club.

The difficulty of choosing between these policies is that we do not know what the future holds for China—democracy, authoritarianism, fragmentation? That is why a sagacious policy toward China must combine the strategies of engagement and balancing. The former approach is already followed by most countries, including the United States, and under successive administrations. If the latter plan of action turns out to be what is required, the United States will not lack for partners, for a problematic China will never be solely an American problem. Some critical partners will not be traditional allies: consider India and Vietnam, both of whom would be threatened were China to turn aggressive. For now, however, China remains far inferior to the United States in the decisive elements of power, and hyping the "China threat" may stoke Chinese nationalism, producing the very China we do not want and reducing the prospects for gaining its support on important issues. Even if a policy of balancing China turns out to be unavoidable, it should be judicious and subtle, not alarmist and ideologically driven. A swaggering strategy will, in fact, reduce the size of a countervailing coalition because it will beget a combative China and increase the risks involved in containing it.

A policy that is attentive to the balance of power among states but that refrains from using military power to rearrange the balance of forces within them need not be a soulless one. The right and the left in

America both agree that advancing democracy abroad is a worthy aim, and there are many ways to act on that consensus without recourse to war. All of them involve "soft power," which has many facets and must be applied with patience and without expectation of dramatic, quick results. The war in Iraq is instructive about the perils of an alternative approach based on hard power. Much of the national debate—to the extent there has been one—on it has involved tactical questions: whether the military force was too small, whether the decision to disband the Iraqi army was sound, whether we were taken in by the rosy reassurances of Iraqi expatriates who had large axes to grind, and so on. The true lesson of the war, however, is that a society cannot be transformed by a mailed fist any more than delicate surgery can be performed with a mallet and saw, and that the complex business of advancing democracy requires many delicate instruments and, even if successful, will take considerable time. Soft power often elicits scoffs—by those who think that it is, well, too soft—but those doing the scoffing are often the very ones who are most dedicated to spreading American democratic values, which themselves are a form of soft power.

Discussions about the extent to which democracy should be a goal of foreign policy quite often extend to military interventions on humanitarian grounds, which the liberal left is quite prepared to endorse despite its general distaste for military power. One facet of humanitarian intervention, disaster relief, is relatively uncomplicated. That is because countries are generally willing to lend their military forces for missions intended to save lives following a natural disaster or a famine, and states that receive such help are invariably grateful (note the Asian tsunami and the Pakistan earthquake). This is not the case when it comes to crafting collective responses to ethnic cleansing, mass killing, and genocide (such as occurred in Cambodia, Rwanda, and are going on in Darfur), and the record of the international community has generally been pathetic, callous, and therefore indefensible.

There is no easy formula for responding to atrocities committed by states or civil wars driven by hatred of "the other," whether the primary marker is ethnicity or religion. As a rule, though, when the United States embarks on such missions, it must do so along with other states, and with UN authorization. Unilateral interventions are beyond America's capacity, if only because there will always be too many instances of such violence against innocents. United Nations bashing is a perennial occurrence in American politics, and sometimes it is justified: the UN is home to many irregularities (most recently involving the oil-for-food program) and absurdities (the spectacle of states infamous for violating human rights serving on its Human Rights Commission). Yet polls show that the American public consistently supports the UN and prefers that America respond to gross and systematic violations of human rights through multilateral means and under UN auspices. Much is asked of the UN, but not much is given to it: its peacekeeping budget of $3.6 billion, for example, has tended to be about what New York City spends on its police and firefighting forces, despite the increasing need for UN peacekeepers. If the United States does not want to bear the principal responsibility for responding to atrocities, but also wants action taken when they occur, it (and others who provide most of the UN's funding) must provide the UN with the necessary resources to amass peacekeeping forces and to keep them in the field.

The difficulty with UN-based solutions to atrocities is that they may never get off the ground because they require approval by the Security Council. If the UN is paralyzed by a veto at a time when innocent people are being abused or killed, the United States, together with other like-minded powers, must take the lead in mustering a diverse union of states that intervenes. But NATO will not be an alternative to the UN when it comes to dealing with such crises. Its European members have no intention of making military interventions beyond the Continent the alliance's new job description; indeed, it is very doubtful that Americans will want to see the alliance transformed to this end given how much NATO depends on U.S. military assets. But even if it were possible to use the alliance for this purpose, a U.S.-led Western force will inevitably arouse suspicions in former colonial lands, producing practical hurdles as a result, and allowing the offending state to redefine the issue by railing against imperialism.

A peacekeeping force must be created from a larger array of states and, when possible, should include troops supplied by states from the region where the killings are taking place. The United States and other major powers should limit themselves to providing financial and logistical support, unless the violence cannot be ended without employing their military forces. Had such as approach been tried early in Darfur, many fewer people would have been slaughtered, raped, and driven from their burned villages. Regional organizations, such as the African Union, claim to want to manage problems in their areas, and the United States should empower them to do so by providing the necessary support and insist that other states provide resources as well.

These are the most practical ways to take the lead in stopping mass murders and gross violations of human rights. There will, of course, inevitably be instances where circumstances make even a well-designed strategy impossible to implement. But refusing to try for that reason amounts to evasion, and the past several decades are littered with instances where the international community took the easy way out. The United States is the world's preeminent power and has unique capabilities to forge collective action, and for that very reason it has a special duty to act.

The end of alliances does not, as I have stressed, mean abandoning cooperation with other states on issues of common interest—that would indeed be isolationism. Consider environmental degradation, economic shocks (such as the 1997 East Asian currency crisis), the management of the global trading and financial system, the narcotics trade, human trafficking, and transnational crime rings. Here, a policy of alignment with states (again, the mix and the size of the grouping will vary depending on the issue at hand), including erstwhile allies, is essential, for these are problems without borders, and despite its overwhelming power, the United States cannot address them alone with any real hope of success. Multilateralism is often sneered at, and collective action can indeed be a maddening process, but the idea that we can deal with problems such those just listed alone, or even in concert with our cold war allies, is a fantasy. America's traditional allies will often be among the states we align with in addressing these issues, but they will not be the only ones, and depending on the particular problem, they may not even be the most important ones.

Even the "war on terror" can only be waged with a large coalition. It is not, to begin with, a war. There is no clear beginning (was it 9/11, the first attack on the World Trade Center, the attack on the American embassies in Kenya and Tanzania, or the ramming of the USS *Cole* in Aden harbor?) Nor, quite often, is there a definitive end: consider how long other states plagued by terrorism—India, Sri Lanka, and Israel, for example—have been fighting it. Alas, terrorism is a problem that sometimes can only be managed, contained, and reduced. The elusiveness of the enemy is among the reasons why terrorism presents a problem quite different from war in the traditional sense. Al-Qaeda, for example, has shown an impressive capacity for regeneration and reconstitution. Moreover, it recruits from multiple regions, infiltrates borders, and uses the world financial system and the Internet with supreme cunning and to deadly effect; the globalization it decries is its biggest asset.[4] Even if al-Qaeda is dismantled, it is certain that clones will emerge, and that raises the depressing question of whether 9/11 will necessarily prove to be a one-time attack. For these reasons, an effective strategy against terrorism will require long-term cooperation on a variety of fronts with a variety of states. The partners will include our cold war allies, but again, some of them, such as Japan and South Korea, will prove to be less important than states with which we have never been formally allied (Indonesia), others with whom our relationship is now strengthening but that once had close ties to the Soviet Union (India), still others that are not formal allies but have long been closely bound to the United States (Israel), and states that we once considered adversaries (Russia).

While terrorism cannot be reduced to single cause, there is little doubt that oil-rich Arab states have been a prime breeding ground—although it's not entirely clear why—and that our profligate consumption of imported oil has filled their coffers. Yet we have done precious little to cure, or even substantially reduce, our dependence on oil. Post-9/11 patriotism has involved much symbolism by, but precious little sacrifice from, civilians (except military families). Cars are festooned with ribbons and flags and just about every politician or official sports a miniature U.S. flag as a lapel pin. Our leaders have, regardless of political party, been utter failures in mobilizing public action because they truck in poll-booth pandering, not straight talk, even though there is one issue that can be addressed by summoning patriotism, and that is our dependence on oil. Much more done can be done on multiple fronts to cut our reliance on oil, but there will be inevitable costs. Whether it is through a tax on gasoline (with rebates to consumers with low incomes); incentives for automobile companies to make fuel-efficient cars and for customers to drive them; stringent fuel efficiency standards (in contrast to the anemic ones that now exist); or ambitious, sustained policies to develop alternatives to oil, a serious energy policy must be an essential element of any sensible grand strategy for the twenty-first century. Our failure to act on this front amounts to gross negligence and a simpleminded compartmentalization that separates prosaic life habits from national security.

While our military presence in the Middle East cannot be reduced to greed for oil, widespread theories to the contrary notwithstanding, cutting our reliance on imported petroleum is nevertheless a way to reduce our profile in that region and our dependence on unsavory regimes (a pattern now being reproduced in the oil-rich Caspian Sea zone). This dependence on undemocratic regimes contradicts the democratic ideals we purport to cherish and invites charges of hypocrisy. More important, by forcing us to rely on unstable and unpopular governments whose repressive and corrupt policies we overlook or disapprove of in the lowest register, it breeds animus toward the United States. The failure to recognize this and to take refuge in self-congratulatory formulations and half-truths that explain away American unpopularity on the grounds that it is produced solely by envy and a dislike for who we are is nothing but evasiveness.

Israel will remain central to our Middle East policy, and our connections with it will and must remain strong and multifaceted, for moral and strategic reasons. Yet we must distinguish between unswerving commitment to Israel's security, undiluted opposition to terrorism against its people, a categorical rejection of those who question its right to exist, and a policy that blesses whatever a given Israeli government does. Unqualified endorsement of Israeli policies is bad for us and bad for Israel. American and Israeli national interests will converge at multiple points, but they will never be identical and will sometimes diverge. We must, therefore, speak out against Israeli policies that ill serve us, be they the expansion of settlements, land confiscations, or collective punishment applied to Palestinians. Oddly enough, on such policies, as well as on options available for reaching a settlement between Israel and the Palestinians, the debate in Israel is far bolder and more creative than it is in America, where official criticism of Israeli policies is rare and the debate narrow and sterile, even though forthrightness ought to be the foundation of true friendship.

Last but not least, comes justice. Opinion polls show consistently that Americans want their country to do good works in the world and to practice the values it professes. One specific way to meet these expectations is for the U.S. government to assume the leadership in assembling a community of wealth and know-how dedicated to reducing global poverty. The assemblage must include states (and not just from the West; the revenue of oil-rich Arab states gives them an unambiguous responsibility), corporations, international organizations, and nongovernmental organizations (NGOs). Its goal must be to make the lives of those living on a dollar a day (estimated to number three billion, or half the planet's population) more livable by providing targeted assistance that is substantial and sustained and has clear criteria for success. Not all of the earth's wretched can be helped through such efforts, but that is no excuse for not doing what is possible to help many.

Africa is the obvious place to focus such an ambitious effort. Skeptics will be quick to present the standard arguments against economic aid: local governments are corrupt, failed economic policies explain the penury, helping failure only perpetuates it, and so on. There's certainly truth in these observations, but the poorest people in Africa have no control over what their governments do and cannot, therefore, change the dysfunctional economic strategies of states. Moreover, withholding aid will certainly not affect the sumptuous lifestyles of those in power, the rich and corrupt, but it will hurt the poor. In principle, it should be possible to fashion a strategy to provide basic needs to the poorest people while ensuring that the resources are not stolen.

Assistance aimed at providing basic necessities can make a difference, and with very little cost. The United States now spends two-tenths of 1 percent of GDP on official development aid, and very few rich states spend more than 1 percent. Much can be done, therefore, without spending very much more—and not through the traditional ways, such as helping to build large economic projects, but by focusing on meeting the most basic needs of the poor. The goal would be to increase what economist Amartya Sen, in a departure from standard theories that link economic development to income, calls the "capabilities" of the poor by providing clean water; basic nutrition and health care; primary education; access to mosquito nets so as to reduce malaria; and access to medicines that eradicate diseases such as river blindness, measles, tuberculosis, and malaria and that contain the ravages of HIV/AIDS.[5] This emphasis on simple needs has been championed by another economist, Jeffrey Sachs, who has helped launch pilot programs in select African villages that have yielded considerable success in a short time.[6] That small steps can equal giant strides is shown by a particularly poignant example. Save the Children revealed in a May 2006 report that four million newborns die annually because clean instruments to cut umbilical cords and other rudimentary paraphernalia and medicines are unavailable. Happily, assistance provided by the U.S. government and by the Bill and Melinda Gates Foundation is making a difference.[7] The bitter truth, however, is that no matter how successful American-led efforts to supply basic human needs may be, they cannot eradicate poverty itself. Its causes are too complex and, therefore, not amenable to external fixes. Still, aid that increases the availability of basic needs can make the lives of millions a bit better. And for the poorest of the poor a little is a lot.

The end of alliances can turn the United States toward a new grand strategy. In what is, and will remain, a world of armed states, this strategy is practical about the necessity of force, yet prudent in its use. It sheds the formal military pacts of containment and employs flexible alignments to promote stability and to address the variety of transnational problems. It employs multilateralism, when possible through the UN, so that realism about power does not become an excuse for cynicism in the face of suffering created by natural disasters, or the cruelties of states toward individuals, or of individuals toward one another. It is sober about the magnitude of poverty and its complicated origins, but helps mobilize resources to sustain a policy aimed at providing as many of the poorest as possible with basics needed for a livable life. In short, this strategy combines realism with principle.

Notes

Preface

1. John Tarrant, *Bring Me the Rhinoceros* (New York: Harmony Books, 2004), 159.
2. Michael Mandelbaum, *The Case for Goliath: How America Acts as the World's Government in the 21st Century* (New York: PublicAffairs, 2006).

Chapter 1: The Impermanence of Paradigms

1. Thomas Kuhn, *The Structure of Scientific Revolutions*, 3rd ed. (Chicago: University of Chicago Press, 1996).
2. Richard Ned Lebow and Janice Gross Stein, *We All Lost the Cold War* (Princeton, N.J.: Princeton University Press, 1995).
3. See Sumner Benson, "Deep-Strike Weapons and Strategic Stability—How New the New Russia?" *Orbis* 40 (Fall 1996): 499–516.
4. See Charles Wolf Jr. et al., *The Costs of Soviet Empire*, R-3073/I-NA (Santa

Monica, Calif.: Rand Corporation, 1983); U.S. Department of Defense, *Soviet Military Power*, 2nd ed. (Washington, D.C., 1983), 88.

5. Andrew Cockburn, *The Threat: Inside the Soviet Military Machine*, rev. and updated ed. (New York: Vintage, 1983).

6. Until 1958, CENTO was called the Baghdad Pact. It was renamed after Iraq withdrew following the overthrow of its pro-Western monarchy that year in a coup mounted by radical military officers.

7. On how Gorbachev's reforms inadvertently led to the collapse of the Soviet Union, see Rajan Menon, "The Perils of Perestroika: The Life and Legacy of Mikhail Gorbachev," *Harriman Review* 10 (Spring 1997): 1–4. For Tocqueville's account, see Alexis de Tocqueville, *The Old Regime and the Revolution in France*, trans. Stuart Gilbert (New York: Anchor, 1983), part 3.

8. See Mikhail Gorbachev, *Memoirs* (New York: Doubleday, 1995), 148–150. On the Gorbachev-Yakovlev discussions on reform, see Thomas Rymer's interview with Canada's then-agriculture minister, Eugene Whelan. "The Farm Visit That 'Changed the World'," Russia Profile.org, October 19, 2005: http://www.russiaprofile.org/politics/2005/10/19/252.wbp.

9. See Paul Kennedy, *The Rise and Fall of the Great Powers: Economic Change and Military Conflict from 1500 to 2000* (New York: Vintage, 1989), chs. 2 and 3.

10. Matthew White, "Selected Death Tolls for Wars, Massacres and Atrocities before the Twentieth Century," http://users.erols.com/mwhite28/war stato.htm#European.

11. The figure for the Seven Years War, the median derived from various estimates, is from Matthew White, "Statistics of Wars, Oppressions and Atrocities of the Eighteenth Century," http://users.erols.com/mwhite28/wars18c.htm#7YrW.

12. Data for the French Revolutionary wars and the Napoleonic wars are from White, "Statistics of Wars, Oppressions and Atrocities of the Nineteenth Century," http://users.erols.com/mwhite28/wars19c.htm.

13. For the number of deaths in World War I and World War II, see Matthew White, "Source List and Detailed Death Tolls for the Twentieth Century Hemoclysm," http://users.erols.com/mwhite28/warstat1.htm#WW1. Again, these numbers are the median from experts' estimates.

14. The most prominent recent example is Robert Kagan, *Of Paradise and Power: America and Europe in the New World Order* (New York: Knopf, 2003).

Chapter 2: Alliances and America's Grand Strategy

1. This is a theme elaborated in Walter A. McDougall, *Promised Land, Crusader State: The American Encounter with the World Since 1776* (Boston: Houghton Mifflin, 1997).

2. See, for example, James Oliver Horton and Lois E. Horton, *Slavery and the Making of America* (New York: Oxford University Press, 2005); and David Brion Davis, *Inhuman Bondage: The Rise and Fall of Slavery in the New World* (New York: Oxford University Press, 2006).

3. V. G. Kiernan, *America, The New Imperialism: From White Settlement to World Hegemony* (London: Verso, 2005), 22–24.

4. See Jonathan Spence, *The Search for Modern China* (New York: Norton, 1990), 158–161; W. Scott Morton, *Japan: Its History and Culture* (New York: McGraw-Hill, 1994), 140–143; Patrick Smith, *Japan: A Reinterpretation*, 3rd ed. (New York: Pantheon, 1997), 57.

5. For the text of the Monroe Doctrine, see Thomas G. Paterson, ed. *Major Problems in American Foreign Policy: Documents and Essays, Volume 1: To 1914* (Lexington, Mass.: D.C. Heath, 1984), 81.

6. J. Reuben Clark, "Memorandum on the Monroe Doctrine," December 17, 1928, in *From Isolation to Containment, 1921–1952: Three Decades of American Foreign Policy from Harding to Truman*, ed. Richard Challener (New York: St. Martin's, 1970), 27.

7. The text of the Roosevelt Corollary appears in Paterson, *Major Problems in American Foreign Policy*, 424–425. The quote appears on p. 424.

8. Akira Iriye, *The Globalizing of America, 1913–1945*, Cambridge History of American Foreign Relations, vol. 3 (Cambridge: Cambridge University Press, 1995), 34–38. It is, true, however, that Wilson developed second thoughts about military intervention in Central America. See John B. Judis, *The Folly of Empire: What George Bush Could Learn from Theodore Roosevelt and Woodrow Wilson* (New York: Scribner, 2004), 84–93.

9. Quoted in Walter LaFaber, *The American Search for Opportunity, 1865–1913*, The Cambridge History of American Foreign Relations, vol. 2 (Cambridge: Cambridge University Press, 1993), 124.

10. William Zimmerman, *First Great Triumph: How Five Americans Made Their Country a World Power* (New York: Farrar, Straus and Giroux, 2002), 7. Cuba was also annexed from Spain but received its independence in 1902, although the Platt Amendment turned it into an exclusive American preserve, and its foreign and domestic policies were to be conducted in ways that the United States deemed acceptable. Accordingly, when civil strife rocked the island in 1906, American troops were dispatched to create order and remained on the island for two years.

11. For the details, see Zimmerman, *First Great Triumph*, 424–437.

12. I am grateful to Michael Lind for impressing upon me the salience of the German factor and for the following citations: Alfred Vagts, "Hopes and Fears of an American-German War, 1870–1915," pt. 1, *Political Science Quarterly* 54, no. 4 (1939): 514–35; and pt. 2, *Political Science Quarterly* 55, no. 1 (1940): 53–76; Holger Herwig, *The Politics of Frustration: The United States in German Naval Planning, 1889–1941* (Boston: Little, Brown, 1976); Hans-Jurgen Schroder, *Confrontation and Cooperation: Germany and the United States in the Era of World War I, 1900–1924* (Providence, R.I.: Berg, 1993).

13. See Manfred Jonas, *Isolationism in America 1935–1941* (Ithaca, N.Y.: Cornell University Press, 1966), esp. chs. 1 and 2.

14. Even a critic of the so-called isolationists concedes this. See Walter Lippmann, *U.S. Foreign Policy: Shield of the Republic* (Boston: Little, Brown, 1943), 45–46.

15. Roger H. Brown, *The Republic in Peril: 1812* (New York: Norton, 1971), esp. 12–15 and ch. 4. See also Bradford Perkins, *The Creation of a Republican Empire, 1776–1865*, Cambridge History of American Foreign Relations, vol. 1 (Cambridge: Cambridge University Press, 1995), 224–228, for three critical events during the Civil War that produced crises between the United States and Britain.

16. Thomas Paine, *Common Sense and Other Writings*, ed. Gordon S. Wood (New York: Modern Library, 2003), 6–19.

17. Ibid., 22.

18. Ibid., 22–23.

19. Ibid., 33–38.

20. "Plan of Treaties with France of 1778," Avalon Project at Yale Law School, http://yale.edu/lawweb/avalon/diplomacy/france/fr1778p.htm.

21. Alexander Hamilton, John Jay, and James Madison, *The Federalist Papers*,

ed. Clinton Rossiter (New York: Signet, 1961), hereafter, *FP*. Hamilton's foreign policy views are set forth in nos. 11, 12, and 24.

22. Ibid., no. 3, 38.

23. Ibid., no. 7, 60.

24. Ibid., no. 8, 64–65.

25. Ibid., no. 11, 85.

26. Ibid., no. 11, 85–86.

27. "George Washington, Farewell Address, September 19, 1796," in *The Declaration of Independence and Other Great Documents of American History, 1775–1865*, ed. John Grafton (Mineola, N.Y.: Dover, 2000). Hereafter, *FA*. For an extended analysis of the address and its wider context, see Alexander DeConde, *Entangling Alliance: Politics and Diplomacy under George Washington* (Durham, N.C.: Duke University Press, 1958).

28. On the background and context of the drafting of the document, see Felix Gilbert, *To the Farewell Address: Ideas of American Foreign Policy* (Princeton, N.J.: Princeton University Press, 1961), ch. 5.

29. *FA*, 56.

30. Ibid., 58.

31. Ibid., 59.

32. Ibid., 59.

33. Here I follow and quote from Richard Brookhiser, *Alexander Hamilton, American* (New York: Simon and Schuster, 1999), 116.

34. Ron Chernow, *Alexander Hamilton* (New York: Penguin, 2004), 435–436.

35. Brookhiser, *Alexander Hamilton, American*, 116.

36. *FA*, 58.

37. Ibid., 57.

38. Ibid., 59.

39. Ibid., 57.

40. Ibid.

41. Ibid., 58.

42. Ibid., 51.

43. "Jefferson's Advice to James Monroe, 1823," in Paterson, *Major Problems*, 78.

44. "John Quincy Adams' Account of the Cabinet Meeting of November 7, 1823," in Paterson, *Major Problems*, 81.

45. For representative examples of these positions, see Samantha Power, *A*

Problem from Hell: America and the Age of Genocide (New York: Basic Books, 2002); and Robert Kagan, *Of Paradise and Power: America and Europe in the New World Order* (New York: Knopf, 2003).

46. Among the canonical texts of American Realism is Hans J. Morgenthau, *In Defense of the National Interest: A Critical Examination of American Foreign Policy* (New York: Knopf, 1952). For debates between realists and neoconservatives that, while focused on the war in Iraq, bring out broader and fundamental differences between the two schools, see Gary Rosen, ed., *The Right War? The Conservative Debate on Iraq* (Cambridge: Cambridge University Press, 2005).

47. On John Quincy Adams's political philosophy and career, see Walter LaFaber, "John Quincy Adams: An Introduction," in Walter LaFaber, ed., *John Quincy Adams and American Continental Empire* (Chicago: Quadrangle, 1965), 13–26. On Adams as a grand strategist (and a progenitor of George W. Bush's conception of preemptive war), see John Lewis Gaddis, *Surprise, Security, and the American Experience* (Cambridge, Mass.: Harvard University Press, 2004), 16–18, 22–27.

48. The text of the address appears in LaFaber, ed., *John Quincy Adams*, 42–46; the words quoted are on p. 45.

49. Akira Iriye, *Globalizing of America*, 19–26.

50. Arthur S. Link, *Woodrow Wilson: Revolution, War, and Peace* (Wheeling, Ill.: Harlan Davidson, 1979), ch. 2. On Wilson's aims for the postwar settlement, see N. Gordon Levin Jr., *Woodrow Wilson and World Politics* (New York: Oxford University Press, 1968).

51. The idea of American mediation was, in fact, House's, and he proposed it to Wilson. David Fromkin, *Europe's Last Summer: Who Started the Great War in 1914?* (New York: Vintage, 2004), 104–110.

52. Michael H. Hunt, *Ideology and U.S. Foreign Policy* (New Haven, Conn.: Yale University Press, 1987), 109–110, 131–132; Andrew J. Bacevich, *American Empire: The Realities and Consequences of U.S. Diplomacy* (Cambridge, Mass.: Harvard University Press, 2002), 115–116; Kiernan, *America*, 172–176; Iriye, *Globalizing of America*, 34–38.

53. H. W. Brands, *T.R.: The Last Romantic* (New York: Basic, 1997), 748–757.

54. Barbara Tuchman, *The Zimmerman Telegram* (New York: Ballantine, 1985).

55. Link, *Woodrow Wilson*, 53.

56. Margaret MacMillan, *Paris 1919: Six Months That Changed the World* (New York: Random House, 2001), 7.

57. I thank Melvyn Leffler for reminding me of this fact.

58. Justus D. Doenecke and John E. Wiltz, *From Isolation to War, 1939–1941*, 2nd ed. (Arlington Heights, Ill.: Harlan Davidson, 1991), 79.

59. FDR quoted in John E. Wiltz, *From Isolation to War, 1931–1941* (Arlington Heights, Ill.: Harlan Davidson, 1968), 69–70.

60. See Selig Adler, *The Isolationist Impulse* (New York: Free, 1957), ch. 11; Justus Doenecke and John Wiltz, *From Isolation to War*, ch.1.

61. Adler, ibid., 222–228. Adler notes the effect on Americans of the weakness shown by the European powers and the League of Nations.

62. On the Nye Committee, see Wayne S. Cole, *Roosevelt and the Isolationists, 1932–45* (Lincoln: University of Nebraska Press, 1983), ch. 11.

63. The first Act prohibited the selling of arms to states at war, the second extended the ban to loans, and the third retained these provisions, while also barring Americans from sailing on the ships of countries at war.

64. For the political battle over the neutrality legislation, see Cole, *Roosevelt*, chs. 12, 15, and 22.

65. Jon Meachem, *Franklin and Winston: An Intimate Portrait of an Epic Friendship* (New York: Random House, 2003), 45–81.

66. For the 1939 fight over revising the Neutrality Act, see Adler, *Isolationist Impulse*, 249–250, 257–258; and Dallek, *Franklin D. Roosevelt and American Foreign Policy, 1939–1945* (New York: Oxford University Press, 1979), 199–205.

67. Susan H. Sperling, "Isolationism in American Foreign Policy from Munich to Pearl Harbor," unpublished M.A. thesis, Department of Political Science, Columbia University, 1965, 94.

68. Dallek, *Franklin D. Roosevelt*, 250; Sperling, ibid., 59, 63.

69. Among the books that trace the evolution of American public opinion on intervention in World War II are Adler, *Isolationist Impulse*, ch. 12; David Reynolds, *From Munich to Pearl Harbor: Roosevelt's America and the Origins of the Second World War* (Chicago: Ivan R. Dee, 2002); Robert Dallek, *Franklin D. Roosevelt*, chs. 5–11. A study that has attracted far less attention, but is splendid nonetheless is Sperling, "Isolationism in American Foreign Policy," esp. 1–2, 14–18, and 26–28.

70. On the genesis of, and calculations behind, FDR's strategy and its aban-

donment after his death, see John Lewis Gaddis, *Strategies of Containment: A Critical Appraisal of American National Security Policy after the Cold War* (New York: Oxford University Press, 2005), 3–15. Also see Daniel Yergin, *The Shattered Peace: The Origins of the Cold War and the National Security State* (Boston: Houghton Mifflin, 1978).

71. The books and articles worth reading on the cold war are too numerous to list here, even in part. An excellent and detailed study is Warren I. Cohen, *America in the Age of Soviet Power, 1945–1991*, Cambridge History of American Foreign Relations, vol. 4 (Cambridge: Cambridge University Press, 1995). A recent, and more general, account is John Lewis Gaddis, *The Cold War: A New History* (New York: Penguin, 2005). For a pointed critique of Gaddis's widely acclaimed, albeit America-centered book, and an alternative narrative, see Tony Judt, "A Story Still to Be Told," review of *The Cold War: A New History*, by John Lewis Gaddis, *New York Review of Books* (March 23, 2006): 11–15.

72. "X" [George F. Kennan], "The Source of Soviet Conduct," *Foreign Affairs* 25 (July 1947), 566–582; text of Kennan's 1946 "Long Telegram" available at http://www.gwu.edu/~nsarchiv/coldwar/documents/episode-1/kennan .htm; text of the 1950 NSC-68, available at http://www.fas.org/irp/ offdocs/nsc-hst/nsc-68.htm.

73. For Kennan's complaint, see George F. Kennan, *Memoirs, 1925–1950* (Boston: Atlantic-Little, Brown, 1967), chs. 11 and 15.

74. For a nuanced reading of Kennan's ideas and the subsequent departures from them by the U.S. government, see Gaddis, *Strategies of Containment*, esp. chs. 1, 2, and 3. A brief but perceptive account is Yergin, *Shattered Peace*, 401–3.

75. Gaddis, *Strategies of Containment*, ch. 4, offers a thorough analysis of NSC-68 and the degree to which it extended the concept of containment in ways fundamentally different from Kennan's conception. A succinct but pointed analysis of NSC-68 and its effects on American strategy is provided in Melvyn P. Leffler, *The Specter of Communism: The United States and the Origins of the Cold War* (New York: Hill and Wang, 1994), 93–96.

76. The United States did not formally join CENTO until 1958, but Britain, its premier ally, was the effective leader and founding member. The pact accorded with the strategy of containment, and American leaders viewed it as such from its inception.

77. Chalmers Johnson, *Sorrows of Empire: Militarism, Secrecy, and the End of the Republic* (New York: Metropolitan, 2004), 24, 32.

78. I rely here on the Pentagon's figures as of December 31, 2002. See table E–3 in U.S. Department of Defense, *2004 Statistical Compendium on Allied Contributions to the Common Defense*, http://www.defenselink.mil/pubs/allied_contrib2004/allied2004.pdf. The figures on U.S. military personnel based overseas can vary because of definitional differences and divergences when it comes to what is counted and what is not and for what year(s). See, for example, data (for the end of 2004) in International Institute for Strategic Studies (IISS), *Military Balance*, 2005–6 (London: IISS, 2005), 31–35; and Johnson, *Sorrows of Empire*, 156–60, for higher figures, which reflect deployments as of 2001. Johnson specifies the distribution as follows: NATO/Europe (262,737), Japan (89,301), South Korea (47,507).

79. A recent example is Johnson, ibid., 2.

Chapter 3: Whither the Atlantic Alliance?

1. I am thankful to Professor Sean Kay for drawing my attention to the role of the British.

2. On the dumbbell strategy, the Brussels Pact, and the WEU, see Hal Gardner, "History Suggests U.S. Needs a More Equal Partnership," *European Affairs* 3 (Summer 2002), http://www.europeanaffairs.org/archive/2002_summer.php4. I have also benefited here from exchanges with Sean Kay.

3. See Elizabeth Pond, *Rebirth of Europe* (Washington, D.C.: Brookings Institution Press, 1999); Ronald Asmus, *Opening NATO's Door: How the Alliance Remade Itself for a New Era* (New York: Columbia University Press, 2002); and Philip H. Gordon and Jeremy Shapiro, *Allies at War: America, Europe, and the Crisis over Iraq* (New York: McGraw-Hill, 2004), ch. 7.

4. Kenneth N. Waltz, "The Emerging Structure of International Politics," *International Security* 18 (Autumn 1993): 76. I owe this reference to Sean Kay.

5. The best analysis of the divisions caused by the Iraq war is by Gordon and Shapiro, *Allies at War*.

6. On the salience of Iraq in the 2005 British parliamentary elections and for Blair's comment on the divisions caused by the war, see BBC News, "Blair Secures Historic Third Term," http://news.bbc.co.uk/go/pr/fr/-/1hi/uk_politics/vote_2005/frontpage/4519863.stm.

7. Tariq Ali, "The Logic of Colonial Rule," *Guardian*, September 23, 2005.

8. CNN.com, "U.S. 'Knew Agent Was Going to Airport'," http://edition.cnn.com/2005/WORLD/Europe/03/09/italy.sgrena/index.html.

9. BBC News, "Italy Plans Troop Pullout," http://news.bbc.co.uk/go/pr/fr/-/2/hi/europe/4352259.stm; Richard Owen and Michael Evans, "Italy to Pull Troops Out of Iraq," *Times* (London), March 16, 2005; Daniel Williams and Carlyle Murphy, "Italy Plans to Pull Troops Out of Iraq," *The Washington Post*, March 16, 2005.

10. For international reactions, see Matthew Clark, "Different Takes on Italy's Iraq Decision," *Christian Science Monitor*, March 16, 2005, http://www.csmonitor.com/2005/0316/dailyUpdate.html.

11. See CNN.com, "Berlusconi 'Tried to Dissuade Bush on Iraq'," http://edition.cnn.com/2005/WORLD/europe/10/31/berlusconi.iraq/.

12. "Italy to Withdraw Its Troops from Iraq by the End of the Year," *The New York Times*, January 20, 2006.

13. Details on the withdrawals from Iraq made by NATO members of the coalition are drawn from Robin Wright and Bradley Graham, "U.S. Works to Sustain Iraq Coalition," *The Washington Post*, July 15, 2005; Robin Wright and Josh White, "U.S. Moves to Preserve Iraq Coalition," *The Washington Post*, February 25, 2005; GlobalSecurity.org, "Non-U.S. Forces in Iraq—15 March, 2005," http://www.globalsecurity.org/military/ops.iraq_orbat_coalition.htm; BBC News," "Hungary Announces Iraq Pull-Out,"http://news.bbc.co.uk/2/hi/europe/3979349.stm; BBC News, "Bulgaria Set for Iraq Withdrawal," http://news.bbc.co.uk/go/pr/fr/-/2/hi/europe/4398019.stm.

14. "New Polish President Approves Iraq Mission to End of 2006," *Deutsche Presse-Agentur*, December 29, 2005, http://news.monstersandcritics.com/europe_printer_1072214.php.

15. This showed that commitments that do stem from compelling interest rarely survive tough times.

16. Quoted in "Polish Troops to Stay in Iraq," CNN.com, http://www.cnn.com/2005/WORLD/europe/12/27/poland.troops.ap/index.html.

17. Williams and Murphy, "Italy Plans to Pull Troops Out of Iraq."

18. Robert Kagan, *Of Power and Paradise: America and Europe in the New World Order* (New York: Knopf, 2003).

19. I am indebted to Sean Kay for this observation.

20. Henry Kissinger, for example, remarked that the fracas over Iraq could prove "catastrophic for the Atlantic alliance," but, perhaps for that very reason, concluded that "in the end, French realism will not permit France to stand aside while its strongest ally—which has stood by it through two world wars and the Cold War—pursues its vital interests with a coalition of the willing." Henry A. Kissinger, "Role Reversal and Alliance Realities," *The Washington Post*, February 10, 2003.

21. Francois Heisbourg, quoted in Michael J. Glennon, "Why the Security Council Failed," *Foreign Affairs* (May/June 2003): 25.

22. See Michael Mandelbaum, *The Dawn of Peace in Europe* (New York: Twentieth Century Fund Press, 1996).

23. Consider Estonia and Lithuania, for example: Estonia provided forty-five troops, most of them specialists in clearing mines and handling explosives; the rest deployed under British command to aid reconstruction in the environs of Mazar-e-Sharif in the north. Estonia also supplied dozens of dogs trained to spot explosives. Lithuania's forces stood at 190 at their peak; most were stationed in western Afghanistan in Chachcharan in Ghor province (a hazard-laden area to be sure) to provide security and to gather intelligence, and in Kabul, while forty-five were operating in the south, the most dangerous part of Afghanistan, under U.S. command. This observation is not meant to denigrate the role of these two states, but to show that their contribution was, in the grand scheme of things, small. See Vladimir Socor, "Baltic Troops in Afghanistan," *Eurasia Daily Monitor* 2 (July 15, 2005), http://jamestown.org/edm/article.php?article_id=2370022.

24. William Pfaff, "What's Left of the Union?," *New York Review of Books*, June 14, 2005.

25. Pew Global Attitudes Project, *"American Character Gets Mixed Review: U.S. Image Up Slightly, But Still Negative"* (June 23, 2005), 5. All subsequent references to this study, cited hereafter as *PGAP*, are to the PDF version, http://pewglobal.org/reports/pdf/247.pdf. See also, EurActiv.com, "Ukraine, Bulgaria to Pull Troops Out of Iraq," http://www.euractiv.com/Article?tcmuri+tcm:29-137189-16&type-News; Wright and Graham, "U.S. Works to Sustain Iraq Coalition." For a comprehensive account of all coalition troops in Iraq and details on planned or implemented pullouts, see U.S./Iraq ProCon.org, "Details of Country Participation in the US-

led Coalition,"http://www.usiraqprocon.org/pop/coalitionuptodate1.htm#albania.

26. *PGAP*, 5.

27. Ibid., 5–6, 34.

28. Ibid., 34.

29. Ibid., 7.

30. Ibid., 6.

31. I owe this point to Sean Kay.

32. *PGAP*, 32. Poland, where 61 percent of respondents supported the war on terrorism, and the Netherlands, where 71 percent did so, are the exceptions, but there is no data supplied for 2002 and it is therefore not possible to assay trends.

33. Ibid., 31.

34. Samuel P. Huntington, *The Clash of Civilizations and the Remaking of World Order* (New York: Simon and Schuster, 1996). The most prominent application of this view to the Middle East is Bernard Lewis, *What Went Wrong? The Clash between Islam and Modernity in the Middle East* (New York: HarperCollins, 2003). For a more recent similar assessment, see, for example, Philip Bobbitt, "Facing Jihad, Recalling the Blitz," *The New York Times*, July 10, 2005.

35. For the rejection of such a link by a leading French expert on Islam, see Olivier Roy, "Why Do They Hate Us? Not Because of Iraq," *The New York Times*, July 22, 2005.

36. For an analysis along these lines by a Belgian scholar, see Rik Coolsaet, "Radicalisation and Europe's Counter-Terrorism Strategy," Dedefensa.org, January 30, 2006, http://www.dedefensa.org/article.php?art_id=2376. Also see the debate between the American scholar Daniel S. Hamilton and Sir Timothy Garden (the former of the Royal Institute of International Affairs), "Should NATO's New Function be Counter-Terrorism?" *NATO Review* (Summer 2002), http://www.nato.int/docu/review/2002/issue2/english/debate.html.

37. On this point, see Tony Judt, *Postwar: A History of Europe Since 1945* (New York: Penguin, 2005), 774–776.

38. Candida Crew, "The Inevitable: We're All on Blair's Front Line Now," *The Washington Post*, July 10, 2005.

39. Anatol Lieven, "Engage Muslims or Lose the War on Terrorism," *Financial Times*, July 13, 2005.

40. On the RIIA report, see Glenn Frankel, "Ties to U.S. Made Britain Vulnerable, Report Says," *The Washington Post*, July 18, 2005; and Alan Cowell, "Britain Assails Critical Report on Role in Iraq," *The New York Times*, July 19, 2005; Robin Cook, "Our Troops Are Part of the Problem," *Guardian* (London), July 15, 2005.

41. "The Iraq Connection," *Guardian* (London), July 20, 2005. The poll was conducted by Guardian/ICM. For poll data, see the ICM Web site, http://www.icmresearch.co.uk/reviews/2005/Guardian%20-%20july/The%20Guardian%20Poll%20-%20july%2005.asp.

42. John Micklethwait and Adrian Wooldridge, "After London, Britain's Doubts," *Los Angeles Times*, July 26, 2005.

43. The statistics of Europe's Muslims are drawn from the country profiles in the Central Intelligence Agency, *World Fact Book*: http://www.cia.gov/publications/geos/da.html; http://www.cia.gov/publications/geos/fr.html; http://www.cia.gov/publications/geos/gm.html; http://www.cia.gov/publications/geos/uk.html; http://www.cia.gov/publications/geos/nl.html; and Nadia Mushtaq Abbasi, "Future of Muslims in Europe," *American Muslim Perspective*, August 27, 2004, http://www.amperspective.com/html/muslims_in_europe_html; and the country briefs in Euro-Islam.info, http://www.euro-islam.info/.

44. Euro-Islam.info, "Belgium," http://euro-islam.info/pages/belgium.html.

45. James Brandon, "A Defiant Islam Rises among Young Britons," *Christian Science Monitor*, July 11, 2005; Quentin Peel, "Rootless Bombers and Faceless Cause," *Financial Times*, July 13, 2005; Hassan M. Fattah, "Anger Burns on the Fringe of Britain's Muslims," *The New York Times*, July 16, 2005; Robert S. Leiken, "Europe's Angry Muslims," *Foreign Affairs* 84 (July/August 2005): 120–135.

46. See Rajan Menon, "Terrorism, Inc." *Los Angeles Times*, August 22, 2004.

47. For examples, see Doug Bandow, "Europe's Unhealthy Security Dependence," in Ted Galen Carpenter and Barbara Conry, eds., *NATO Enlargement: Illusions and Reality* (Washington, D.C.: Cato Institute, 1998), 210–211.

48. Jeffrey Sachs, *The End of Poverty: Economic Possibilities for Our Time* (New York: Penguin, 2005).

49. The international community failed to stop Pol Pot's campaign of mass murder or the slaughter of 800,000 Tutsis in Rwanda, but when the Serbian government launched an offensive aimed at driving the Kosovars from Kosovo, NATO intervened, even though many more people died in Cambodia and Rwanda than in Kosovo.

50. See http://www.capitals.com/rankorder/2034rank.html.

51. See William Richard Smyser, "American Might Is Sailing Away from Europe," *Financial Times*, March 2, 2003. Smyser does not, however, believe that this portends the end of NATO.

52. Rowan Scarborough, "NATO Allies Cut Military Since 9/11," *The Washington Times*, February 15, 2006.

53. "Analysis: 'Zombie' NATO Springs to Life," United Press International, December 9, 2005, http://www.terradaily.com/reports/Analysis_Zombie_NATO_NATO_Springs_To_Life.html.

54. Aznar quote from United Press International, "Analysis." For Reid's observation, see Scarborough, "NATO Allies Cut Military Since 9/11."

55. David Calleo, *Rethinking Europe's Future* (Princeton, N.J.: Princeton University Press, 2001), 304–309. Calleo notes that the Europeans' operation in Bosnia was "painfully inept" (p. 305) and that they "were confused about their own purposes and divided among themselves" (pp. 305–306). See also Sean Kay, *NATO and the Future of European Security* (Lanham, Md.: Rowman and Littlefield, 1998), 74–87. On the reluctance of Britain and France, see Judt, *Postwar*, 683.

56. William Anthony Hay and Harvey Sicherman, "Europe's Rapid Reaction Force: What, Why, and How?" *Watch on the West* (A Newsletter of FPRI's [Foreign Policy Research Institute's] Center for the Study of America and the West) vol. 2, no. 2 (February 2001), http://www.fpri.org/ww/0202.200102.haysicherman.europerapidreaction.html. Hay and Sicherman base their statement on the remarks made to Congress by General Wesley Clark, then NATO's Supreme Commander.

57. Judt, *Postwar*, 787.

58. Calleo, *Rethinking Europe's Future*, 360.

59. See ibid., 360–361.

60. Mandelbaum, *Dawn of Peace*, 27–28.

61. For the troop contributions of NATO and non-NATO members for ISAF and the history of the operation, see the following NATO documents: "NATO in Afghanistan Factsheet," http://www.nato.int/issues/afghanistan/040628-factsheet.htm#troop_contributions; and http://www.afnorth.nato.intISAF/about/about_hostory.htm.

62. NATO, "Briefing, Helping Secure Afghanistan's Future," http:// www.nato.int/docu/briefing/afghanistan2/html_en/afghanistan02.html; and Reuters, "NATO Forces Take over West Afghan Duty from U.S.," May 31, 2005.

63. "A Glass Half Full," *Economist*, September 17, 2005.

64. Carlotta Gall, "NATO to Expand Force and Task in Afghanistan," *The New York Times*, October 7, 2005; Vladimir Socor, "NATO Expanding Its Role in Afghanistan," *Eurasia Daily Monitor* 2 (September 8, 2005).

65. Socor, "NATO Expanding Its Role in Afghanistan"; Ahmed Rashid, "Afghanistan Faces Uncertainty After Its Landmark Vote," Eurasianet.org, http://www.eurasianet.org/departments/insight/articles/eav091605_pr.shtml.

66. *The New York Times*, December 31, 2005, and February 1, 2006.

67. "Southward, Ho," *Economist*, November 5, 2005.

68. Ann Scott Tyson, "NATO Far from Relieving U.S. Forces in Afghanistan," *Christian Science Monitor*, December 9, 2003.

69. Robert Cooper, *The Breaking of Nations* (New York: Grove, 2003), 161, 162.

70. See David S. Yost, *NATO Transformed: The Alliance's New Roles in International Security* (Washington, D.C.: United States Institute of Peace Press, 1998), ch. 5; Pond, *Rebirth of Europe*, 79.

71. The phrase is that of Timothy Garton Ash in "How the West Can Be One," *New York Times Magazine*, April 27, 2003, 14.

72. Professor Sir Timothy Garden, "The Future of ESDP: Defense Capabilities for Europe," *International Spectator*, 38 (July–September 2003), http://www.tgarden.demon.co.uk/writings/articles/2003/03815intspec.htm.

73. For an excellent discussion, see Sean Kay, "Putting NATO Back Together Again," *Current History* 102 (March 2003): 106–112. Also, Tony Judt, "Europe Finds No Counterweight to American Power," *The New York Times*, April 20, 2003.

74. Garden, "The Future of ESDP."

75. Judt, *Postwar*, 787.

76. See Rajan Menon, "Fitting the Military to Reality," *Los Angeles Times*, July 16, 2004.

77. Bandow, "Europe's Unhealthy Security Dependence," 210–11.

Chapter 4: A Japan That Can—and Will—Do More

1. Marc Gallichio, "Occupation, Dominion, and Alliance: Japan in American Security Policy, 1945–1969," in Akira Iriye and Robert A. Wampler, eds. *The United States and Japan 1951–2001* (Tokyo: Kodansha, 2001), 115–117.

2. The term is Richard Rosecrance's. See his *Rise of the Trading State: Commerce and Conquest in the Modern World* (New York: Basic Books, 1998).

3. On Mishima, see Henry Scott Stokes, *The Life and Death of Yukio Mishima* (New York: Penguin, 1985).

4. My thanks to Jim Auer for bringing this to my attention.

5. Gallichio, "Occupation, Dominion, and Alliance," 120–121.

6. Figures from Chalmers Johnson, *Japan: Who Governs? The Rise of the Developmental State* (New York: Norton, 1995), 267 (table 12).

7. U.S. Department of Defense, "2004 Statistical Compendium on Allied Contributions to the Common Defense," http://www.defenselink.mil/pubs/allied_contrib2004/allied2004.pdf.

8. For a discussion, see Robert W. Barnett, *Beyond War: Japan's Concept of Comprehensive National Security* (Washington, D.C.: Pergamon-Brassey's, 1984).

9. On these aspects of U.S.-Japan economic relations, see Robert Gilpin, *The Challenge of Global Capitalism in the 21st Century* (Princeton, N.J.: Princeton University Press, 2000), ch. 9.

10. The difference in terminology was pointed out to me by Dick Samuels.

11. Some details are in order in the interests of accuracy and currency. The director general holds the rank of minister of state and the post has cabinet rank. Thanks to Jim Auer and Dick Samuels for these details.

12. The text of Japan's 1947 constitution is available at http://www.solon.org/Constitutions/Japan/English/english-Constitution.html. I am grateful for Jim Auer, Robyn Lim, and Dick Samuels for guidance on the points discussed in this paragraph.

13. For a subtle analysis that examines the link between culture and norms

and national security policy in Japan, while viewing them as contingent and contested, and thereby avoiding an essentialist conception of Japan, see Peter J. Katzenstein, *Cultural Norms and National Security: Police and Military in Postwar Japan* (Ithaca, N.Y.: Cornell University Press), 1996. Despite his acuity, Katzenstein, in my view, gives culture and norms far more significance than they deserve relative to shifts in Japan's (or for that matter, other countries') security environment.

14. International Institute for Strategic Studies (IISS), *Military Balance*, 2005–2006 (London: Routledge, 2006), 270, 279.

15. For a more detailed discussion, see Rajan Menon, "Japan: The Once and Future Superpower," *The Bulletin of the Atomic Scientists* 53 (January–February 1997): 29–34; and Glenn D. Hook, *Militarization and Demilitarization in Contemporary Japan* (London: Routledge, 1996).

16. The discussion in this paragraph of Japan's military policy and capabilities during and after the cold war draws heavily on Menon, "Japan," 29–34.

17. On Japan's World War II submarine fleet, see "Submarines of the Imperial Japanese Navy," http://www.combinedfleet.com/htm. This study notes that "Japan had what was easily the most diverse submarine fleet of any nation in the Second World War." It adds, "during the Second World War, there were 56 submarines larger than 3,000 tons in the entire world, and 52 of these were Japanese."

18. On AIP, see the Wikipedia entry for "Air-Independent Propulsion," http://en.wikipedia.org/wiki/Air-independent_propulsion; and Don Walsh, "Air-Independent Propulsion: An Idea Whose Time Has Come?" http://www.navyleague.org/seapower/aip_alternative.htm. AIP has benefited from technological improvements that have removed some of the significant disadvantages that have encumbered it since it was first developed during World War II.

19. International Institute for Strategic Studies (IISS), *Military Balance, 2005–2006* (London: Routledge, 2006), 279–282; Kenji Hall, "Japan Takes Steps to Boost Military," The Associated Press, May 15, 2003.

20. Richard J. Samuels, *"Rich Nation, Strong Army": National Security and the Technological Transformation of Japan* (Ithaca, N.Y.: Cornell University Press, 1994), 319–340.

21. On this, see Michael J. Green, *Arming Japan: Defense Production, Alliance*

Politics, and the Postwar Search for Autonomy (New York: Columbia University Press, 1995). METI was previously known as the Ministry for International Trade and Industry (MITI).

22. Axel Berkofsky, "Shigeru Ishiba: Japan's Hawk in Chief," *Asia Times Online*, April 10, 2003, http://www.atimes.com/atimes/Japan/ED10Dh01.html; Menon, "The End of Alliances," 13; Eugene A. Matthews, "Japan's New Nationalism," *Foreign Affairs*, vol. 82, no. 6 (November/December 2003): 74–75; Chalmers Johnson, "Some Thoughts on the Nanjing Massacre," *JPRI Critique*, vol. 7, no. 1 (January 2000), http://www.jpri.org/publications/critiques/critique_VII_1.html.

23. "Japan Mulls Strike on North Korea," CBSNews.com, http://www.cbsnews.com/stories/2006/07/09/world/main1786517.shtml.

24. This point is made in Richard Samuels's book, *Securing Japan* (Ithaca, N.Y.: Cornell University Press, forthcoming, 2007).

25. "New Hawks Bloom under Korea Threat," *The Age*, April 5, 2003, http://www.theage.com.au/articles/2003/04/04/1048962932191.html.

26. The term *fissile cores* is used by William M. Arkin and William Burr in "How Much Did Japan Know?" *Bulletin of the Atomic Scientists* 56 (January/February 2000): 11–13, 78–79, a detailed assessment of the extent to which the United States emplaced nuclear weapons in Japan during the cold war. Based on their extensive research into declassified U.S. government documents, Arkin and Burr also conclude that operational nuclear weapons were also stationed on the Japanese islands of Chichi Jima, Iwo Jima, and Okinawa at various points while they were under American occupation. For an extensive review of Japan's record of denial, see Hans M. Kristensen, "Japan under the Nuclear Umbrella: U.S. Nuclear Weapons and Nuclear Planning in Japan during the Cold War," Working Paper, Nautilus Institute, July 1999. Also see the numerous sources listed in "Japan FOIA Documents," Nuclear Strategy Project, http://www.nautilus.org/archives/library/security/foia/japanindex.html.

27. These programs totaled $243.5 million in 2001 alone, according to the U.S. Department of Defense, "Allied Contributions." Dick Samuels pointed out to me the fact that actual transfers have been few in number.

28. Yoichiro Sato, "Japan's Naval Dispatch Expands the Envelope," *PacNet Newsletter*, no. 04A, January 24, 2003.

29. Dan Blumenthal, "The Revival of the U.S.-Japanese Alliance," American Enterprise Institute for Public Policy Research, *Asian Outlook*, February 25, 2005, http://www.aei.org/publications/pubID.22027/pub_detail.asp.

30. See Yuki Tatsumi, "First Steps to a National Security Strategy," *Japan Times*, October 23, 2004; Asia-Pacific Center for Security Studies, "Japan's FY 2005 National Defense Program," *Asia-Pacific Security Studies* 4 (March 2005), http://www.apcss.org/Publications/APSSS/Japans%20FY2005%20National-%20Defense%20Program%20Outline.pdf.

31. I thank Jim Auer for bringing this derisive acronym to my attention.

32. See Matake Kamiya, "Nuclear Japan: Oxymoron or Coming Soon," *Washington Quarterly* 26 (Winter 2002–3): 63–75.

33. Selig Harrison, "Japan and Nuclear Weapons," in Selig Harrison, ed., *Japan's Nuclear Future: The Plutonium Debate and East Asian Security* (Washington, D.C.: Carnegie Endowment for International Peace, 1996), 7, 10, 17–18.

34. Ibid., 8, 10.

35. See "Greenpeace Calls for Cancellation of 'Peaceful' Nuclear Cooperation with Japan as a Special Diet Committee Debates Nuclear Weapons Policy," July 10, 2002, http://archive.greepeace.org/pressreleases/nuclear/2002jun10.html; and Matthews, "Japan's New Nationalism," 76.

36. Quoted in Frank Barnaby and Shawn Burnie, "Thinking the Unthinkable: Japanese Nuclear Power and Proliferation in East Asia," JapanFocus.org, http://japanfocus.org/article.asp?id=391.

37. For example, following North Korea's launch of a satellite with its intercontinental-range Taepodong ballistic missile in 1998, Shingo Nishimura, the vice minister of Japan's defense agency, called for the acquisition of nuclear weapons in a 1999 interview, and was forced from office as a result.

38. Harrison, "Japan and Nuclear Weapons," 18–21.

39. Details on Japan's plutonium stocks from the Federation of American Scientists, "A Call on Japan to Strengthen the Non-Proliferation Treaty by Indefinitely Postponing Operation of the Rokkasho Spent Fuel Reprocessing Plant," http://www.ucsusa.org/global_security/nuclear_terrorism/japan-strengthen-the-nonproliferation-treaty.html; Barnaby comments in Barnaby and Burnie, "Thinking the Unthinkable"; Joseph Cirincione, "The Asian Nuclear Reaction Chain," *Foreign Policy*, no. 118 (Spring 2000): 125–126.

40. On the rockets produced by Japan's space program, see the entry for Japan

in Federation of American Scientists, "Missile Program," http://www.fas.org/nuke/guide/japan/missile; and *Encyclopedia of Astrobiology, Astronomy, and Space Flight*, "H Series (Japanese rockets)," http://www.daviddarling.info/encyclopedia/H/H_series.html.

41. See Ayako Doi, "Unforeseen Consequences: Japan's Emerging Nuclear Debate," *Japan Times*, March 12, 2003; and Robyn Lim, "Toward a Nuclear Japan?" *Japan Times*, September 29, 2005.

42. Harrison, "Japan and Nuclear Weapons," 16–17.

43. This is essentially the position taken by Kamiya, "Nuclear Japan."

44. For the full text, see the Web site of the Japan Ministry of Foreign Affairs, http://www.mofa.go.jp/region/n-america/us/q&a/ref/1.html.

45. U.S. Department of Defense, *Quadrennial Defense Review Report*, February 6, 2006, http://www.defenselink.mil/qdr/report/Report20060203.pdf.

46. See Rajan Menon, "Fitting the Military to Reality," *Los Angeles Times*, July 16, 2004. "Stop-loss" refers to the extension of service contracts beyond the time frame for which they were originally signed.

47. Yoichiro Sato, "Japan's Naval Dispatch Expands the Envelope," *PacNet Newsletter*, no. 04A, January 24, 2003; BBC News, "Japan Extends Its Military Reach," http://news.bbc.co.uk/go/pr/fr/-/1/hi/world/asia-pacific/4078815.stm; "Japan's Koizumi Faces a 'Tony Blair Bind' on Iraq," *Christian Science Monitor*, March 4, 2003; "Worldwide Protests Mark Iraq War," BBC News, March 20, 2005, http://news.bbc.co.uk/2/hi/middle_east/4364305.stm.

48. Christopher Griffin, "Transforming the U.S.-Japan Alliance," *Armed Forces Journal* (March 19, 2006), http://www.armedforcesjournal.com/story.php?F=1230066_1205.

49. The 2005 announcement stated that 7,000 marines would be moved, but an additional 1,000 were added in February 2006. See the Agence-France Press dispatch, "U.S. to Ship Out Marines from Okinawa: Report," in *DefenseNews.com*, February 27, 2006, http://www.defensenews.com/story.php?F=156277&C=landwar.

50. See Tom Shanker, "U.S., Japan Announce Major Changes to Military Alliance," *The New York Times*, October 30, 2005; Griffin, "Transforming the U.S.-Japan Alliance."

51. On Japan's fear of such entanglement, see Hirotoshi Sako, "All Tied Up: Alliance Anxiety," *Asahi Shimbun*, April 19, 2003.

52. For Japan's contribution to the American military presence, see "2004 Statistical Compendium on Allied Contributions." For an example of critiques of the "subsidy," see "Toward a New Relationship with Japan," *CATO Handbook for Congress*, http://www.cato.org/pubs/handbook/hb105-47.html. Also see Doug Bandow, "No One Benefits from U.S. Presence in Japan," February 9, 1998, http://www.cato.org/cgi-bin/scripts/pritntech.cgi/dailys/2-09-98.html.

53. These points are made with cogency and eloquence in Ted Galen Carpenter, "Paternalism and Dependence: The U.S. Japan Security Relationship," *Cato Policy Analysis*, no. 244 (November 1, 1995).

54. The figure on support among Americans for bases in Japan is taken from "40% in U.S. Say Bases Unnecessary," *Japan Times*, September 30, 2004.

55. See the *Economist*, "The World in 2006," http://www.economist.com/theWorldIn/unitedstates/displayStory.cfm?story_id=5134029&d=2006.

56. For a transcript of a Defense Department briefing on the report given by Nye and his response to questions, see "February 27, 1995 Defense Department Briefing," http://link.lanic.utexas.edu/~bennett/__338/us_nye.htm.

57. For an argument along these lines, see Richard Armitage (former deputy secretary of state in President George W. Bush's administration), "Insights into the World—China the Emerging Power," *Daily Yomiuri* (Tokyo), August 14, 2005, http://www.yomiuri.co.jp/dy/world/20050814TDY04002.htm.

58. There is a substantial body of scholarship on the democratic peace theory. A particularly comprehensive and rigorous item is Bruce Russett, *Grasping the Democratic Peace: Principles for a Post-Cold War World* (Princeton, N.J.: Princeton University Press, 1993).

59. For an excellent discussion of this possibility—one rarely discussed by China watchers—and the conditions that make it likely, see Gordon G. Chang, *The Coming Collapse of China* (New York: Random House, 2001). The Warring States era was marked by China's balkanization and conflict among the various fragments; it ended when the Qin dynasty—one of the participants in the wars and based in the western region—enforced unification in 221 BCE.

60. Martin Fackler, "Japan Casts Relations with China in Bolder Terms," Post-Gazette.Com, June 28, 2005, http://www.post-gazette.com/pg/pp/05179/529696.stm, reprinted from *The Wall Street Journal*. For a balanced discus-

sion of generational change and its current and future effects on Japanese foreign policy, see John H. Miller, "Will the Real Japan Please Stand Up," *World Policy Journal* 22 (Winter 2005/06): 36–46.

61. For recent examples, see Masashi Nishihara, "Japan Needs to Protect Itself against North Korea," *International Herald Tribune*, March 4, 2003; Richard Lloyd Parry and Robert Thomson, "Japan Seeks Parasol in Shade of U.S. Umbrella," *The London Times*, February 26, 2003; Robin Gedye and Colin Joyce, "Tokyo Threat Marks End of Pacifism," http://www.telegraph.co.uk/core/Content...s%2F2003%2f02%f15%2Fwkor114.xml&site=5; "Debate: Should the 'Peace' Constitution Be Revised?" *Asahi Shimbun*, April 28, 2003; Richard Lloyd-Parry and Robert Thomson, "Japan to Review Defence Policy to Cope with New Threats," *The London Times*, February 26, 2003; Ayako Doi, "Unforeseen Consequences: Japan's Emerging Nuclear Debate," *PacNet*, no. 12, March 13, 2003; Gillian Tett and Alexandra Harney, "Japan's Defence Role Scrutinized," *Financial Times*, June 13, 2001; Sebastian Moffett, "Japan Begins to Doubt Its Defense Capabilities," *The Wall Street Journal*, March 12, 2003.

62. "Koizumi Visits Shrine, As He Pledged," *The New York Times*, October 17, 2005.

63. On the EEZ dispute, see "Oil and Gas in Troubled Waters," *Economist*, October 8, 2005.

64. Gregory Clark, "Reviving the China Threat," JapanFocus.org, http://japanfocus.org/article.asp?id=497.

65. See "Japan FM's 'China Threat' Remarks Criticized," ChinaDaily.com, http://www.chinadaily.com.cn/english/doc/2005-12/23/content_505846.htm.

66. For a survey of the differences among Japanese leaders and experts on the alliance, and on Japan's future military course, see Kiyoshi Sugawa, "Time to Pop the Cork: Three Scenarios to Refine Japanese Use of Force," Working Paper, Brookings Institution, Center for Northeast Asian Policy Studies, July 2000.

67. Moffett, "Japan Begins to Doubt Its Defense Capabilities." I have also benefited from discussions with Paul Giarra on Japanese perceptions of post–cold war national security.

68. On Japan's nationalists, see Mayumi Itoh, "Japan's Neo-Nationalism: The Role of the Kimigayo and Hinomaru Legislation," Japan Policy Research

Institute [JPRI] Working Paper, no. 79 July 2001, http://www.jpri.org/publi-cations/workingpapers/wp79.html; Johnson, "Some Thoughts on the Nanjing Massacre"; Brian McVeigh, "Postwar Japan's 'Hard' and 'Soft' Nationalism," JPRI Working Paper, no. 73 January 2001, http://www.jpri.org/publications/workingpapers/wp73.html; David McNeill, "Media Intimidation in Japan," *Electronic Journal of Contemporary Japanese Studies, Discussion Paper*, no. 1 (March 2001), http://www.japanesestudies.org.uk/discussionpapers/McNeill.html.

69. Eugene A. Matthews, "Japan's New Nationalists," *Far Eastern Economic Review*, December 20, 2001.

70. From 1998 through 2005, between 21 and 27 percent of those surveyed said that U.S.-Japan relations were "good" (in two years, 2001 and 2005, the percentages were somewhat higher: 29.5 percent and 31.8 percent, respectively), 50 percent said they were "okay," while between 16 percent and 19 percent said that they were "not so good" or "not good." For the latest poll (October 2005), see the Mansfield Foundation's Web site, which provides an English translation: http://www.mansfieldfdn.org/polls/poll-05-12.htm. For the remaining years, 1998 through 2004, see the Japanese Cabinet Office's Web site, http://www8.cao.go.jp/survey/h17/h17-gaikou/images/z02.gif. I thank Erica De Bruin for arranging the translation of the latter polls. Of course, the questions asked in polls, even on similar topics, can bring different results. Thus when Japanese were asked not about their country's relationship with the United States, but about whether they have an "affinity" toward the United States (a rather different query), about 75 percent of them answered in the affirmative from 1978 thorough 2005, according to the data provided by the Mansfield Foundation: http://www.mansfieldfdn.org/polls/poll-05-12.htm.

71. "Japan to Deploy 18 Advanced Ballistic Missiles By 2011," *Hindu* (Madras), October 10, 2005.

Chapter 5: Korea: Coming of Age

1. The treaty was signed in October 1953 and entered into force in November 1954.

2. On South Korea's gross national product (GNP) and its ranking, see *The Economist, Pocket World in Figures* (London: Profile, 2005), 26.

3. On South Korea's economic transformation, see Alice Amsden, *Asia's Next*

Giant: South Korea and Late Industrialization (New York: Oxford University Press, 1989).

4. On the lead-up to the Korean War and the skirmishes initiated by South Korea, see Bruce Cumings's superb *Korea's Place in the Sun: A Modern History* (New York: Norton, 1997), 247–264.

5. *OECD in Figures: Statistics on Member Countries* (Paris: OECD Publications, 2005), table 1, 70–71.

6. Paul Kennedy, *Rise and Fall of the Great Powers: Economic Change and Military Conflict from 1500 to 2000* (New York: Vintage, 1987).

7. "North Korea Wants New Treaty with Russia," *RFE/RL* (Radio Free Europe/Radio Liberty), 89, part 1 (May 1996); Shigeru Aoyama, "Changing North Korea's Strategies, Policies and Their Perspective," http://www.drc-jpn.org/AR-6E/aoyama-e02.htm. By the time the new treaty was signed, Vladimir Putin had replaced Yeltsin as president.

8. Russian arms sales to Seoul have included amphibious transport aircraft, helicopters, and air-to-air missiles. International Institute for Strategic Studies, *Military Balance, 2005–2006* (London: Routledge, 2005), table 34, 312.

9. "Russian Speed Bump on the Road to Pyongyang," *Asia Times Online*, June 14, 2000 (reprinted from stratfor.com, Global Intelligence Update, June 13, 2000), http://atimes.com/c-asia/BF14Ag01.htm.

10. See Rajan Menon, "The Strategic Convergence between Russia and China," *Survival* 39, no. 2 (Summer 1997): 101–125.

11. On this concept, see Rajan Menon, *Soviet Power and the Third World* (New Haven, Conn.: Yale University Press, 1986), ch. 1.

12. On the Bush administration's plans, see Kathleen T. Rhem, "U.S. Realigning, Redeploying Military Forces in South Korea," U.S. Forces Information Service, *News Articles*, September 2, 2004, http://www.defenselink.mil/news/Sep2004/n09022004_2004090207.html.

13. Among the few persistent critics, and one who is very perceptive, is Doug Bandow. See, for example, his "Free Rider: South Korea's Dual Dependence on America," *Cato Policy Analysis* 308 (May 19, 1998) and, more recently, "Making Dangerous Enemies," *In the National Interest*, http://www.inthenationalinterest.com/Articles/Vol2Issue23/Vol2iss23Bandow.html.

14. International Institute for Strategic Studies, *Military Balance, 2005–2006*, 33–34, 287.

15. On the origin and history of "Team Spirit" and of American nuclear weapons in South Korea, see Don Oberdorfer, *Two Koreas: A Contemporary History* (New York: Basic Books, 1997), 76–77, 256–260, 264, 272–274.

16. "Rumsfeld and South Korean Defense Chief Agree to Keep Status Quo," *The New York Times*, October 22, 2005.

17. Oberdorfer, *Two Koreas*, 259.

18. My discussion of the developments related to U.S. forces in Korea under the Nixon, Ford, and Carter presidencies is based closely on Oberdorfer, *Two Koreas*, 84–94, 101–108; and Ted Galen Carpenter and Doug Bandow, *The Korean Conundrum: America's Troubled Relations with North Korea and South Korea* (New York: Palgrave Macmillan, 2004), 107–110.

19. For a notable exception, see Michael O'Hanlon, "Stopping a North Korean Invasion: Why Defending South Korea Is Easier Than the Pentagon Thinks," *International Security* 22, no. 4 (Spring 1998): 135–170.

20. The data on the relative economic strength of the two Korean states are from International Institute for Strategic Studies, *Military Balance, 2005–2006*, 282–284.

21. Jeffrey Chamberlin, *Comparison of U.S. and Foreign Military Spending: Data from Selected Public Sources* (Washington, D.C.: Congressional Research Service, January 24, 2004), table 1, 8. The report compares countries using 1999 data from the U.S. State Department's Bureau of Arms Control and 2002–2003 figures from the International Institute for Strategic Studies. I refer here to the more recent data from IISS.

22. International Institute for Strategic Studies, *Military Balance, 2005–2006*, 282–287.

23. On the tank forces of North Korea and South Korea, see: http://www.fas.org/man/dod-101/sys/land/row/t-34.htm (T-34); http://www.fas.org/man/dod-101/sys/land/row/t54tank.htm (T-54/55); http://www.fas.org/man/dod-101/sys/land/row/t80tank.htm (T-80); http://www.globalsecurity.org/military/world/rok/type-88-mbt.htm (Type 88 K1); http://www.fas.org/man/dod-101/sys/land/m1.htm (M1 A1); and http://www.army-technology.com/projects/t80/ (T-80).

24. For the aircraft comparisons, see the entries on the Web site of the Federation of American Scientists: http://www.fas.org/man/dod-101/sys/ac/row/mig-21.htm; and on the Web site of GlobalSecurity.org: http://www.globalsecurity.org/military/world/china/j-5.htm, http://www.globalsecurity

.org/military/world/china/j-6.htm, http://www.globalsecurity.org/military/
rok/fx-rok.htm, and http://www.globalsecurity.org/military/systems/air
craft/f-4d.htm. The numerical balance in airpower is from International
Institute for Strategic Studies, *Military Balance 2005–2006*, 284, 286.

25. For a comparison of North Korean and South Korean surface ships and
submarines, see the entries on the following Web sites of GlobalSecurity
.org: http://www.globalsecurity.org/military/world/rok/navy.htm; http://
www.globalsecurity.org/military/world/rok/ffk-951.htm; http://www.global
security.org/world/dprk/navy.htm; and http://www.globalsecurity.org/mili
tary/world/rok/kdx-1.htm; the Center for Nonproliferation Studies; http://
cns.miis.edu/research/submarines/skorea/; and "World Navies Today,"
http://www.hazegray.org/worldnav/asiapac/n_korea.htm. The numerical
balance in naval power is from International Institute for Strategic Studies,
Military Balance, 2005–2006, 283–85.

26. Keith Jacobs, "Korean Security and the KDX-III DDG Programme," *Naval
Forces* 24 (2003), http://proquest.umi.com/pqdweb?did=535005291&sid=4
&Fmt=4&clientld=1566&RQT=309&VName=PQD.

27. See the table in "Emerging-Market Indicators," *Economist*, December 17,
2005.

28. Seung-Hwan Kim, "Anti-Americanism in Korea," *Washington Quarterly* 26
(Winter 2002–2003): 109–122; Nahal Toosi, "South Koreans Chafe Under
U.S. Ties," *Milwaukee Journal Sentinel*, December 21, 2003.

29. David I. Steinberg, Summary Report of the Conference on "Korean Attitudes toward the United States: The Enduring and Endured Relationship,"
January 30–February 1, 2003 10, 11. The conference was organized by
Georgetown University's School of Foreign Service in cooperation with
the Pacific Studies Institute.

30. On varieties of anti-Americanism, see Yongshik Bong, "*Yongmi*: Pragmatic
Anti-Americanism in South Korea," *Brown Journal of World Affairs* 10
(Winter/Spring 2004): 153–165.

31. For these and other qualifications, see "Public Opinion on Korea-U.S.
Ties," *Korea Times*, November 4, 2005.

32. See, for example, the editorial written in response to the call by conservative American *New York Times* columnist William Safire for a withdrawal
of U.S. troops from Korea, "Warning against Theory of USFK With-

drawal," *Tong-a Ilbo*, December 28, 2002 (in Korean), http://toolkit
.dialog.com.ezproxy.lib.lehigh.edu/intranet/cgi/present?STYLE=739318018
&PRESENT=DB=985,AN=164200650,FM=9,SEARCH=MD.Generic
Search; and "USFK Withdrawal?" *Choson Ilbo*, December 9, 2002.

33. Kim, "Anti-Americanism in Korea," 109–11.

34. These apt and cautionary points are made in an excellent study prepared
by researchers from the RAND Corporation. See Eric V. Larson, Norman
D. Levin, Senhae Baik, and Bogdan Savych, *Ambivalent Allies: Study of
South Korean Attitudes toward the U.S.* (Santa Monica, Calif.: RAND Corporation, 2004), 51–58.

35. Ibid., figure 3.10, 56. The authors contend that the results showing that only
a very small majority of those favoring withdrawal want it to happen right
away are reassuring. What is more striking to me, however, is that in two of
the five years at least half of all South Koreans favored a withdrawal and that
the proportion of those who did so in the remaining three years remained
strikingly high, ranging from 30 percent (1990) to 40 percent (2003).

36. These poll results are reported in "Majority Opposes U.S. Troop Presence",
JoongAng Ilbo, September 22, 2005, http://joongangdaily.joins.com/200509/
21/200509212243265579900090309031.html; http://toolkit.dialog.com.ezp
roxy.lib.lehigh.edu/intranet/cgi/present?STYLE=739318018&PRESENT=D
B=985,AN=168500755,FM=9,SEARCH=MD.GenericSearch; http://toolkit.
dialog.com.ezproxy.lib.lehigh.edu/intranet/cgi/present?STYLE=739318018
&PRESENT=DB=985,AN=122951210,FM=9,SEARCH=MD.GenericSearch.

37. Larson et al., *Ambivalent Allies*, table 3.1, 50.

38. These poll results are reported in "Koreans Cast Wary Eye on the World,"
JoongAng Ilbo, October 15, 2005, http://joongangdaily.joins.com/200510/
14/200510142210035839900090409041.html; and "Survey Shows Japan Is
Seen as Leading Threat," *JoongAng Ilbo*, April 18, 2005, http://joongang
daily.joins.com/200504/17/200504172206552209900090309031.html.

39. See the results of a poll involving one thousand respondents conducted by
Korea Times and Media Research, Inc., as reported in "Economy, Close
U.S. Ties Top New Year's Wish List," *Korea Times*, January 1, 2003.

40. Results of a Gallup Korea poll, as reported in "Poll Finds Pragmatic Patriotism among the Young," *Chosun Ilbo*, August 15, 2005, http://english
.chosun.com/cgi-bin/printNews?id=200508140019.

41. *JoongAng Ilbo* poll results reported in "42 Percent of Koreans Say Another War Is Possible Here," *JoongAng Ilbo*, June 25, 2005, http://joongangdaily .joins.com/200506/24/200506242326421109900090409041.html. The finding that a higher proportion of young Koreans consider the United States rather than North Korea a threat emerged in a 2004 poll, which is noted in Larry Niksch, "Korea—U.S.-Korean Relations—Issues for Congress," CRS Issue Brief for Congress (updated August 18, 2004), 14–15, http://shelby .senate.gov/legislation/NorthK.pdf.

42. "S. Koreans Oppose Military Action against N. Korea: Poll" (English), *Yonhap*, May 13, 2005, http://toolkit.dialog.com.ezproxy.lib.lehigh.edu/ intranet/cgi/present?STYLE=739318018&PRESENT=DB=985,AN=207500 267,FM=9,SEARCH=MD.GenericSearch.

43. See the firsthand account of Suki Kim, a Korean American who returned to South Korea after immigrating to the United States in the 1980s: "Korea's New Wave," *The New York Times*, May 10, 2003.

44. The poll was conducted by *JoongAng Ilbo* and Sungkyunkwan University's Survey Research Center. Results reported in "Warm Feelings Increase for North Korea," *JoongAng Ilbo*, June 23, 2006, http://joongangdaily.joins .com/200512/22/200512222218174309900092309231.html.

45. *Yonhap* (English), December 20, 2005, reporting on a poll conducted by Metrix. In this survey, 55 percent of the one thousand South Korean respondents in 2005 stated that North Korea was a partner with whom they favored cooperation, in comparison to 34 percent in the previous year. Similarly, from 2004 to 2005, the percentage declaring that North Korea was an enemy fell from 50.1 percent to 25.7 percent. See http://toolkit.dialog.com.ezproxy.lib.lehigh.edu/intranet/cgi/present?STY LE=739318018&PRESENT=DB=985,AN=218550148,FM=9,SEARCH=MD. GenericSearch.

46. David Steinberg, "Miguk Naemse—Smell of Americans," *Korea Herald*, March 2, 2003, http://times.hankooki.com/lpage/opinion/200303/kt2003 030217021511600.htm.

47. A 2005 poll conducted by Korea Gallup from November 23, 2004, through December 4, 2004, showed that 64.7 percent of those polled believed that South Korea should adhere to an independent foreign policy and communicate its positions to the United States on that basis. In the same survey, only 35.4 percent opined that the alliance and friendship with the United

States should be made stronger. See "Poll on ROK Administrations, Relations with Foreign Countries, View on DPRK," *Choson Ilbo*, January 3, 2005 (in Korean), http://toolkit.dialog.com.ezproxy.lib.lehigh.edu/intra net/cgi/present?STYLE=739318018&PRESENT=DB=985,AN=201000476,F M=9,SEARCH=MD.GenericSearch.

48. On the significance of generational change, see Charles K. Armstrong, "South Korea and the United States Sixty Years On," JapanFocus.org, http://www.japanfocus.org/article.asp?id=297.

49. For example, a June–July 2005 poll of 101 South Korean professors, experts in private public policy research centers, and government officials taken by the *JoongAng* newspaper showed strong support for the alliance and blamed the current left-leaning government of President Roh Moo-hyun for its deterioration. Even in this group, however, only 13.9 percent of those polled said that there should be no reduction in the number of U.S. troops in South Korea. By contrast, 59.4 percent favored a partial withdrawal (but opposed a total disengagement), while 23.8 percent supported only a minimum presence, and 1 percent supported a total pullout. "Monthly JoongAng Survey Research on U.S.-Korea Alliance," http://www.mansfieldfdn.org/polls/poll-05-5.htm.

50. Median age of South Koreans provided in U.S. Central Intelligence Agency, *World Factbook*, http://www.cia.gov/cia/publications/factbook/geos /ks.html.

51. See Bruce Cumings, *Korea's Place in the Sun*, esp. ch. 6; Chalmers Johnson, *Blowback: The Costs and Consequences of American Empire* (New York: Metropolitan, 2000), ch. 4; and Don Oberdorfer, *The Two Koreas: A Contemporary History* (New York: Basic Books, 1997).

52. On some of these episodes and issues, see Johnson, ibid.; "Why Anti-U.S. Sentiment," in *Taehan Maeil*, December 13, 2002, http://toolkit.dialog. com.ezproxy.lib.lehigh.edu/intranet/cgi/present?STYLE=739318018&PRE-SENT=DB=985,AN=163451342,FM=9,SEARCH=MD.GenericSearch; *Yonhap* (English), December 12, 2002, http://toolkit.dialog.com.ezproxy.lib. lehigh.edu/intranet/cgi/present?STYLE=739318018&PRESENT=DB=985, AN=163401389,FM=9,SEARCH=MD.GenericSearch; Meredith Woo-Cumings, "South Korean Anti-Americanism," Working Paper no. 93, Japan Policy Research, July 2003, http://www.jpri.org/publications/workingpapers/wp93.html.

53. Kim, "Anti-Americanism in Korea," 109–111; Bong, "*Yongmi*," 157–158; Kim Seung-hwan, "A Dormant Volcano? Korean Sentiment towards United States," *Korea Times*, May 9, 2004.

54. For example, a public opinion poll conducted by Media Research and the *Korean Times* showed that 46.1 percent of South Koreans favored keeping aid to North Korea at current levels while 16.9 percent supported an increase. Only one-third advocated a reduction. "6 in 10 Support Assistance to N.K.," *Korea Times*, March 31, 2004.

55. This increases the possibility of a widening of the gap between the United States and South Korea on how to deal with North Korea. A demonstration that this could happen occurred in March 2003, when North Korean jets tried to force a U.S. surveillance plane, operating in international airspace, to land, a move that suggested that Pyongyang was planning to hold the crew hostage. Roh's insistence that the United States proceed cautiously despite this incident did not please Washington. Robyn Lim, "South Korea: The Yanks May Go Home," *International Herald Tribune*, March 12, 2003.

56. "North Korean Counterfeiting Complicates Nuclear Crisis," *The New York Times*, January 29, 2006.

57. See, for example, Marcus Noland (of the Institute for International Economics), "North Korea and the South Korean Economy," paper presented to the Roh Government Transition Team, February 24, 2003, http://www.iie.com/publications/papers/paper.cfm?researchid=242. Also see the assessments noted in Catherine Lee, "The Economics of Korean Reunification," *Yale Economic Review* (Fall 2005), http://yaleeconomic review.com/issues/fall2005/korea.php.

58. "Hi-Rise, DMZ View: Seoul's Hot Property," *International Herald Tribune*, January 15, 2001.

59. "Statement of General Thomas A. Schwartz, Commander-in-Chief, United Nations Command/Combined Forces Command, and Commander, United States Forces Korea before the Senate Armed Services Committee," March 27, 2001, http://armedservices.senate.gov/statement/2001/010327ts.pdf.

60. For an analysis that disputes the prevalent view that it is essential to station U.S. troops in Korea, see Carpenter and Bandow, *Korean Conundrum*, esp. ch. 4.

61. On the cost of U.S. deployment in South Korea and U.S.-South Korean negotiations over this issue, see "S.K., U.S. Face Tough Talks Again on How to Share Military Costs," *YonhapNews*, March 23, 2006, http://bbs.yonhapnews.co.kr/ynaweb/printpage/EngNews_Content.asp; Larry Niksch, "Korea—U.S.-South-Korean Relations—Issues for Congress," *CRS Issue Brief for Congress* (March 5, 2002), 1; and "South Korea, U.S. Making Progress toward Military Cost-Sharing Agreement" *Stars and Stripes*, February 27, 2005.

62. Chicago Council on Foreign Relations, *Worldviews 2002: American Public Opinion and Foreign Policy*, figure 3.11, http://www.worldviews.org/detail-reports/usreport.pdf. The rest of the study at various points documents strong public support for our alliances and an active global role by the United States, but also shows clearly the importance Americans place on multilateralism and working through the United Nations.

63. Victor D. Cha, "Focus on the Future, Not on the North," *Washington Quarterly* 26, no. 1 (Winter 2002–2003): 95.

64. "U.S. to Redeploy Troops in South Korea," CNN.com, http://www.cnn.com/2003/WORLD/asiapcf/east/06/05/korea.usa/index.html; "U.S. Plans Major Cut of Forces in Korea," *The Washington Post*, June 8, 2004.

65. "After U.S. Military Relocation, Security Vacuum Must Be Prevented" (Korean), *Tong-a Ilbo*, November 28, 2003, http://toolkit.dialog.com.ezproxy.lib.lehigh.edu/intranet/cgi/present?STYLE=739318018&PRESENT=DB=985,AN=180950675,FM=9,SEARCH=MD.GenericSearch.

66. Cha, in "Focus on the Future, Not on the North," offers many creative ideas for reshaping the alliance.

67. On the economic crisis and famine of the 1990s, see Andrei Lankov, "The Natural Death of North Korean Stalinism," *Asia Policy* 1 (January 2006): 97, 109–111.

68. On North Korea's increasing ties with the outside world, see ibid., 100–114.

69. Among those who predicted that the Soviet Union would collapse because of a war with China was the Soviet dissident Andrei Amalrik. See his *Will the Soviet Union Survive until 1984?* (New York: Harper & Row, 1970).

70. On China as the next threat, see, among others, John J. Mearsheimer, *Tragedy of Great Power Politics* (New York: Norton, 2001), 360–402; and

Aaron L. Friedberg, "The Struggle for Mastery in China," *Commentary* 4 (November 2000): 17–26.

71. Kim, "Anti-Amercanism in Korea," 116.

Chapter 6: Conclusion

1. U.S. Department of Defense, *2004 Statistical Compendium on Allied Contributions to the Common Defense,* http://www.defenselink.mil/pubs/allied_contrib2004/allied2004.pdf.

2. The data that follow comparing U.S. and allied contributions in various categories are drawn from ibid., tables C-3, C-4, C-5, D-1, D-2, D-4, and D-5.

3. See Rumsfeld's remarks at a May 4, 2006, speech in Atlanta, Georgia, as reported by CNN.com, May 4, 2006, http://www.cnn.com/2006/POLITICS/05/04/rumsfeld.ap/index.html.

4. See Rajan Menon, "Terror, Inc.," *Los Angeles Times,* August 22, 2004.

5. See, for example, Amartya Sen, *Development as Freedom* (New York: Oxford University Press, 1999). This work is among his many writings stressing the importance of "capabilities" over income.

6. See Marc Lacey, "Kenyan Village Serves as Test Case in Fight on Poverty," *The New York Times,* April 4, 2005; Jeffrey D. Sachs, "Net Gains," *The New York Times,* April 29, 2006. Sachs offers an extended analysis of the roots of poverty and an ambitious program for reducing it through a series of coordinated simple steps in *The End of Poverty: Economic Possibilities for Our Time* (New York: Penguin, 2005), chs. 10–17.

7. Celia W. Dugger, "Infants Dying for Lack of Basics, Report Says," *The New York Times,* May 9, 2006.

Index

alliances
    activism without, 24–29
        Atlantic, 53–99 (*See also* North
            Atlantic Treaty Organization
            (NATO))
        as bad practice, 34–36, 182, 191
        cold war, 8, 10–11, 182, 187, 196
        constructive reasons for, 185, 188
        as contextual and contingent, 56–57,
            60–61, 74
        for economic development, 185–186,
            188, 192
        for military strength, 8–9, 107, 183
        for technological creativity, 7–8
    of U. S.
        as dangerous, 61–62, 78–79, 130, 166,
            172, 176
        post-World War II, 45–51, 101–105
        pre-World War II, 23–45, 53
        shift in, 16–17, 45, 182, 185–188,
            199–200
altruism, 54
America First Committee, 44
Anglo-French Entente Cordiale (1904),
    14
Annan, Kofi, 84
annexations, 49–50
anomie, escape from, 81
anti-Americanism
    in Europe, 70, 72–73
    media coverage of, 163, 171, 176
    in South Korea, 162–168
anti-communism, NATO practices for, 75,
    79
anti-immigration movements, 82
anti-interventionists, 54
anti-terrorism
    beginnings of, 58, 60, 74–75, 79, 196
    intelligence sharing for, 79–80, 83
    NATO practices for, 75–83, 97–98
antinuclear movements, 102, 123–124
antiterrorist organization, 83
ANZUS, 8, 49
appeasement, 15–16

Arab-Israeli dispute, 77
Arab states
    for global poverty reduction efforts,
        198–199
    as terrorist breeding ground, 196–197
Arabian Peninsula, U. S. military forces in,
    77
Araki Commission, 119
armament. *See* arms *entries;* weapons
armies. *See* military forces/troops
arms embargo, during World War II,
    43–44
arms limitations
    for Japan, 105–106, 111
    multilateral efforts for, 29, 141, 188
    nuclear, 123, 125–126
arms sales
    by Japan, 111, 114–116, 118
    by Russia, 153–154
    by U. S., 161–162
Article IX, of Japan's constitution,
    106–107, 110–111, 113, 118–119
    revision of, 137–139
Article V, of NATO charter, 95, 97
Articles of Confederation, 32
Asia-Pacific
    balance of power in, 127, 130–132
    regional security systems for, 140–141,
        176–177
assemblies, for global poverty defeat,
    198–199
atomic weapons. *See* nuclear weapons
atrocities, 86
    military interventions against, 193,
        195
    UN-based solutions to, 193–194
Australia, alliance with U. S., 8, 49
Austria-Hungary, in Triple Alliance, 14
authoritarianism
    in China, 192
    in South Korea, 145, 149, 169–170
"axis of evil," 171
Axis Powers, 23–24, 44–45
Aznar, José María, 59–61, 89

balance of power
    Britain's twists and turns in, 12–17
    during cold war, 8–9, 11, 57–58, 182
    in East Asia, 49, 69, 74, 90, 93, 192
        shifts in, 106, 120–123, 134–135, 155,
        161
    in North Pacific, 127, 140–141
    post-World War II, 45–49, 54–55, 106
    twenty-first century, 67, 69, 88, 178,
        187, 192–193
Balkans
    NATO's role in, 70, 95
    Russian designs on, 14–15
Baltic States
    in Iraq War, 63–64, 68, 70
    in NATO, 70–71, 97
Barnaby, Frank, 126
Basque separatist group, 60
BBC poll, on Iraq War, 175–176
Beijing
    position on Korea, 152–154
    Pyongyang competition with, 177–
        179
Belgium, 67–68, 183
Berlin Crisis, 47–48
Berlusconi, Silvio, 59, 61–62
bilateralism
    to combat terror, 83
    in trade, 105–110, 136, 140–141, 154
Bill and Melinda Gates Foundation, 199
bin Laden, Osama, 76–77, 191
Black Death, 18
Black Ships, 25, 104
Blair, Tony, 58–59, 62, 76, 78
Bolshevik Party, 9–10
Bolshevik Revolution, 7, 9, 104
Bosnia, 86, 89–91, 94
Brandt, Willy, 67, 102
Britain
    alliance with France, 14
    alliance with Japan, 15
    alliance with Russia, 14–15
    alliance with U. S., 8, 16–17
    appeasement policy of, 15–16

    defense policy of, 71, 86, 88, 92
    in Iraq War, 58–60, 62, 64, 68, 70–71
    power struggle with France, 12–14,
        33–34
    strategic twists and turns of, 12–17
    terror attacks in, 59, 74, 76, 78–79, 81
    in Triple Alliance, 14
    in World War I, 38–40
    in World War II, 43–45, 54
British monarchy, 32
    rejection of, 26, 30
British National Front, 82
Brussels Pact, 55
budgets, defense. *See* defense spending
Bulgaria, 63, 68, 97
bureaucracy, of post-cold war alliances,
    56–57
Bush, George H. W., 156
Bush, George W., 58, 64, 72, 76, 98
    Korean states and, 154, 158, 170–171,
        175–176

Calipari, Nicola, 61–62
Calleo, David, 90
Cambodia, civil war in, 193
Camp Zama, 131
Canada, 25, 86, 92
capital, in economic development, 7, 53
capitalism
    in China, 133, 135
    communism as alternative to, 9–10
    as terrorist target, 76, 82
Caribbean, U. S. military interventions in,
    39–40, 49
Carter, Jimmy, 102–103, 157–158, 175
Central America
    U. S. military interventions in, 39–40,
        49
    U. S. vs. European presence in, 25–28
Central Treaty Organization (CENTO), 8,
    49, 56
Chamberlain, Neville, 16, 42
Cheju massacre, 169
Cheney, Dick, 59

community of comity, 58
community of peace, 98, 185
community of wealth, for global poverty
    defeat, 198–199
"comprehensive security," 109
computer revolution, 7
concessions, 35
confidence-building, in U. S. and Japan
    realignment, 140–141
Conservative Party, British, 58–59
constitution
    of European Union, 71–72, 87–88
    of Japan, 105–107, 110–111, 113,
        118–119
        Article IX revision, 137–139
containment
    as grand strategy, 6–10, 181
    impact on Soviet Union, 8–10
    as security, 10–12, 192
    as U. S. strategy, 28, 46–51, 133
context, of alliances, 56–57, 60–61, 74,
    76
contingency, of alliances, 56–57, 60–61,
    74, 76
    Japan and U. S., 120–123
    South Korea and U. S., 168
Cook, Robin, 78
Cooper, Robert, 94
corporations
    and global poverty reduction efforts,
        199
    industrial
        of Japan, 107–108, 116
        of South Korea, 151
Council on Security and Defense Capabil-
    ity, of Japan, 119
counterfeiting, of American currency,
    171
counterinsurgency missions, 186
    by NATO, 84–86, 91–92
creativity. See technology
crime rings, transnational, 195
Cuba, 10, 27
    alliance with Soviets, 7–8
Cuba, crisis over, 47

cultural diversity
    in America, 103–104
    of Muslim communities, 79–82
cultural exchanges, of South and North
    Korea, 167, 172
Cultural Revolution, of China, 152
currency counterfeiting, 171
cynicism, 200
Czechoslovakia/Czech Republic, 9, 42,
    97
    in Iraq War, 64–65

Darfur, civil war in, 84, 86, 186, 193, 195
decision making, in NATO, 97
defense policy
    of Britain, 71, 86, 88, 92
    of European Union, 71, 86, 95, 98
    of Japan, 107, 111–112, 185
        asymmetrical gains with, 128–133
        catalysts for, 120–123, 155
        discourse shift in, 116–119
        fresh thinking about, 139–143
        public opinion on, 111–112, 139
        U. S. contract for, 102–106, 109
    of South Korea
        commitment vs. continuance of,
            155–158, 164
        U. S. provisions for, 24, 154, 185–
            187
    of U. S., 29, 38, 175, 190 (*See also* U. S.
        foreign policy)
defense spending
    by Canada, 86, 92
    by France, 86, 88, 92
    by Germany, 92, 183
    inequity of, 71, 86, 96, 184–185
    by Japan, 107–108, 110–111, 113–114,
        183–184
        breech of, 118, 120–123, 129
        U. S. expenditures and, 131–133
    9/11 impact on, 118, 129, 158, 174,
        183
    by North Korea, 150–151, 159
    by South Korea, 147–148, 159, 161,
        173–174, 183–184

security for, 24, 127, 176–177, 183–187, 189, 196
South Korea's role in, 147–149, 155, 161, 164
U. S. military force reconfiguration in, 129, 131–133, 156, 164
East Asia Strategy Report (1995), 132
East Central Europe. *See also specific country*
in NATO, 70–71, 73, 97
economic aid, to poor countries, 198–199
NATO's future role in providing, 84–85
economic development
in Afghanistan, 91
in Africa, 198–199
alliances for, 185–186, 188, 192
in China, 74, 133–135
EU defense policy and, 71, 96
Japan's superiority in, 101, 103, 107–110, 121–122
American protection and Japan's achievements in, 107–110
leading powers club for, 151
NATO provisions for, 84, 91–92
in North Korea, 150–151, 177
in South Korea, 145–148, 150–151, 161
crisis bailout for, 169–170
North Korea zone for, 172
in Southeast Asia, 109
in Soviet Union, 6–7, 9–10, 54
as terrorism target, 81
economic shocks, 195
education programs, NATO interventions for, 84
Egypt, in Gulf War, 90
Eighty Years War, 18
Eisaku Sato, 124
Eisenhower, Dwight, 156
elections, alliance politics and
in England, 58–59, 65
in Italy, 62
in Poland, 63
in Spain, 60–61

in Ukraine, 64
in U. S., 39, 45
electronic warfare, 152
empowerment, for human rights implementation, 195
energy
nuclear, 125–126, 167
oil, 96, 126, 129, 140, 197–198
undersea fields of, 137–138
energy policy, need for, 137, 197
engagement
with alliance (*See* world engagement)
as security, 133, 173, 192
of South Korea, with North Korea, 167, 169–170, 172
without alliance, 28–29
England. *See* Britain
entanglement, U. S. position on
post-World War II, 45–51, 55
pre-World War II, 23–45
shift in, 19–21, 45, 182, 187–188, 199–200
during World War I, 38–41
environmental degradation, 195
equality, as terrorist target, 76, 82
Estonia, 97
ethics, of genetics, 5
Ethiopia, 10
ethnic cleansing, interventions against, 37, 84–86, 193
ethnicity
atrocities related to, 193–194
diverse
in America, 103–104
of Muslim communities, 79–80
homogeneous, of Japan, 104
Eurasia, post-World War II, 47–49, 58
Eurocorps, 94
Franco–German, 87
Europe
America's separation from, 29–38, 42
demoralization post-World War II, 54, 96

in Iraq War, 58, 65–70, 73, 90
nationalism in, 16
NATO security for, 73–74
naval power of, 28
Nazi (*See* Nazi Germany)
power source of, 14, 19
in Triple Alliance, 14
World War I demands, 38–40
world wars blamed on, 19
Ghana, 145
glasnost, 10
global leadership, U. S. public opinion on,
198–199
global peacekeeping, NATO role in,
84–86, 186
global policing, 182, 186, 193–194
global poverty reduction, 198–200
NATO agenda for, 84–85, 96
global terrorism, 82–83
global trading, 195. *See also* trade
go-it-alone policy, 20
good works, U. S. public opinion on,
198–199
goodwill, 70–72, 165
Gorbachev, Mikhail, 10
government institutions, alliances' influence on, 36
grand strategy
America's
post-World War II, 45–51
pre-World War II, 23–45
shift in, 19–21, 45, 182, 187–188,
199–200
Britain, shifts in, 10–17
containment as, 6–10 (*See also* containment)
energy policy as, 137, 197
Japan's capacity for, 140–143
security policy as, 96–99, 109
Great Depression, 42
Great Leap Forward, 152
Great War. *See* World War I
Greece, 86, 183
gross domestic product (GDP)

of China, 161
defense spending and, 71, 86, 96, 183
comparisons, 113–114, 159
of North Korea, 150–151, 158–159, 177
of South Korea, 145–147, 158–159, 161,
173
of Taiwan, 161
of U. S. vs. allies, 114, 183–184
gross national product (GNP)
of Japan, 106, 108, 111, 113
of Soviet Union, 7
ground troops. *See* military forces/troops
Guam, 27
U. S. military forces in, 131–132, 141
Gulf War, 77, 90, 107, 129, 191
Guyana, British, 26

Haider, Jorg, 82
Hamilton, Alexander, 30–32, 34
Hapsburgs, 13, 87
Hawaii, 27–28
Hay, John, 32
Hay-Pauncefote Treaty (1901), 27
health programs, 84–85, 199
hegemony, 13, 90, 135
Helsinki Accords, 10
Hinomaru flag, 138–139
Hiroshima, 121, 123–124
hit-and-run tactics, 93
Hitler, Adolf
appeasement impact on, 15
Munich deal with, 42
territorial claims of, 15–16, 42–44
HIV epidemic, NATO aid to combat, 84
Hobbesian international system, 188
Holy Alliance, 36
homegrown terrorism, 79, 82
homeland security. *See* national security
Hosei Norota, 117
"host nation support," 110, 131
hostage-takings, in Iraq, 61
House, Colonel, 39
House of Commons, British, 58
human cloning, 5

liberty
   as terrorist target, 76, 82
   U. S. embodiment of, 30–38
lifestyle, American, as terrorist target, 76,
      82
Lippmann, Walter, 55
Lithuania, 64, 86, 97
Lodge, Henry Cabot, 28
logistics/logistical support, military
   Japan's participation in, 118–119, 130
   for peacekeeping, 195
   U. S. vs. NATO, 148, 174–175, 184
London Naval Treaty, 29
London Underground, terror attacks on,
      59, 74, 76, 78, 81
"Long Telegram" (Kennan), 47
loss of life, in European wars, 18
Louis XIV, 13, 87
Lusitania, sinking of, 39
Luxembourg, 71, 183

Maastricht Treaty, 87
MacArthur, Douglas, 105–107
Machtpolitik, 111
Madison, James, 30, 3
Madrid commuter rail system, terror at-
      tacks on, 59–61, 74, 76, 81
Manchuria, Japan's invasion of, 43–44
Maoist ideology, 133, 152
Marcos, Ferdinand, 56
Maritime Safety Agency, of Japan, 107, 141
marketplace, global, 195. *See also* trade
Marshall Plan, 47–48, 54
Marxist ideology, 152
mass killing
   military interventions against, 85–86,
      193
   peacekeeping forces for, 194–195
   by Saddam Hussein, 190–191
Masyoshi Ohira, 124
maximalism, 46
Mecca, 77
media coverage, of anti-Americanism,
      163, 171, 176

Medina, 77
Meiji period, in Japan, 112
merchant vessels
   security for, 31
   World War I attacks on, 39–40
Mexico, U. S. vs. European presence in, 25,
      27, 40
Middle East
   equilibrium of, 66
   U. S. military presence in, 66, 197–198
militant Islam, 60, 74, 76, 78–82
military bases, U. S., in South Korea,
      162–167, 169, 174–175, 178
military expenditures. *See* defense
      spending
military forces/troops
   American (*See* U. S. military troops)
   coalition, in Iraq War, 58–65
   early British, 32
   European
      deployment of, 12–13, 17
      independent joint, 68, 70, 87
   of Japan, 103–104, 106–107, 110
      autonomous evolution of, 136–139
      modern potential of, 113–116, 118,
         129
      support missions by, 118–119, 130
   of Nazi Germany, 43
   of Russia, 185
   of South vs. North Korea, 159–161
   total NATO, 184
military-industrial complex, of Soviet
      Union, 7
military power, 19, 21
   alliances for, 8–9, 71, 75, 104–105
   of Britain, 12–13
   of China, 125, 127, 135
   to combat terror, 79–80, 83
   of Germany, 16
   for humanitarianism, 85–86, 94, 193
   of Japan, 106–107, 112, 185
      as ample for self–defense, 128–133
      catalysts for, 120–123
      paper tiger vs. real capacity, 113–116

military power (*continued*)
  nonmilitary policy vs., 48
  for peacekeeping, 86–87, 90–91, 94–95
  preventive use of, 66, 190–191
  for security, 19, 182, 188
  of South vs. North Korea, 150–153,
    157
    ever–widening gap in, 158–162
  of U. S. vs. NATO, 67, 183–184
military technology
  atomic (*See* nuclear weapons)
  modern development of, 111, 114–116,
    122, 184
minimalism, 20–21, 46
  in Japan, 112, 122, 128, 185
missile defense programs, 127, 171
  Japan capabilities for, 126–127, 129
  technology for, 116–117, 119, 121, 126
modernization reforms
  in Japan, 104
  in South vs. North Korea, 146, 150
Moldova, 63–64
monarchy, British, 32
  rejection of, 26, 30
Monroe, James, 36–37
Monroe Doctrine (1823), 25–26, 37, 40,
    49
morality/moralizing
  in developmental assistance programs,
    84–85
  in security programs, 96
Moscow
  position on Korea, 153–154
  post-World War II, 54, 69
multilateralism
  for arms limitations, 29
  to combat terror, 79–80, 83
  for humanitarianism, 94, 194, 200
  post-World War I, 16–17
  for security organizations, 140–141, 174
Munich Deal (1938), 42
Muslims in Europe
  appeal of radicalism Islam among,
    81–82

socioeconomic status of, 77–78
  population data on, 80–81
Mutual Defense Treaty (1954), 145

Nagasaki, 121, 123–124
Napoleonic Empire, 13, 18, 36, 87
narcotics trade, 195
nation building, 70
national defense budget. *See* defense
    spending
National Defense Program Outline
    (2005), of Japan, 119
National Guard units, U. S., 98, 129
National Police Reserve, of Japan, 107
National Reserve forces, U. S., 98
national security
  in Japan
    asymmetrical gains from, 128–133
    catalysts of, 120–123
    discourse shift in, 116–119
    nuclear threats and, 123–127
    policy on, 107, 111–112, 185
    U. S. contract for, 102–106, 109
  NATO vs. U. S. position on, 73–74, 89,
    92, 95–96
  post-cold war, 55–57
  in South Korea
    commitment vs. continuance of,
      155–158, 164
    military capacity for, 158–162
    policy changes on, 167–171
    public opinion about, 162–168, 172
    reform proposals for, 172–177
    U. S. provisions for, 24, 154, 185–187
  in U. S., 29, 38, 175, 190
nationalism
  alliances based on, 19–20
  anti-colonial, 17
  in China, 133–135, 192
  in Germany, 16
  in Japan, 106, 112, 120–123, 185
    Gaullist, 136–139
  in Korea, 178–179
  of Muslim communities, 79–80

North Atlantic Treaty Organization
(NATO) (*continued*)
pact with South Korea, 129, 155,
186–187
peacekeeping role, 84–86, 186
perceptions and politics of, 69–75
Pew public opinion survey on, 71–74
poverty alleviation agenda of, 84–85
precursors to, 53–55
reshaping of, 55–57, 82–83, 90–95, 101
unanimity rule, 97
U. S. protection benefits with, 96–99
weapons of, Soviets' vs., 8–9
North Korea
apprehension about, 120–123, 127,
163–164
defense spending by, 150–151, 159
economic development in, 150–151,
158–159, 177
in Korean War, 146–147
nuclear weapons of, 116–117, 121, 124,
127, 189
South Korea's position on, 152, 156,
167, 170–171
worsening strategic position of,
149–154
reforms failure in, 146, 150
mortality emerging from, 177–179
Seoul's attitude changes toward,
167–171
socialism in, 10
solidarity with China, 152–153
economic challenges of, 177–179
South Korea protection against
modern influences on, 155–158
policy changes on, 167–171
public opinion about, 162–168,
172
reform proposals for, 172–177
by self, 158–162
U. S. provisions for, 24, 154, 185–
187
technology development in, 150–
153

North Pacific
balance of power in, 127, 130–132
modern security systems for, 140–141,
176–177
Norway, 62–63, 183
NSC-68 document, 48
nuclear energy/reactors, 123, 125–126, 167
Nuclear Non-Proliferation Treaty (NPT),
123, 125–126
nuclear weapons, 48, 67, 188–189
of China, 125, 127, 142
Japan's position on, 123–127, 139,
141–142
limitations agreements for, 102,
105–106, 111, 188
of North Korea, 116–117, 121, 124, 127,
189
South Korea's position on, 152, 156,
167, 170–171
U. S. deployment of, 69, 102–103, 117,
156–157
nutrition programs, NATO interventions
for, 84
Nye, Gerald P., 43
Nye, Joseph, 132
Nye Committee, 43

oil
Japan dependence on, 129, 140
nuclear energy vs., 126
undersea fields of, 137–138
U. S. dependence on, 96, 197–198
oil-rich states
global poverty reduction efforts,
198–199
as terrorist breeding ground, 196–197
Okinawa, 131, 139
Olney, Richard, 26–27
"omoiyari yosan," 110
opinion polls. *See also* public opinion
BBC, on Iraq War, 175–176
on global leadership, 198–199
Pew, of U. S., NATO, and EU, 71–74
opium trafficking, 25

South Korean's public opinion on, 166–167

U. S. position vs., 172–177

Quadrennial Defense Review (QDR), 129

radical Islam, 60, 74, 76, 78–82
Reagan, Ronald, 6, 10
realignment, of U. S. and Japan alliance, 140–141
realism, American
  early Republic, 33–35, 37
  modern, 66
  post-World War II, 54
Realpolitik, 54, 70, 109, 149
reciprocity, in U. S. and Japan alliance, 131, 139–140
"reconciliation euphoria," of South and North Korea, 172–173
recruiting, by terrorist organizations, 82–83
Red Army, 182
reflexive agreement, of NATO and U. S., 96
reforms
  modernization
    in Japan, 104
    in South vs. North Korea, 146, 150
  progressive, of New Deal, 42
  for U. S. alliance with South Korea, 172–177
"regime change"
  in Iraq, 58, 62, 66, 68, 75
  in Soviet Russia, 104
regions
  oil-rich, 197–199
  peacekeeping forces for, 195
  post-World War II wars, 47
  remaking by U. S., 190–191
  security systems for, 140–141
Reid, John, 89
religion, atrocities related to, 193–194

reorientation, of world engagement, 3, 19–21
Republic of America. *See* United States (U. S.)
Republic of Korea. *See* South Korea
research and development (R&D), military
  by Japan vs. U. S., 116, 118–119, 184
  by South vs. North Korea, 150–153
revisionist regimes, 20
Revolution in Military Affairs (RMA), 151–152
revolutionary idealism, 29–30, 33, 37
revolutions. *See also specific revolution*
  change resulting from, 4, 10, 190
right-wing politics
  in America, 192–193
  in South Korea, 163
robotics, 7
Roh Moo-hyun, 170–171
Rokassho-mura, Japanese plutonium reprocessing plant, 126
Romania, 68, 97
Roosevelt, Franklin
  battle against neutrality, 41–45
  strategy for Soviet Union, 46–47
Roosevelt, Theodore, 28, 40
Roosevelt Corollary (1904), 26, 49
Root, Elihu, 28
Royal Institute of International Affairs (RIIA), 78
Rumsfeld, Donald, 58, 63, 69, 72–73, 184
Russia
  alliance with Britain, 14–15
  diplomacy with South Korea, 153–154, 164
  in Iraq War, 67–70
  military forces of, 93, 185
  political transformation in, 4, 70, 74, 90, 104, 152
  post-World War II recovery of, 54
  "strategic relationship" with China, 153–154
Rwanda, civil war in, 84, 186, 193

Sachs, Jeffrey, 84, 199
Samoa, 28
San Francisco Peace Treaty (1951), 103, 107, 111, 114, 187
sanitation programs, in Africa, 199
Saudi Arabia, in Gulf War, 90
Save the Children, 199
Schmidt, Helmut, 69, 102
Schroeder, Gerhard, 58, 65, 96
science, change exemplified in, 4–5
sea-lanes, Japan's defense of, 118–119, 129, 148 141
sealift capabilities, of NATO, 87–88
search-and-destroy operations, against terrorists, 92
secrecy, in terrorism, 80
secularism, as terrorist target, 76, 81
security
    alliances for, 31, 185–188
        NATO and US, 73–74, 89, 92, 96, 98
        post-World War II, 45–51, 103, 107
        pre-World War I, 53–54
    "comprehensive," 109
    for East Asia, 24, 127, 183–187, 189, 196
    homeland (*See* national security)
    for trade, 30–32, 38, 105, 141–142
Security Council, UN
    atrocities solutions approval, 193–194
    nuclear weapons arsenals of, 189
sedition, 30
self–defense
    as inherent right, 111, 114, 117
    Japan's resources for, 107, 110–112, 123, 128–133
    as NATO mission, 95
    South Korea's resources for, 158–162
        generational influences on, 167–171
Self–Defense Force, of Japan, 107, 110–111
    military capacity of, 113–116, 118–119
self–determination, 26
self–interest, in developmental assistance programs, 84–85, 95, 199
Sen, Amartya, 199

Seoul
    attitude changes toward North Korea, 167–171
    Pyongyang competition, 146, 153–154, 156
    Washington alliance with, 145–150, 153, 155, 163, 166–168, 170, 173–174
Serbian military offensive, 89–90, 95
Seven Years War (1763), 5, 11–12, 18
Sgrena, Giuliana, 61
Shigeru Ishiba, 117, 121
Shingo Nishimura, 125
Shintaro Ishihara, 124
Shinzo Abe, 117, 121, 124–125
ships
    passenger, World War I attacks on, 39–40
    war (*See* naval power)
Sierra Leone, 86
Sino-Soviet frontier, 8–9
skepticism, 5
slave trade, 24–25
Slovakia, 97
Slovenia, 97
socialism, 9–10
Socialist Workers' Party (PSOE), Spanish, 60
society(ies)
    remaking by U. S., 190, 193
    U. S., alliances' influence on, 36
socioeconomics, terrorism related to, 81
"soft power," 109, 193
solidarity
    of NATO and U. S., 71, 74, 96–97
    of North Korea and China, 152–153
    in Poland, 9
    symbolism of, 97–98
South America, U. S. vs. European presence in, 25–26
South Korea, 145–179
    alliance with U. S., 8, 10–11, 49, 129, 182, 187